# GREEN LANTERNS
## GHOSTS OF THE PAST

writers
**TIM SEELEY**
**AARON GILLESPIE**

artists
**RONAN CLIQUET \ V KEN MARION**
**ROGE ANTONIO \ SANDU FLOREA**

colorists
**HI-FI \ DINEI RIBEIRO**

letterer
**DAVE SHARPE**

collection cover artists
**BRETT BOOTH, NORM RAPMUND**
and **ANDREW DALHOUSE**

SUPERMAN created by JERRY SIEGEL and JOE SHUSTER
By special arrangement with the Jerry Siegel family

VOL.
**8**

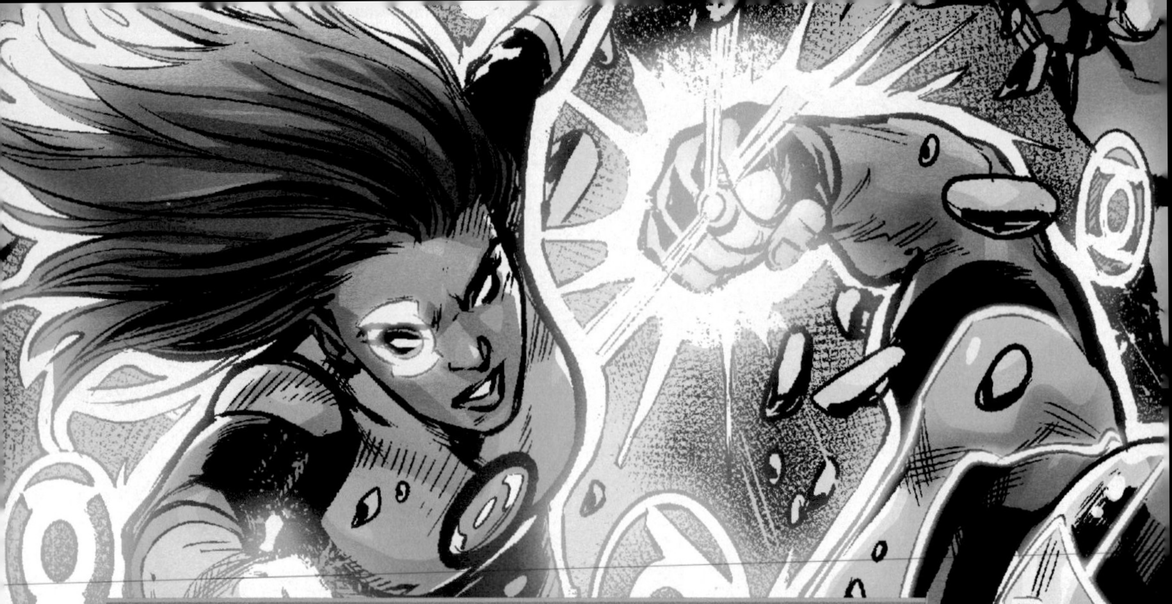

**BRIAN CUNNINGHAM** Editor – Original Series
**ANDREW MARINO** Assistant Editor – Original Series
**JEB WOODARD** Group Editor – Collected Editions
**ROBIN WILDMAN** Editor – Collected Edition
**STEVE COOK** Design Director – Books
**MONIQUE NARBONETA** Publication Design

**BOB HARRAS** Senior VP – Editor-in-Chief, DC Comics
**PAT McCALLUM** Executive Editor, DC Comics

**DAN DiDIO** Publisher
**JIM LEE** Publisher & Chief Creative Officer
**AMIT DESAI** Executive VP – Business & Marketing Strategy, Direct to Consumer & Global Franchise Management
**BOBBIE CHASE** VP & Executive Editor, Young Reader & Talent Development
**MARK CHIARELLO** Senior VP – Art, Design & Collected Editions
**JOHN CUNNINGHAM** Senior VP – Sales & Trade Marketing
**BRIAR DARDEN** VP – Business Affairs
**ANNE DePIES** Senior VP – Business Strategy, Finance & Administration
**DON FALLETTI** VP – Manufacturing Operations
**LAWRENCE GANEM** VP – Editorial Administration & Talent Relations
**ALISON GILL** Senior VP – Manufacturing & Operations
**JASON GREENBERG** VP – Business Strategy & Finance
**HANK KANALZ** Senior VP – Editorial Strategy & Administration
**JAY KOGAN** Senior VP – Legal Affairs
**NICK J. NAPOLITANO** VP – Manufacturing Administration
**LISETTE OSTERLOH** VP – Digital Marketing & Events
**EDDIE SCANNELL** VP – Consumer Marketing
**COURTNEY SIMMONS** Senior VP – Publicity & Communications
**JIM (SKI) SOKOLOWSKI** VP – Comic Book Specialty Sales & Trade Marketing
**NANCY SPEARS** VP – Mass, Book, Digital Sales & Trade Marketing
**MICHELE R. WELLS** VP – Content Strategy

GREEN LANTERNS VOL. 8: GHOSTS OF THE PAST



DC Comics, 2900 West Alameda Ave., Burbank, CA 91505
Printed by LSC Communications, Kendallville, IN, USA. 12/28/18. First Printing.
ISBN: 978-1-4012-8590-6

Library of Congress Cataloging-in-Publication Data is available.

PEFC Certified
This product is from sustainably managed forests and controlled sources
PEFC
PEFC/29-31-337
www.pefc.org

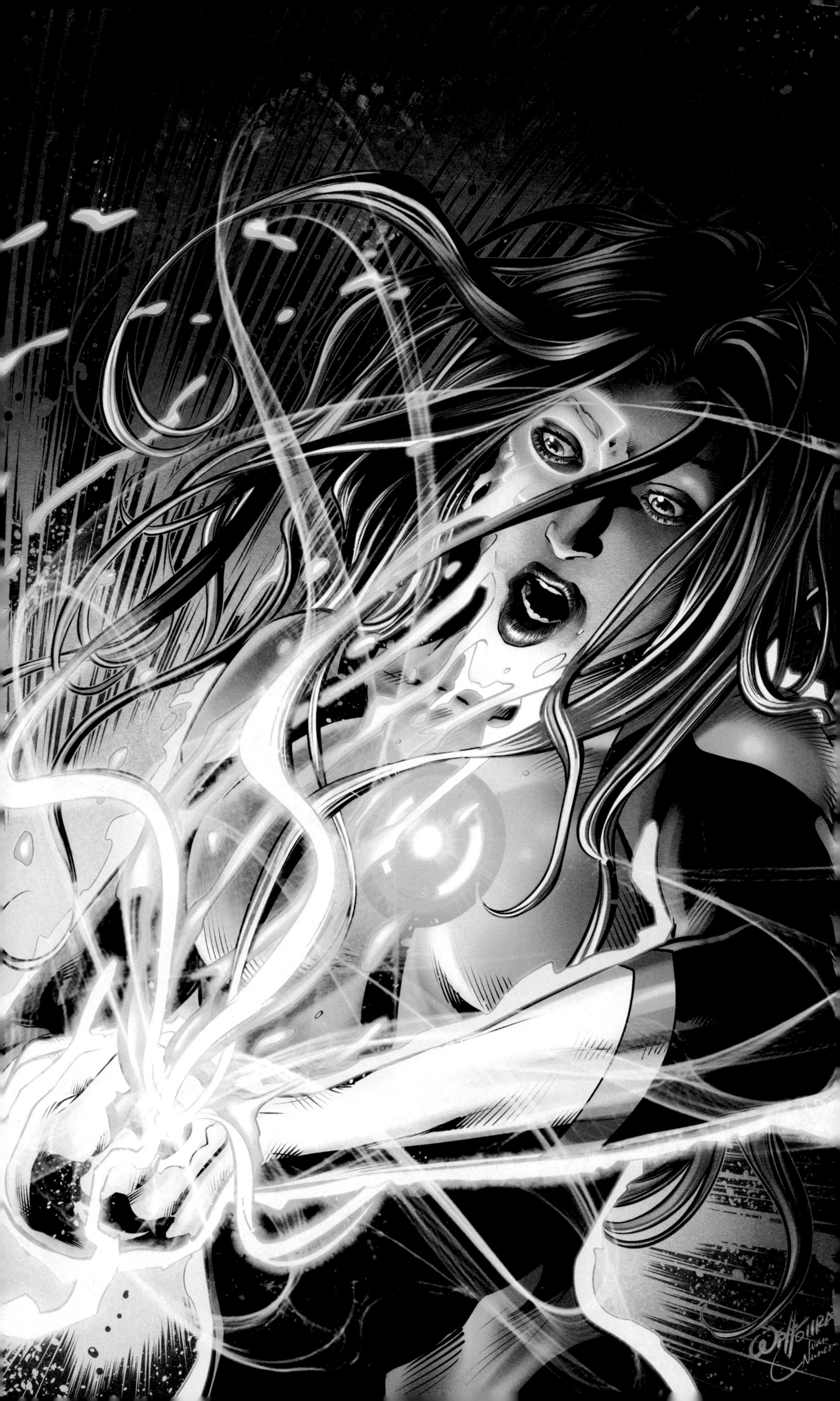

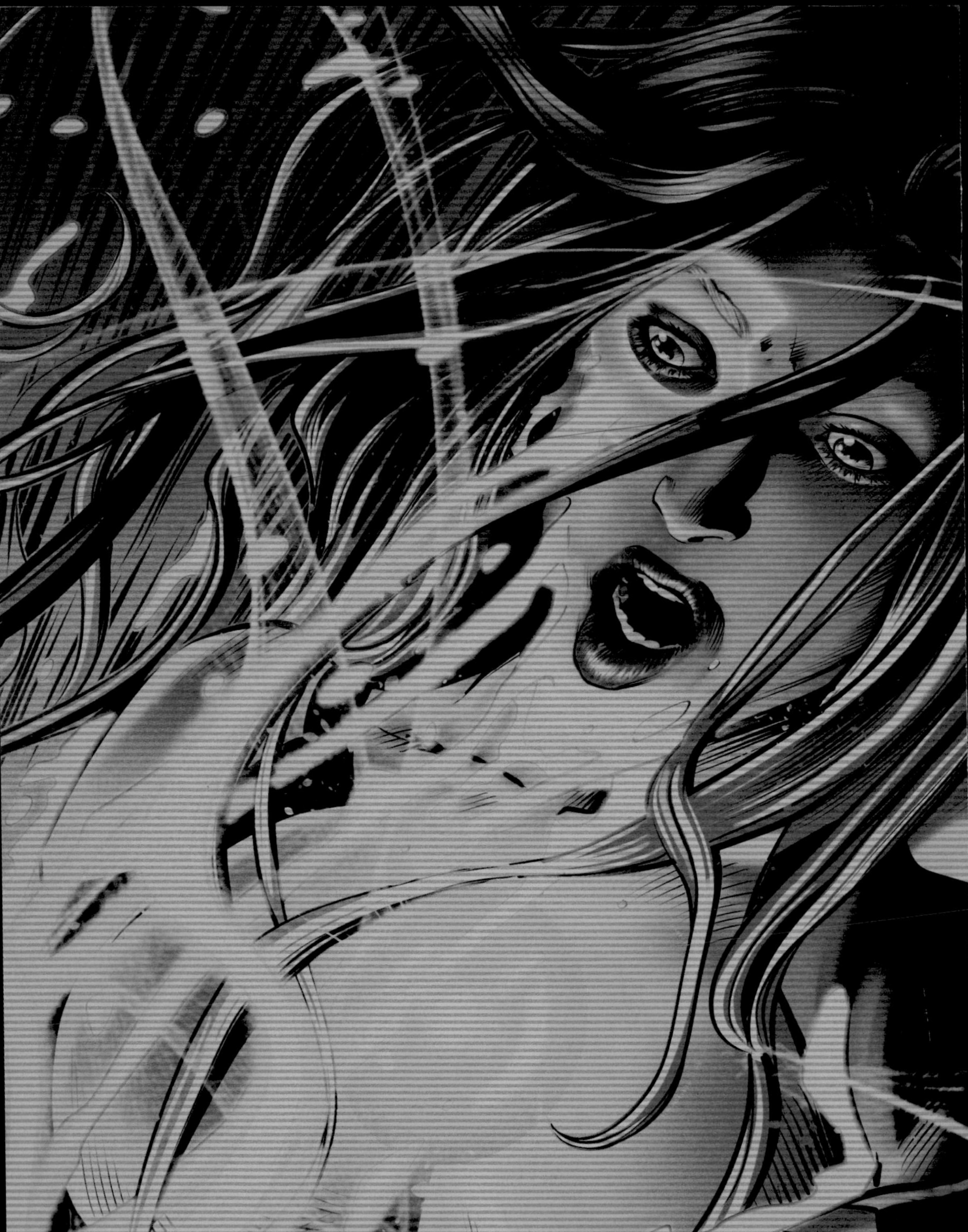

# GREEN LANTERNS
#44

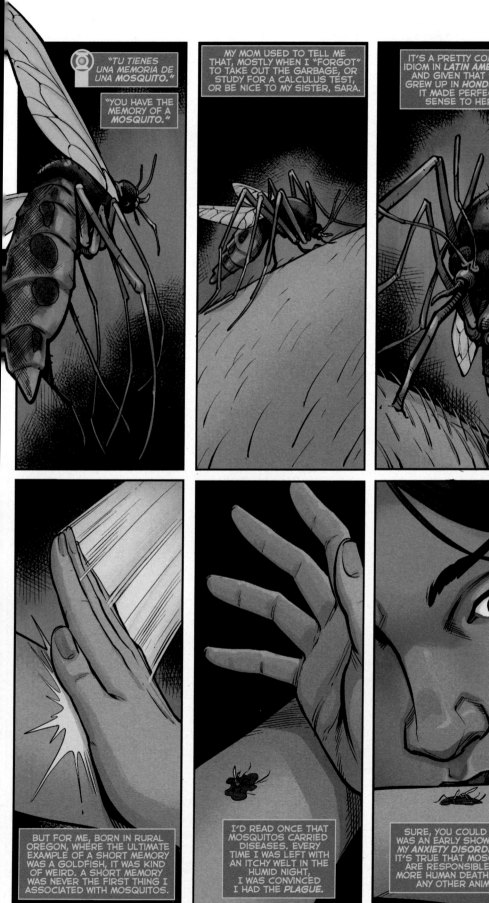

"*TU TIENES UNA MEMORIA DE UNA MOSQUITO.*"

"YOU HAVE THE MEMORY OF A *MOSQUITO.*"

MY MOM USED TO TELL ME THAT, MOSTLY WHEN I "FORGOT" TO TAKE OUT THE GARBAGE, OR STUDY FOR A CALCULUS TEST, OR BE NICE TO MY SISTER, SARA.

IT'S A PRETTY COMMON IDIOM IN *LATIN AMERICA,* AND GIVEN THAT SHE GREW UP IN *HONDURAS,* IT MADE PERFECT SENSE TO HER.

BUT FOR ME, BORN IN RURAL OREGON, WHERE THE ULTIMATE EXAMPLE OF A SHORT MEMORY WAS A GOLDFISH, IT WAS KIND OF WEIRD. A SHORT MEMORY WAS NEVER THE FIRST THING I ASSOCIATED WITH MOSQUITOS.

I'D READ ONCE THAT MOSQUITOS CARRIED DISEASES. EVERY TIME I WAS LEFT WITH AN ITCHY WELT IN THE HUMID NIGHT, I WAS CONVINCED I HAD THE *PLAGUE.*

SURE, YOU COULD SAY IT WAS AN EARLY SHOWING OF MY *ANXIETY DISORDER,* BUT IT'S TRUE THAT MOSQUITOS ARE RESPONSIBLE FOR MORE HUMAN DEATHS THAN ANY OTHER ANIMAL.

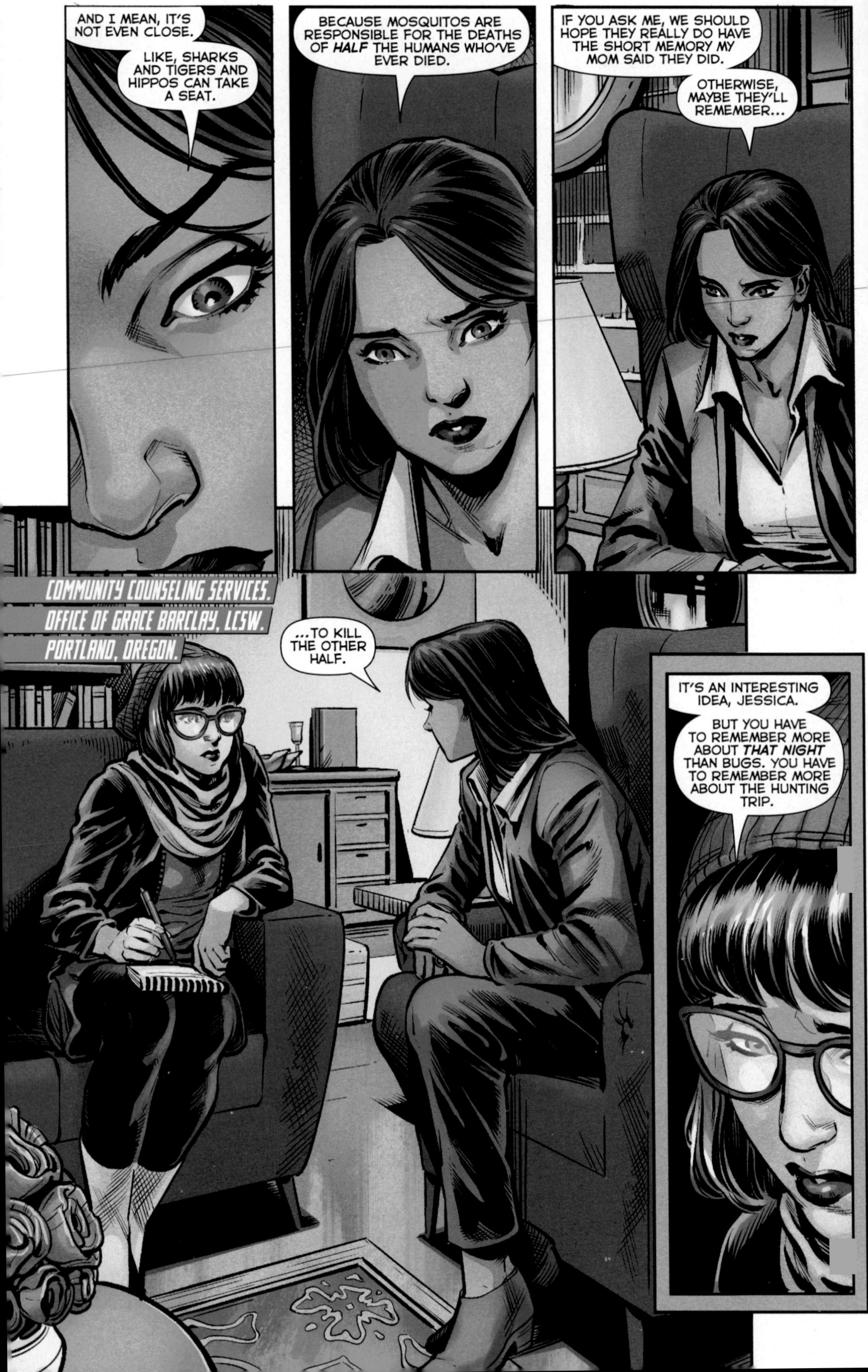
AND I MEAN, IT'S NOT EVEN CLOSE.
LIKE, SHARKS AND TIGERS AND HIPPOS CAN TAKE A SEAT.
BECAUSE MOSQUITOS ARE RESPONSIBLE FOR THE DEATHS OF HALF THE HUMANS WHO'VE EVER DIED.
IF YOU ASK ME, WE SHOULD HOPE THEY REALLY DO HAVE THE SHORT MEMORY MY MOM SAID THEY DID.
OTHERWISE, MAYBE THEY'LL REMEMBER...
COMMUNITY COUNSELING SERVICES.
OFFICE OF GRACE BARCLAY, LCSW.
PORTLAND, OREGON.
...TO KILL THE OTHER HALF.
IT'S AN INTERESTING IDEA, JESSICA.
BUT YOU HAVE TO REMEMBER MORE ABOUT THAT NIGHT THAN BUGS. YOU HAVE TO REMEMBER MORE ABOUT THE HUNTING TRIP.

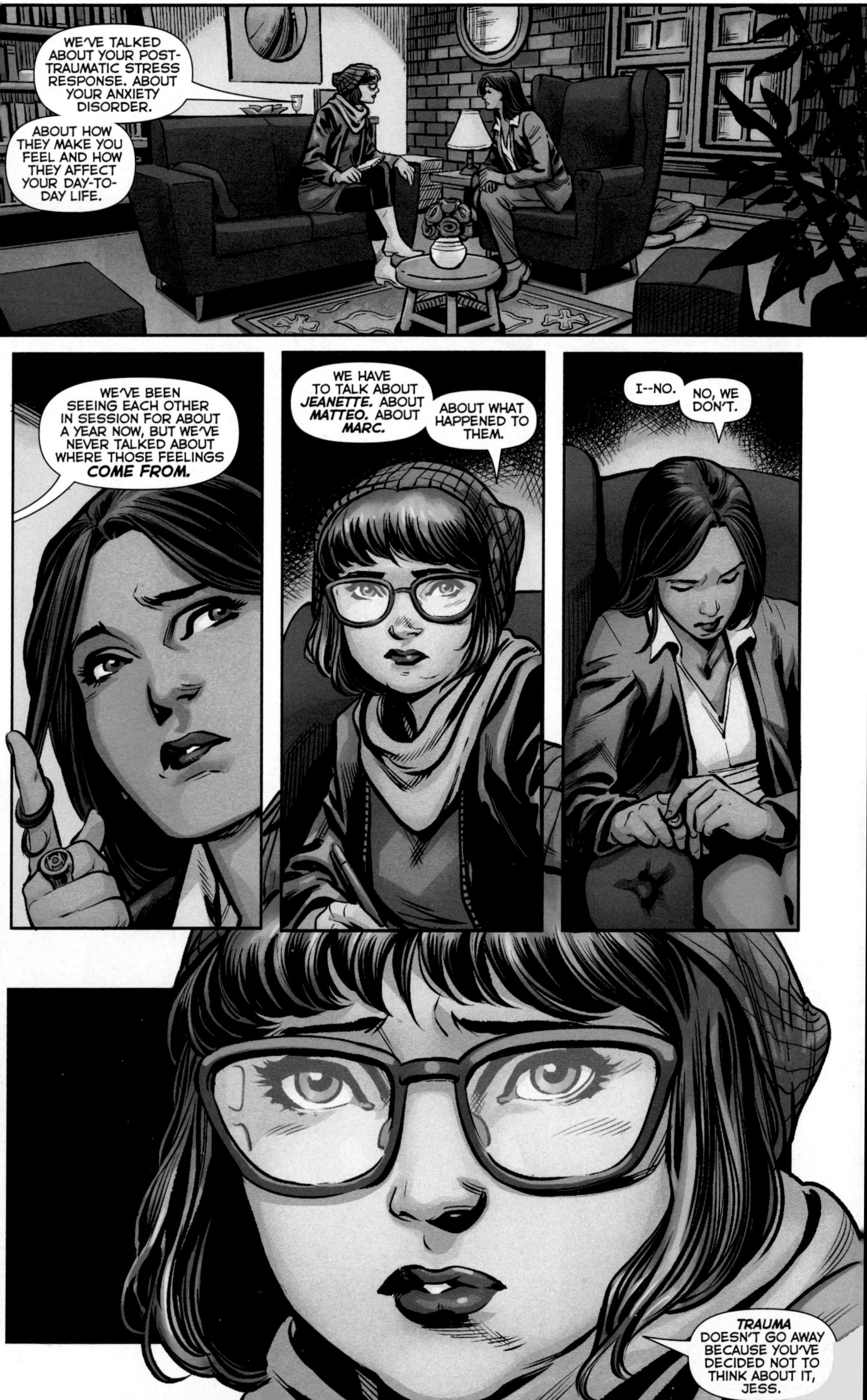

WE'VE TALKED ABOUT YOUR POST-TRAUMATIC STRESS RESPONSE. ABOUT YOUR ANXIETY DISORDER.
ABOUT HOW THEY MAKE YOU FEEL AND HOW THEY AFFECT YOUR DAY-TO-DAY LIFE.
WE'VE BEEN SEEING EACH OTHER IN SESSION FOR ABOUT A YEAR NOW, BUT WE'VE NEVER TALKED ABOUT WHERE THOSE FEELINGS **COME FROM.**
WE HAVE TO TALK ABOUT ***JEANETTE.*** ABOUT ***MATTEO.*** ABOUT ***MARC.***
ABOUT WHAT HAPPENED TO THEM.
I--NO.
NO, WE DON'T.
***TRAUMA*** DOESN'T GO AWAY BECAUSE YOU'VE DECIDED NOT TO THINK ABOUT IT, JESS.

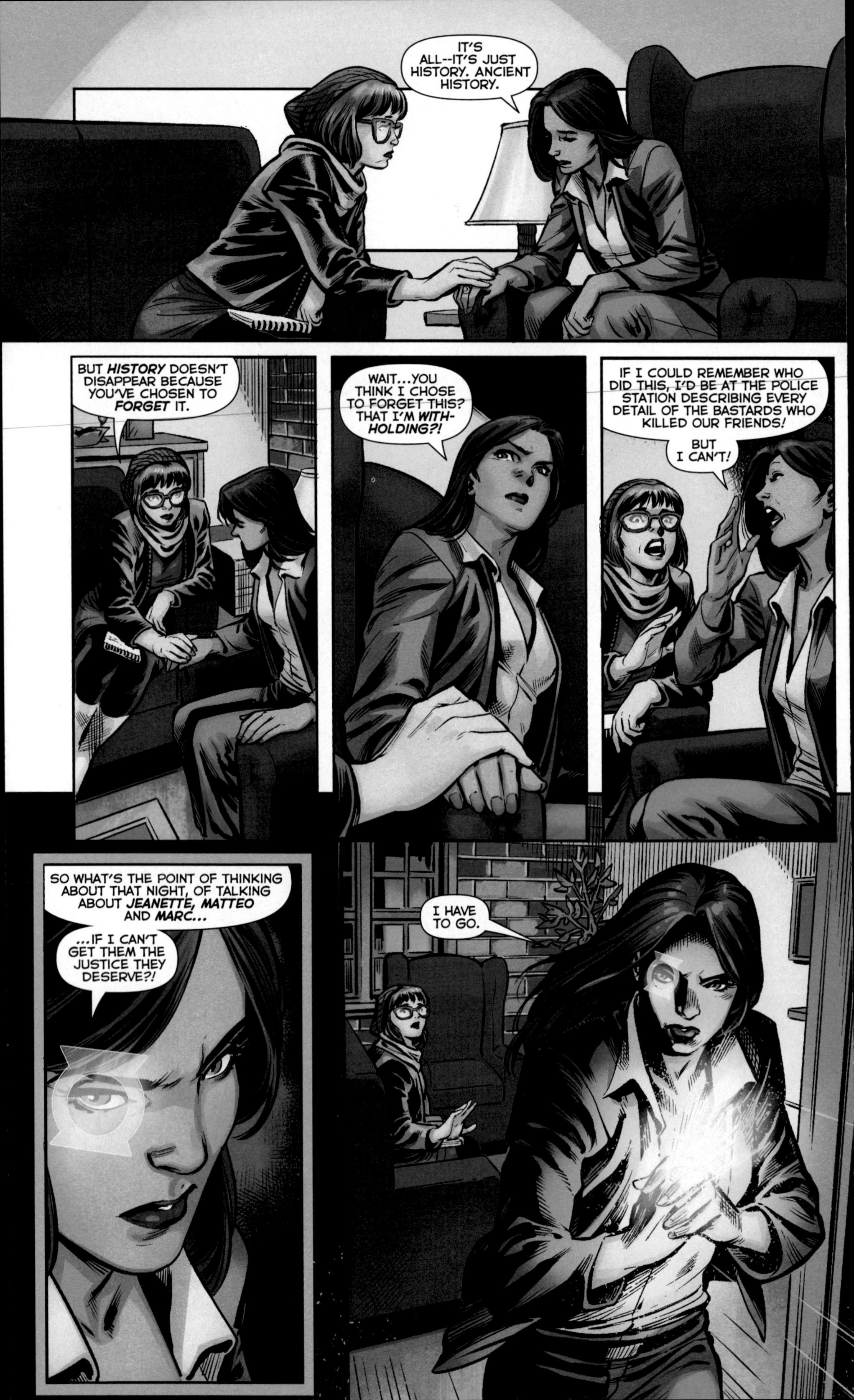
IT'S ALL--IT'S JUST HISTORY. ANCIENT HISTORY.
BUT HISTORY DOESN'T DISAPPEAR BECAUSE YOU'VE CHOSEN TO FORGET IT.
WAIT...YOU THINK I CHOSE TO FORGET THIS? THAT I'M WITH-HOLDING?!
IF I COULD REMEMBER WHO DID THIS, I'D BE AT THE POLICE STATION DESCRIBING EVERY DETAIL OF THE BASTARDS WHO KILLED OUR FRIENDS!
BUT I CAN'T!
SO WHAT'S THE POINT OF THINKING ABOUT THAT NIGHT, OF TALKING ABOUT JEANETTE, MATTEO AND MARC...
...IF I CAN'T GET THEM THE JUSTICE THEY DESERVE?!
I HAVE TO GO.

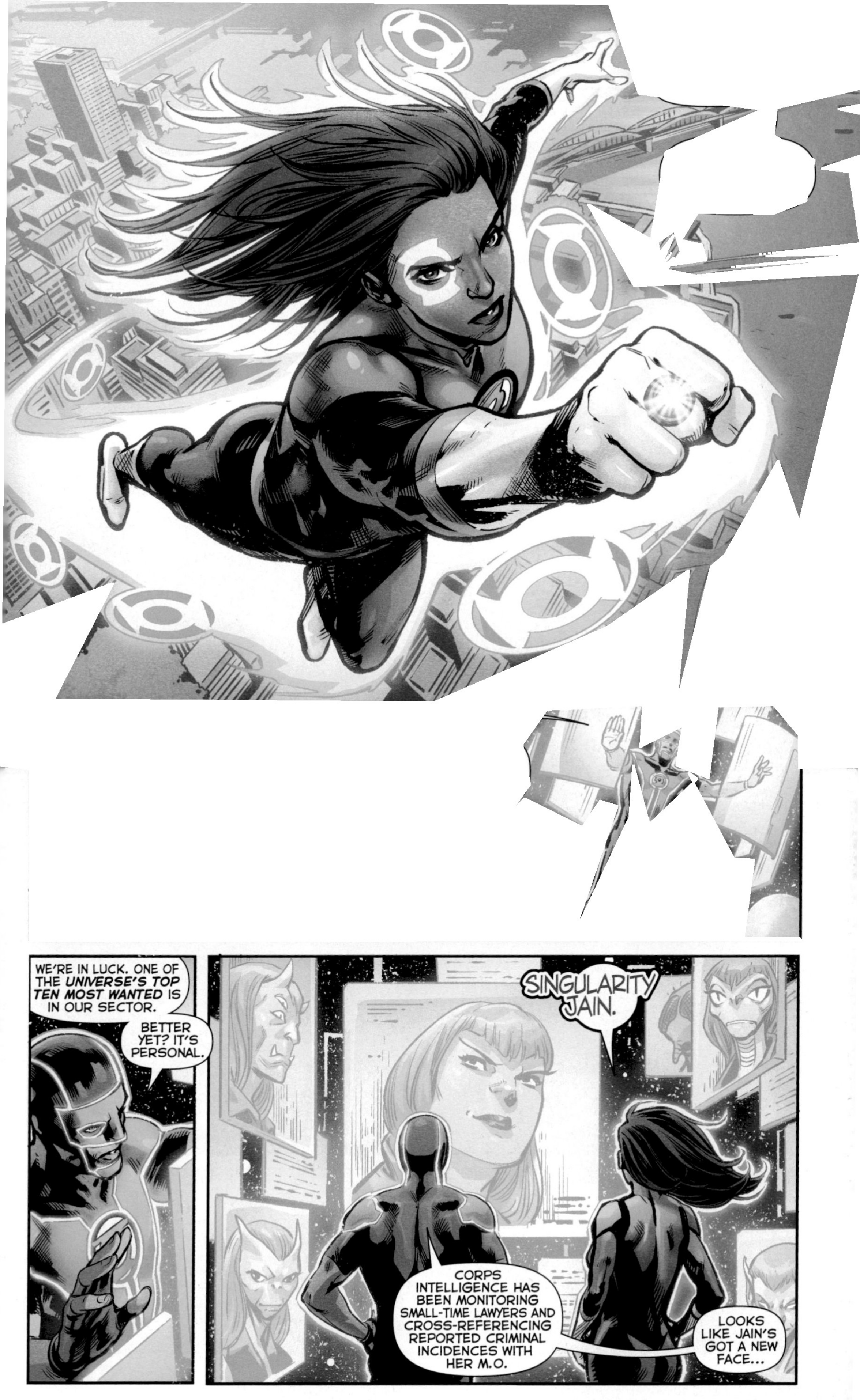
WE'RE IN LUCK. ONE OF THE UNIVERSE'S TOP TEN MOST WANTED IS IN OUR SECTOR.
BETTER YET? IT'S PERSONAL.
SINGULARITY JAIN.
CORPS INTELLIGENCE HAS BEEN MONITORING SMALL-TIME LAWYERS AND CROSS-REFERENCING REPORTED CRIMINAL INCIDENCES WITH HER M.O.
LOOKS LIKE JAIN'S GOT A NEW FACE...

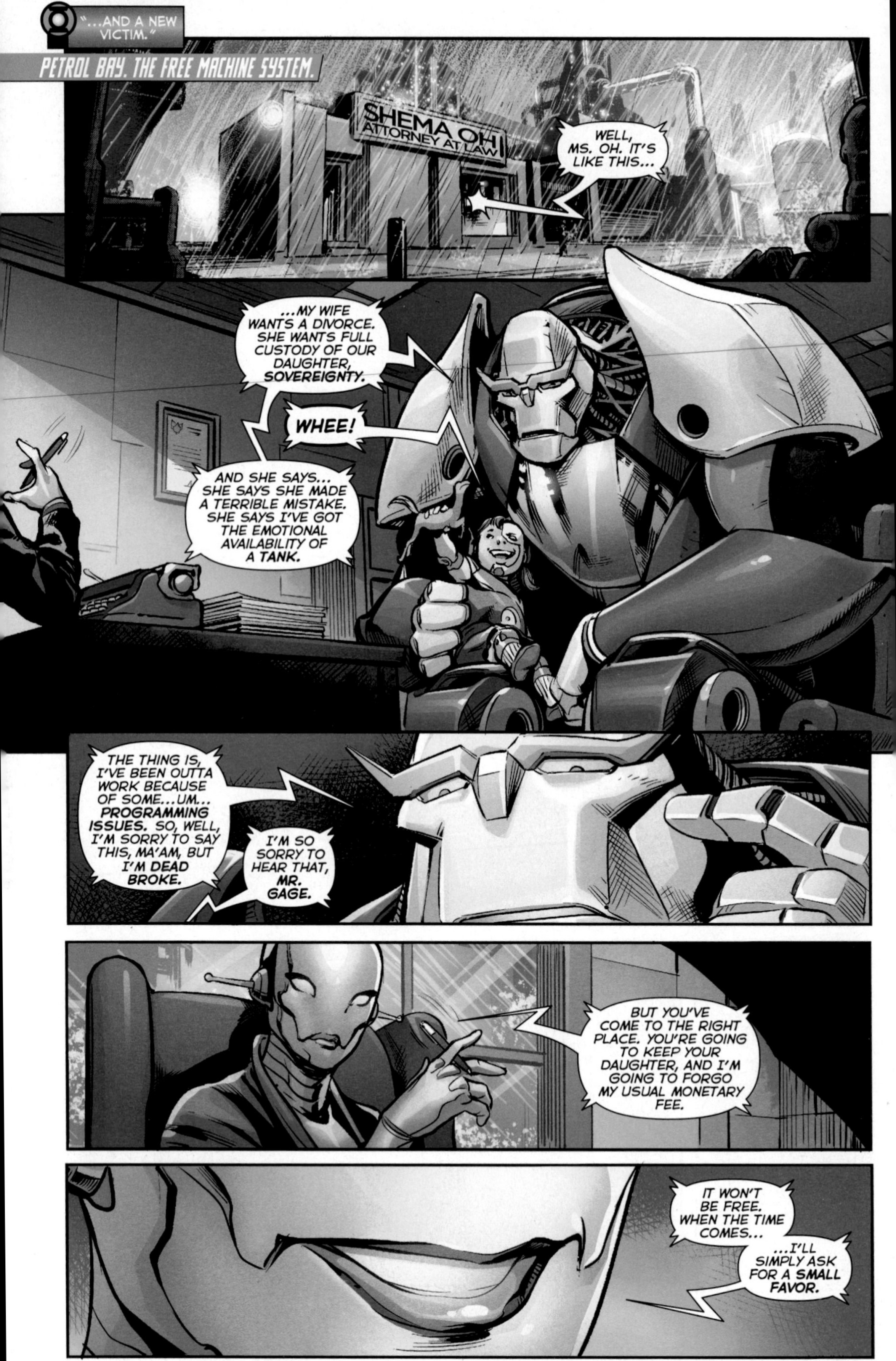
"...AND A NEW VICTIM."
PETROL BAY. THE FREE MACHINE SYSTEM.
SHEMA OH ATTORNEY AT LAW
WELL, MS. OH. IT'S LIKE THIS...
...MY WIFE WANTS A DIVORCE. SHE WANTS FULL CUSTODY OF OUR DAUGHTER, SOVEREIGNTY.
WHEE!
AND SHE SAYS... SHE SAYS SHE MADE A TERRIBLE MISTAKE. SHE SAYS I'VE GOT THE EMOTIONAL AVAILABILITY OF A TANK.
THE THING IS, I'VE BEEN OUTTA WORK BECAUSE OF SOME...UM... PROGRAMMING ISSUES. SO, WELL, I'M SORRY TO SAY THIS, MA'AM, BUT I'M DEAD BROKE.
I'M SO SORRY TO HEAR THAT, MR. GAGE.
BUT YOU'VE COME TO THE RIGHT PLACE. YOU'RE GOING TO KEEP YOUR DAUGHTER, AND I'M GOING TO FORGO MY USUAL MONETARY FEE.
IT WON'T BE FREE. WHEN THE TIME COMES...
...I'LL SIMPLY ASK FOR A SMALL FAVOR.

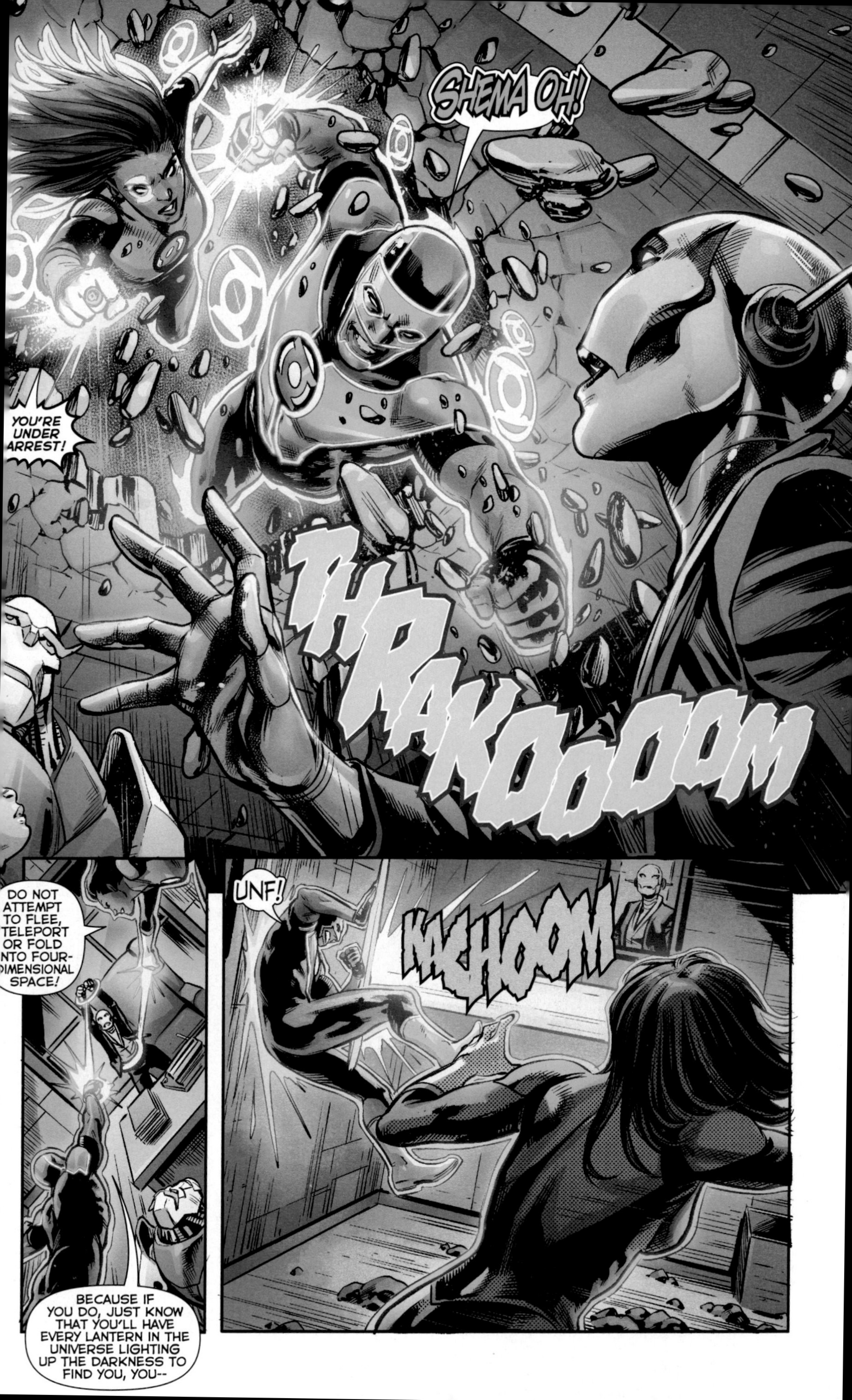
SHEMA OH!
YOU'RE UNDER ARREST!
THRAKOOOOOM
DO NOT ATTEMPT TO FLEE, TELEPORT OR FOLD INTO FOUR-DIMENSIONAL SPACE!
UNF!
KACHOOM
BECAUSE IF YOU DO, JUST KNOW THAT YOU'LL HAVE EVERY LANTERN IN THE UNIVERSE LIGHTING UP THE DARKNESS TO FIND YOU, YOU--

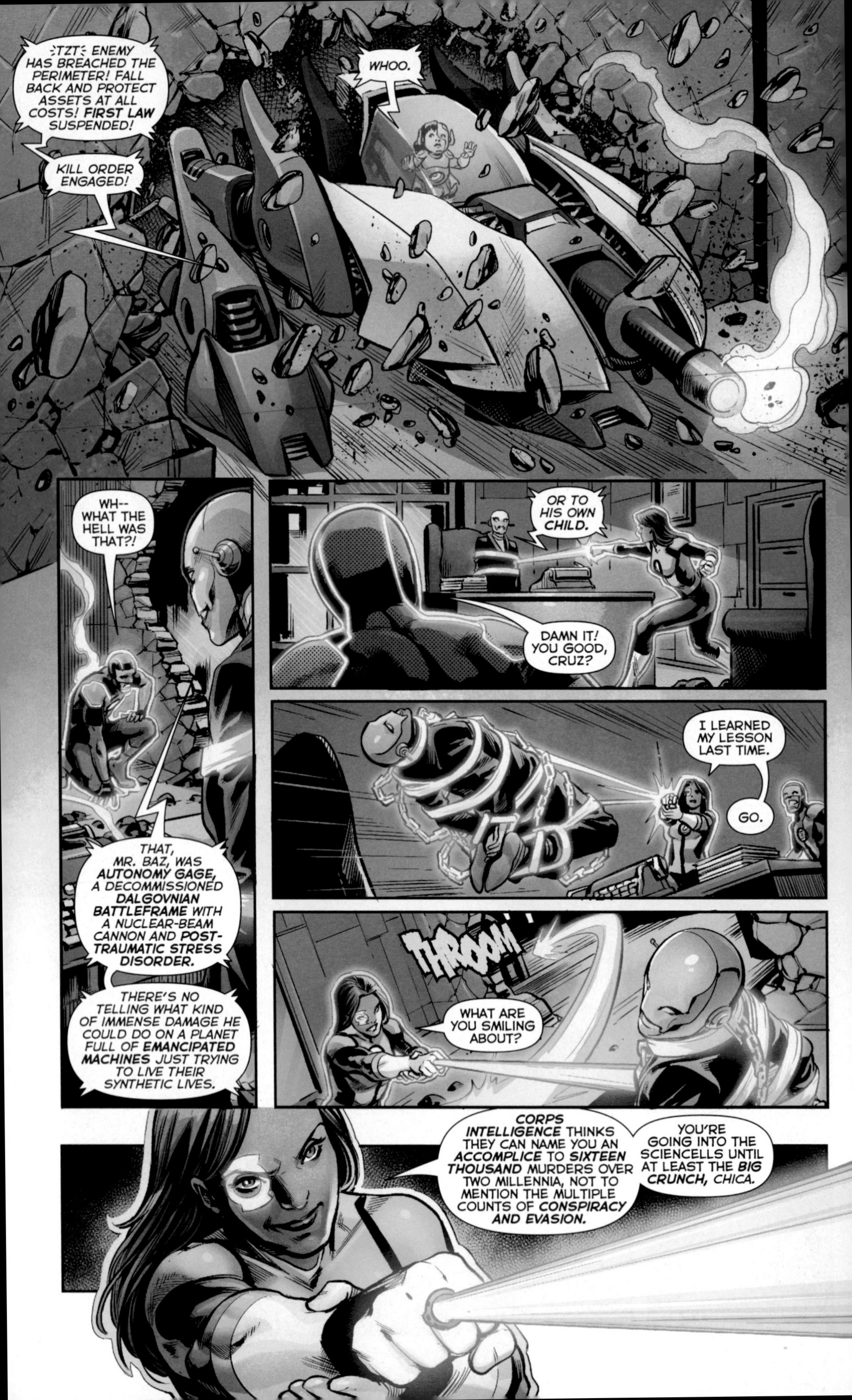

:TZT: ENEMY HAS BREACHED THE PERIMETER! FALL BACK AND PROTECT ASSETS AT ALL COSTS! FIRST LAW SUSPENDED!
KILL ORDER ENGAGED!
WHOO.
WH-- WHAT THE HELL WAS THAT?!
OR TO HIS OWN CHILD.
DAMN IT! YOU GOOD, CRUZ?
THAT, MR. BAZ, WAS AUTONOMY GAGE, A DECOMMISSIONED DALGOVNIAN BATTLEFRAME WITH A NUCLEAR-BEAM CANNON AND POST-TRAUMATIC STRESS DISORDER.
THERE'S NO TELLING WHAT KIND OF IMMENSE DAMAGE HE COULD DO ON A PLANET FULL OF EMANCIPATED MACHINES JUST TRYING TO LIVE THEIR SYNTHETIC LIVES.
I LEARNED MY LESSON LAST TIME.
GO.
THROOM
WHAT ARE YOU SMILING ABOUT?
CORPS INTELLIGENCE THINKS THEY CAN NAME YOU AN ACCOMPLICE TO SIXTEEN THOUSAND MURDERS OVER TWO MILLENNIA, NOT TO MENTION THE MULTIPLE COUNTS OF CONSPIRACY AND EVASION.
YOU'RE GOING INTO THE SCIENCELLS UNTIL AT LEAST THE BIG CRUNCH, CHICA.

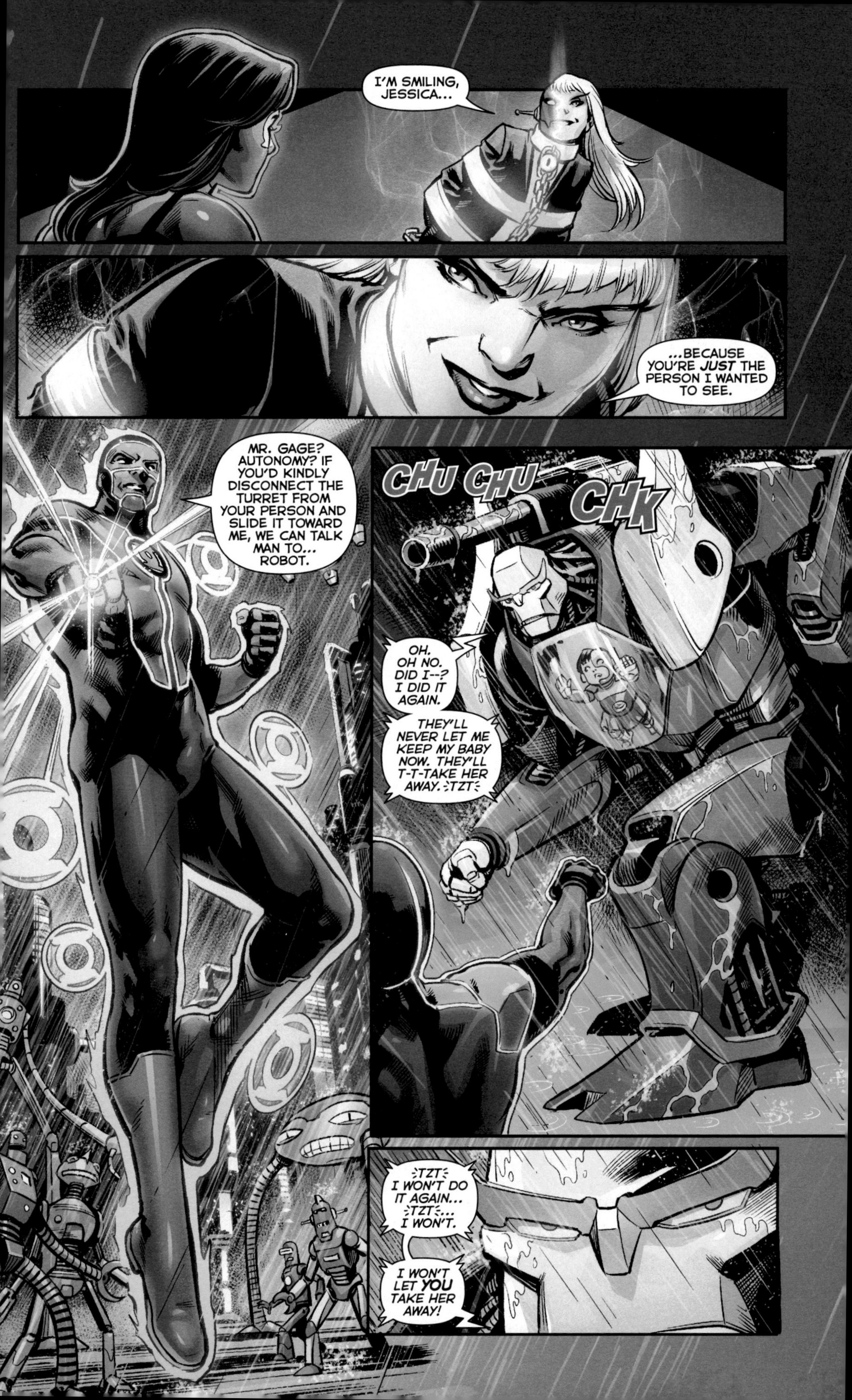
I'M SMILING, JESSICA...
...BECAUSE YOU'RE *JUST* THE PERSON I WANTED TO SEE.
MR. GAGE? AUTONOMY? IF YOU'D KINDLY DISCONNECT THE TURRET FROM YOUR PERSON AND SLIDE IT TOWARD ME, WE CAN TALK MAN TO... ROBOT.
CHU CHU CHK
OH. OH NO. DID I--? I DID IT AGAIN.
THEY'LL NEVER LET ME KEEP MY BABY NOW. THEY'LL T-T-TAKE HER AWAY. TZT
TZT I WON'T DO IT AGAIN... TZT... I WON'T.
I WON'T LET **YOU** TAKE HER AWAY!

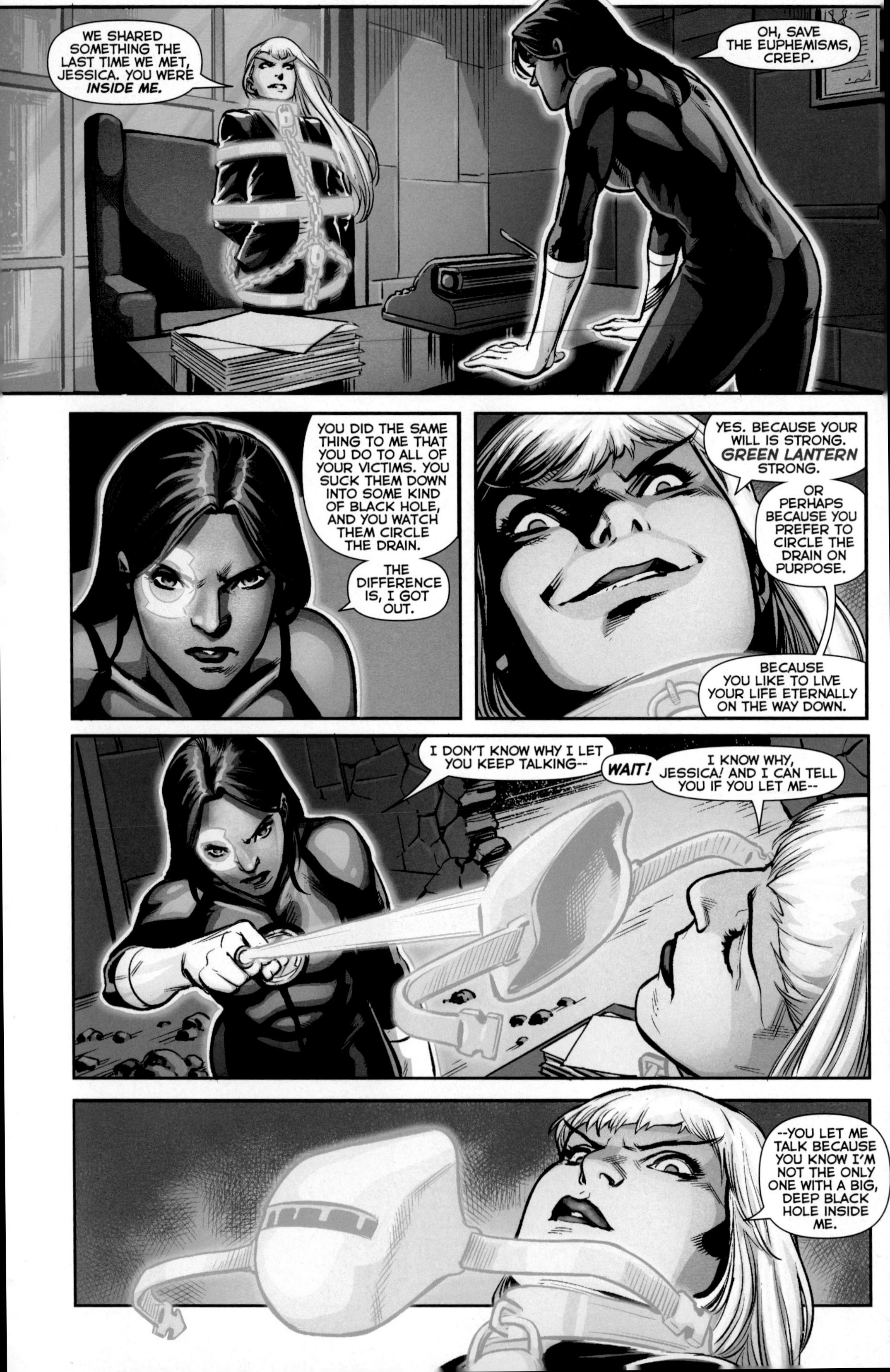
WE SHARED SOMETHING THE LAST TIME WE MET, JESSICA. YOU WERE *INSIDE ME.*
OH, SAVE THE EUPHEMISMS, CREEP.
YOU DID THE SAME THING TO ME THAT YOU DO TO ALL OF YOUR VICTIMS. YOU SUCK THEM DOWN INTO SOME KIND OF BLACK HOLE, AND YOU WATCH THEM CIRCLE THE DRAIN.
THE DIFFERENCE IS, I GOT OUT.
YES. BECAUSE YOUR WILL IS STRONG. *GREEN LANTERN* STRONG.
OR PERHAPS BECAUSE YOU PREFER TO CIRCLE THE DRAIN ON PURPOSE.
BECAUSE YOU LIKE TO LIVE YOUR LIFE ETERNALLY ON THE WAY DOWN.
I DON'T KNOW WHY I LET YOU KEEP TALKING--
*WAIT!*
I KNOW WHY, JESSICA! AND I CAN TELL YOU IF YOU LET ME--
--YOU LET ME TALK BECAUSE YOU KNOW I'M NOT THE ONLY ONE WITH A BIG, DEEP BLACK HOLE INSIDE ME.

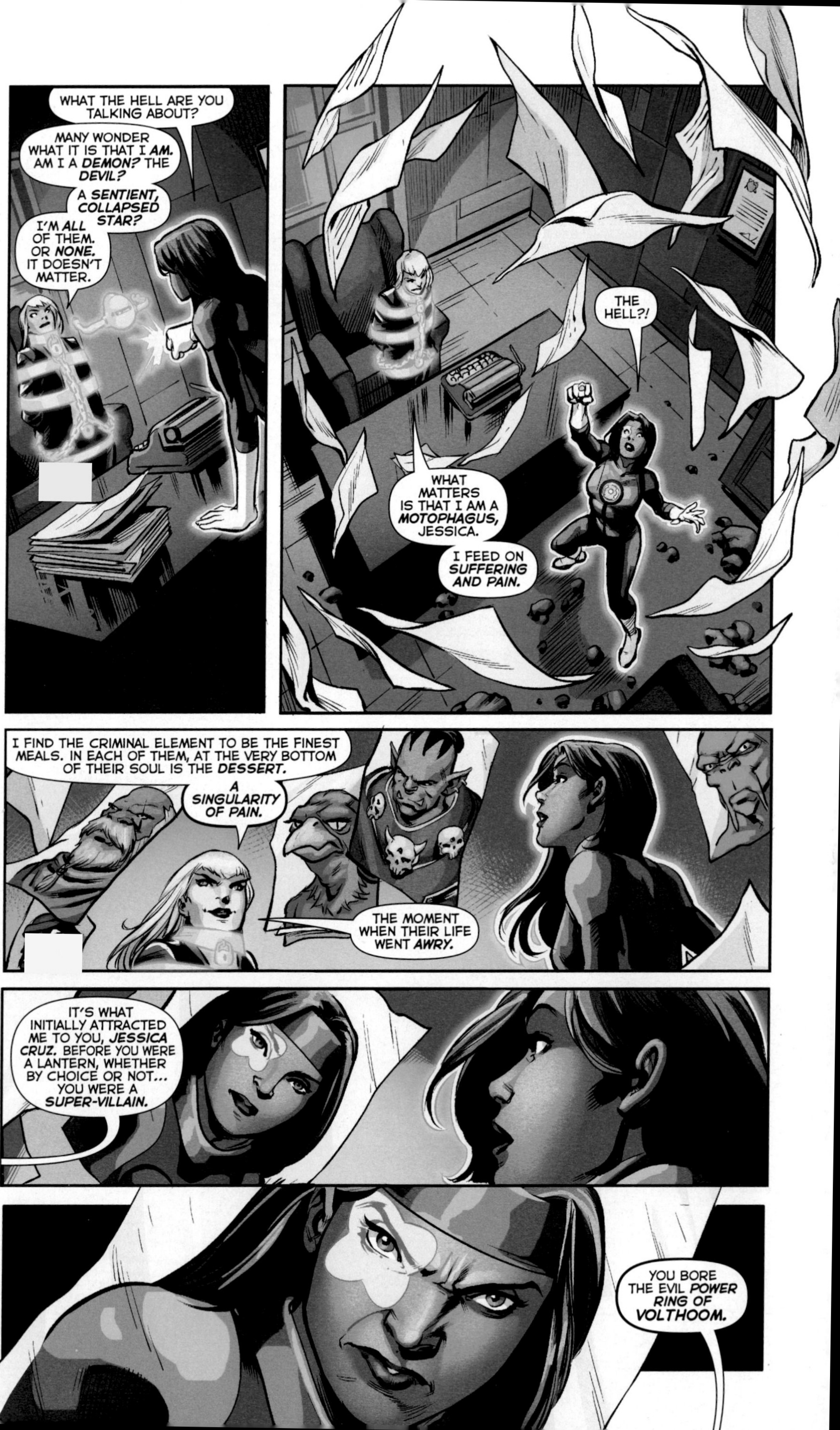

WHAT THE HELL ARE YOU TALKING ABOUT?
MANY WONDER WHAT IT IS THAT I **AM.** AM I A **DEMON?** THE **DEVIL?**
A **SENTIENT, COLLAPSED STAR?**
I'M **ALL** OF THEM. OR **NONE.** IT DOESN'T MATTER.
THE HELL?!
WHAT MATTERS IS THAT I AM A **MOTOPHAGUS,** JESSICA.
I FEED ON **SUFFERING AND PAIN.**
I FIND THE CRIMINAL ELEMENT TO BE THE FINEST MEALS. IN EACH OF THEM, AT THE VERY BOTTOM OF THEIR SOUL IS THE **DESSERT.**
**A SINGULARITY OF PAIN.**
THE MOMENT WHEN THEIR LIFE WENT **AWRY.**
IT'S WHAT INITIALLY ATTRACTED ME TO YOU, **JESSICA CRUZ.** BEFORE YOU WERE A LANTERN, WHETHER BY CHOICE OR NOT... YOU WERE A **SUPER-VILLAIN.**
YOU BORE THE EVIL **POWER RING OF VOLTHOOM.**

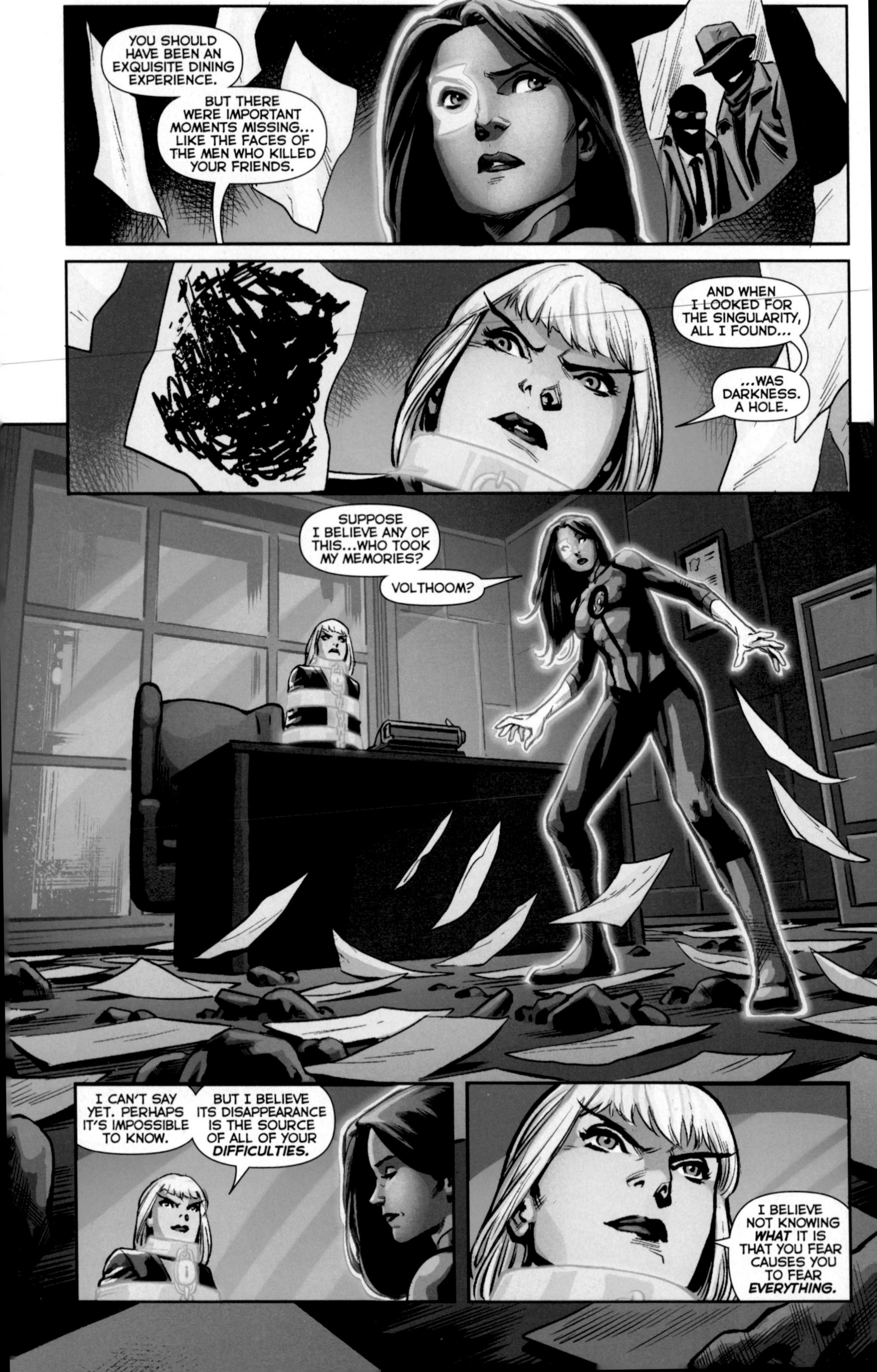

YOU SHOULD HAVE BEEN AN EXQUISITE DINING EXPERIENCE.
BUT THERE WERE IMPORTANT MOMENTS MISSING... LIKE THE FACES OF THE MEN WHO KILLED YOUR FRIENDS.
AND WHEN I LOOKED FOR THE SINGULARITY, ALL I FOUND...
...WAS DARKNESS. A HOLE.
SUPPOSE I BELIEVE ANY OF THIS...WHO TOOK MY MEMORIES?
VOLTHOOM?
I CAN'T SAY YET. PERHAPS IT'S IMPOSSIBLE TO KNOW.
BUT I BELIEVE ITS DISAPPEARANCE IS THE SOURCE OF ALL OF YOUR *DIFFICULTIES.*
I BELIEVE NOT KNOWING *WHAT* IT IS THAT YOU FEAR CAUSES YOU TO FEAR *EVERYTHING.*

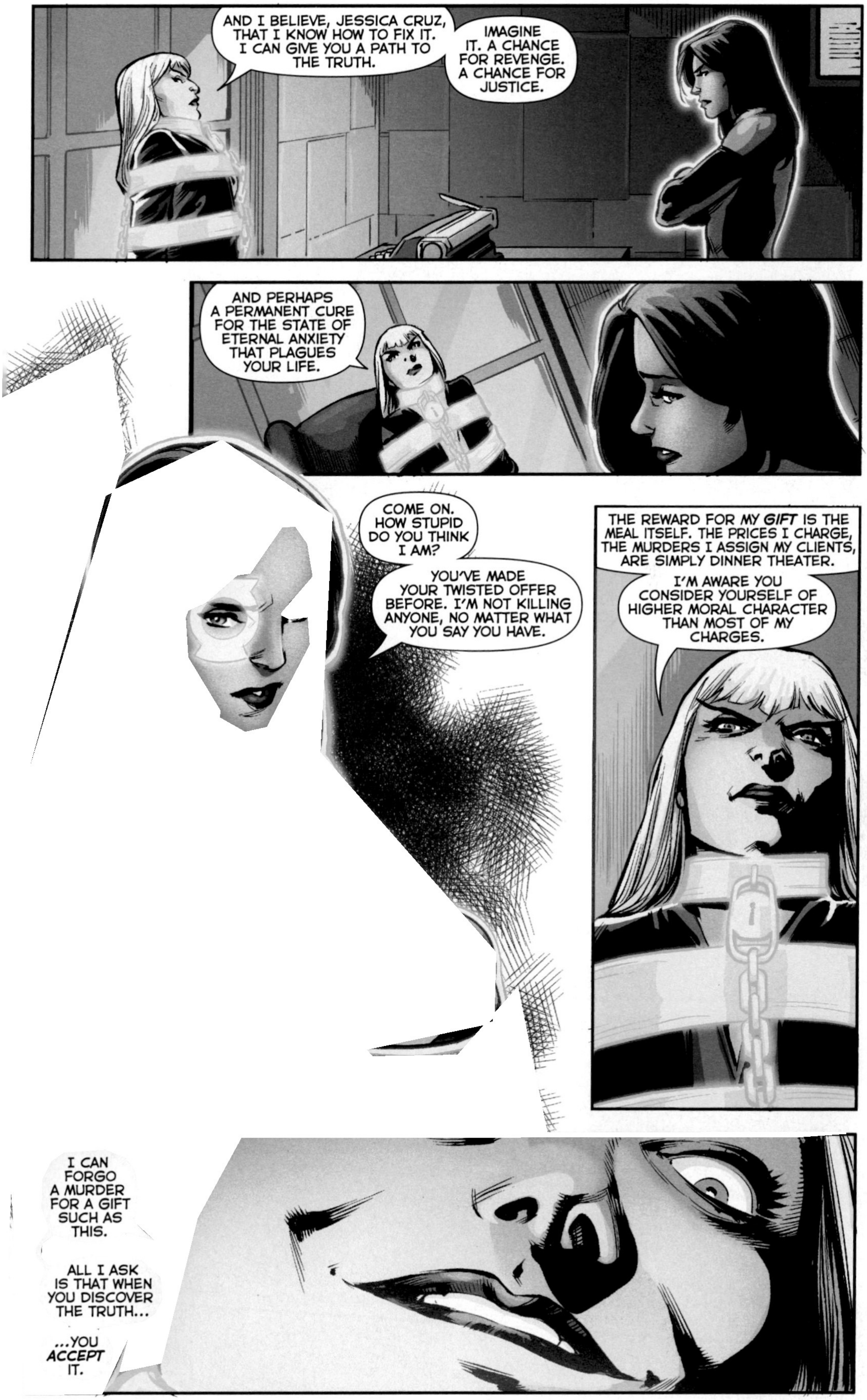

AND I BELIEVE, JESSICA CRUZ, THAT I KNOW HOW TO FIX IT. I CAN GIVE YOU A PATH TO THE TRUTH.
IMAGINE IT. A CHANCE FOR REVENGE. A CHANCE FOR JUSTICE.
AND PERHAPS A PERMANENT CURE FOR THE STATE OF ETERNAL ANXIETY THAT PLAGUES YOUR LIFE.
COME ON. HOW STUPID DO YOU THINK I AM?
YOU'VE MADE YOUR TWISTED OFFER BEFORE. I'M NOT KILLING ANYONE, NO MATTER WHAT YOU SAY YOU HAVE.
THE REWARD FOR MY *GIFT* IS THE MEAL ITSELF. THE PRICES I CHARGE, THE MURDERS I ASSIGN MY CLIENTS, ARE SIMPLY DINNER THEATER.
I'M AWARE YOU CONSIDER YOURSELF OF HIGHER MORAL CHARACTER THAN MOST OF MY CHARGES.
I CAN FORGO A MURDER FOR A GIFT SUCH AS THIS.
ALL I ASK IS THAT WHEN YOU DISCOVER THE TRUTH...
...YOU *ACCEPT* IT.

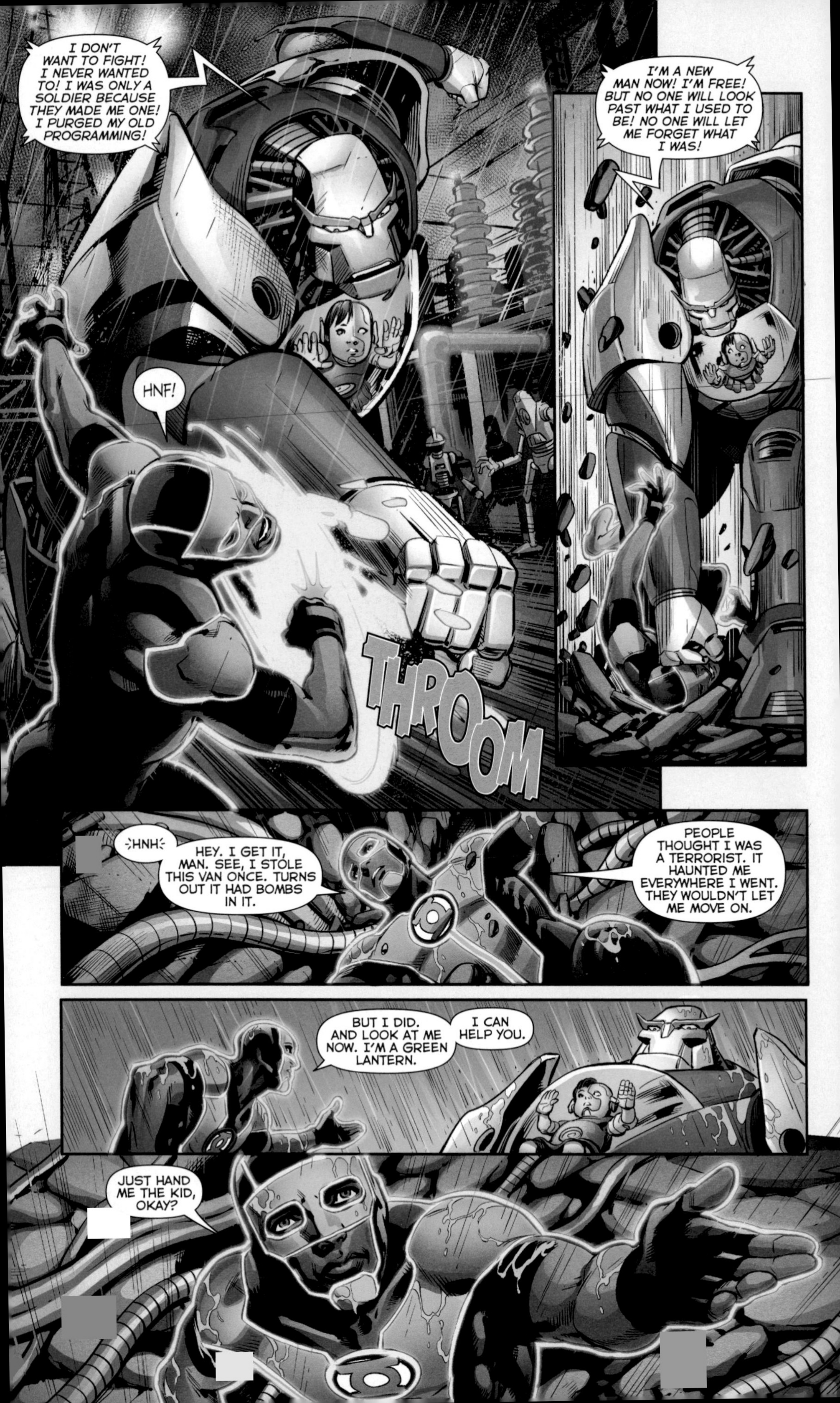
I DON'T WANT TO FIGHT! I NEVER WANTED TO! I WAS ONLY A SOLDIER BECAUSE THEY MADE ME ONE! I PURGED MY OLD PROGRAMMING!
HNF!
THROOM
I'M A NEW MAN NOW! I'M FREE! BUT NO ONE WILL LOOK PAST WHAT I USED TO BE! NO ONE WILL LET ME FORGET WHAT I WAS!
HNH
HEY. I GET IT, MAN. SEE, I STOLE THIS VAN ONCE. TURNS OUT IT HAD BOMBS IN IT.
PEOPLE THOUGHT I WAS A TERRORIST. IT HAUNTED ME EVERYWHERE I WENT. THEY WOULDN'T LET ME MOVE ON.
BUT I DID. AND LOOK AT ME NOW. I'M A GREEN LANTERN.
I CAN HELP YOU.
JUST HAND ME THE KID, OKAY?

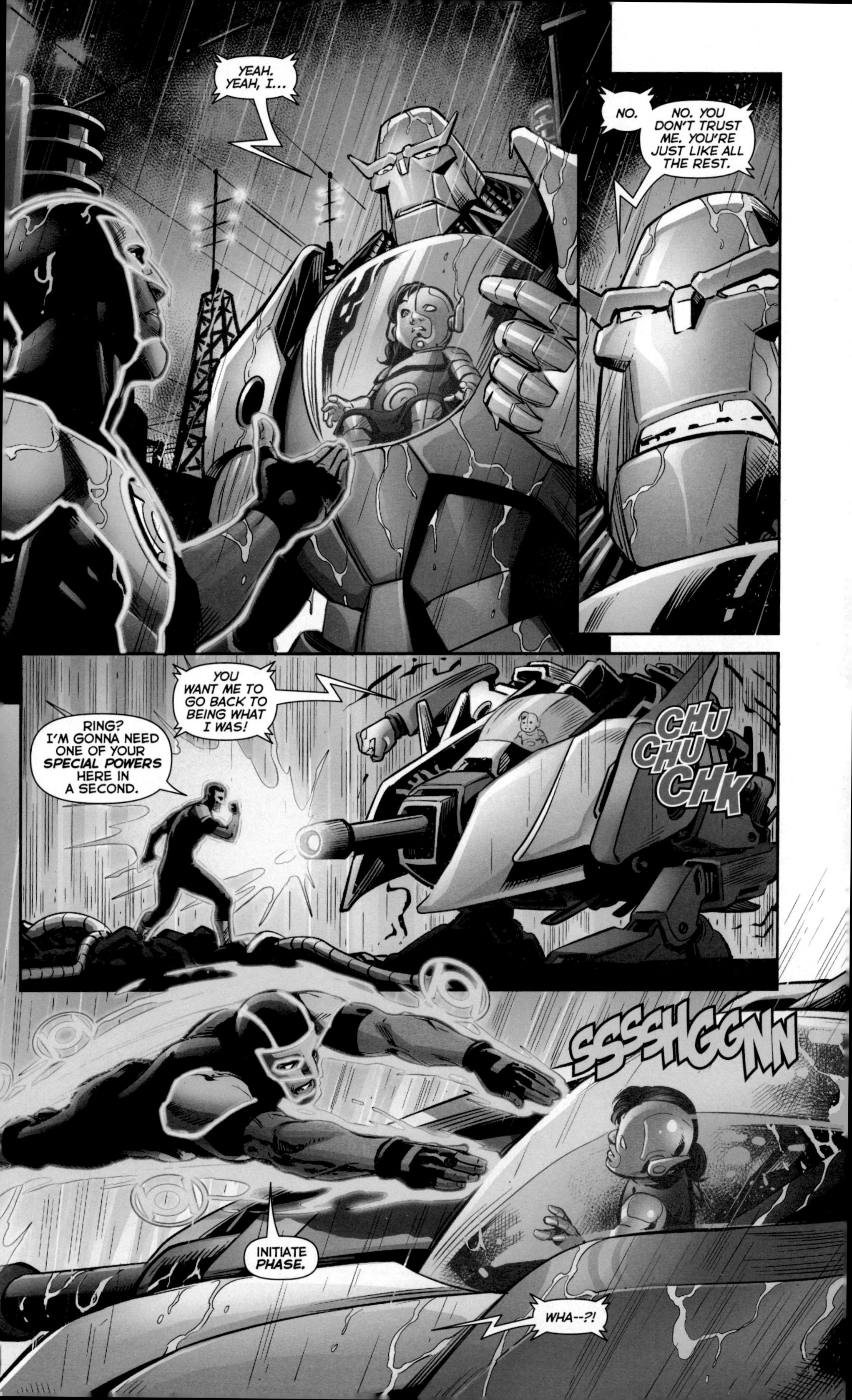
YEAH. YEAH, I...
NO.
NO. YOU DON'T TRUST ME. YOU'RE JUST LIKE ALL THE REST.
YOU WANT ME TO GO BACK TO BEING WHAT I WAS!
RING? I'M GONNA NEED ONE OF YOUR SPECIAL POWERS HERE IN A SECOND.
CHU CHU CHK
SSSSHGGNN
INITIATE PHASE.
WHA--?!

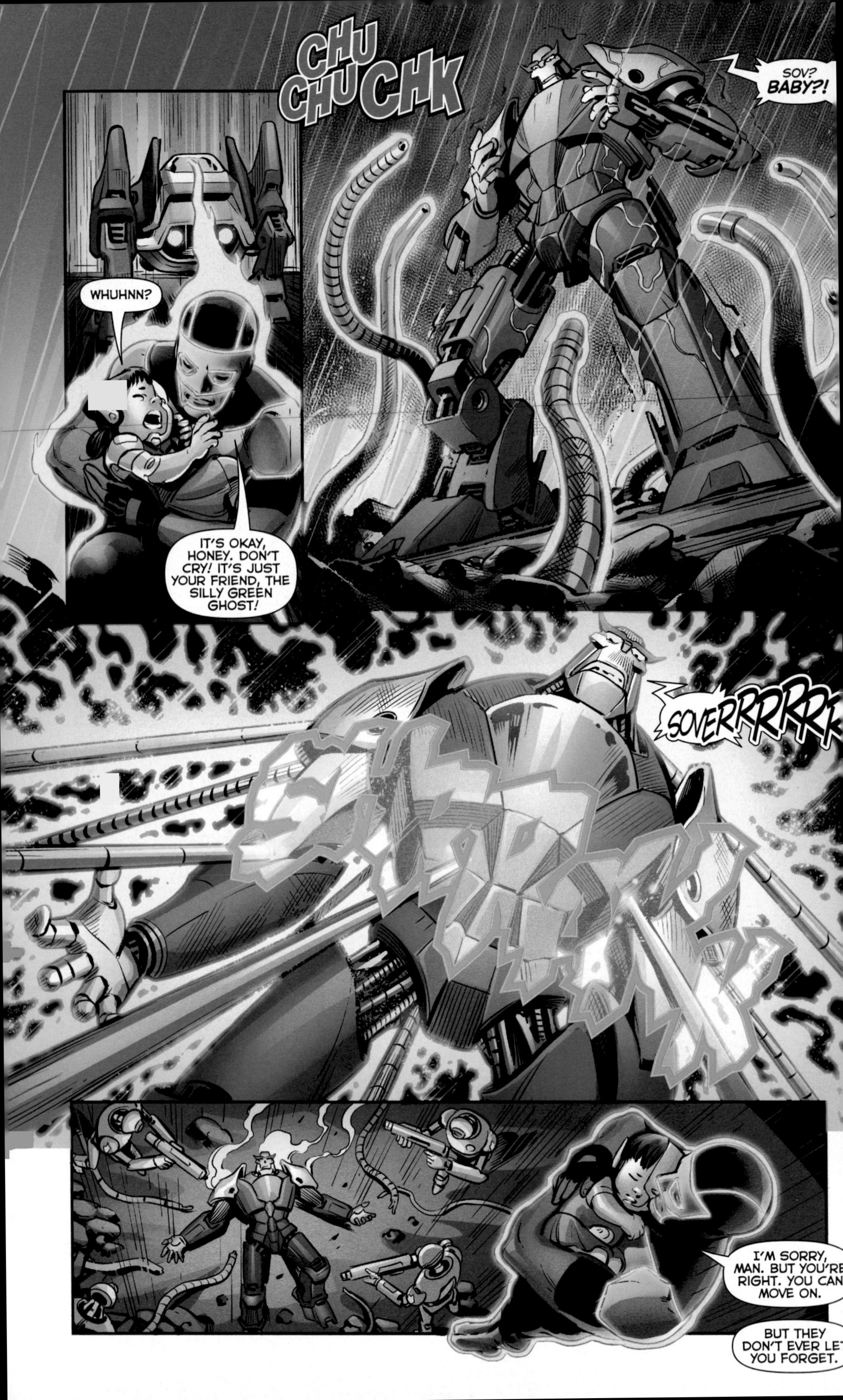
CHU CHU CHK
SOV? BABY?!
WHUHNN?
IT'S OKAY, HONEY. DON'T CRY! IT'S JUST YOUR FRIEND, THE SILLY GREEN GHOST!
SOVERRRRR
I'M SORRY, MAN. BUT YOU'RE RIGHT. YOU CAN MOVE ON.
BUT THEY DON'T EVER LET YOU FORGET.

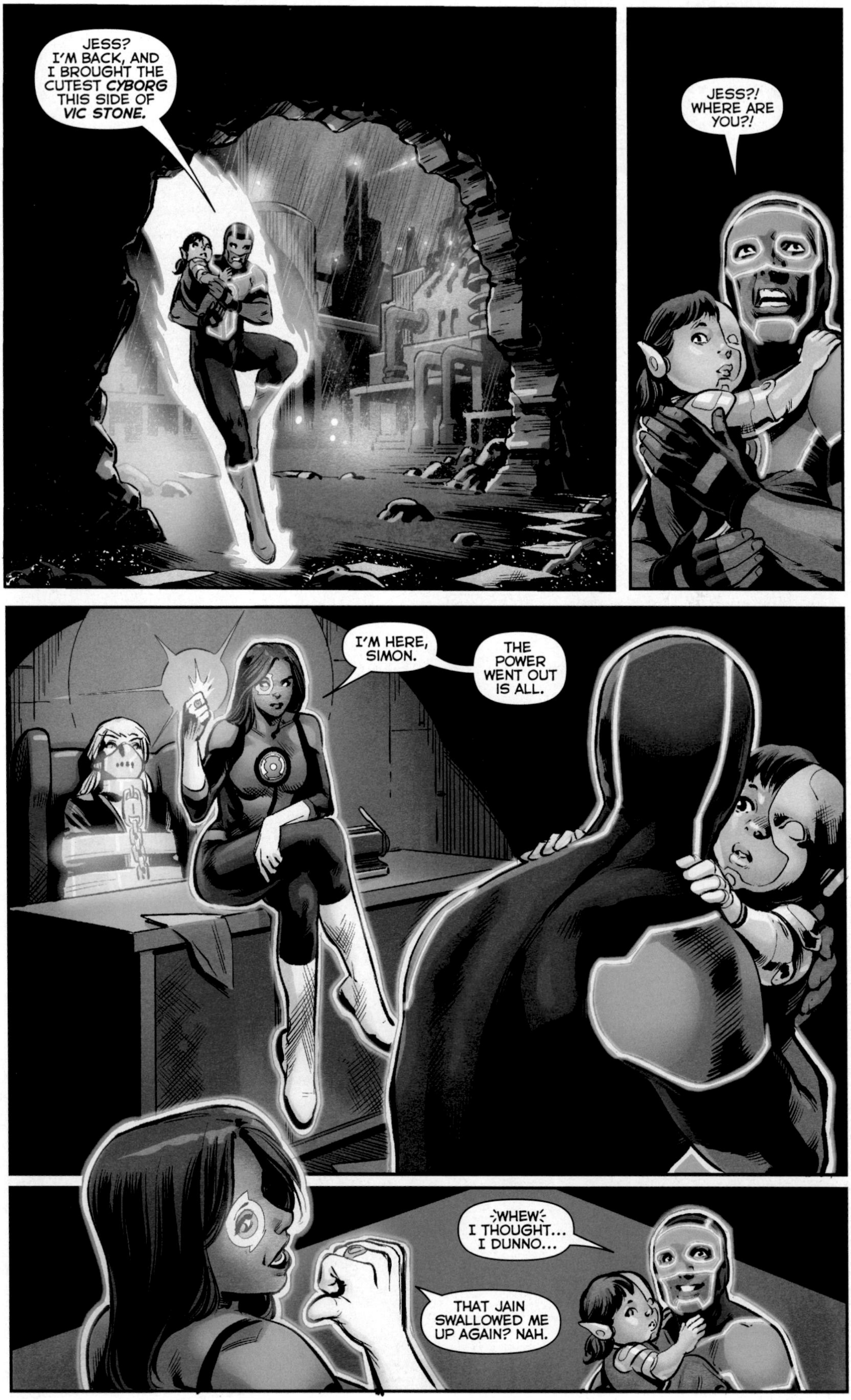
JESS? I'M BACK, AND I BROUGHT THE CUTEST *CYBORG* THIS SIDE OF *VIC STONE.*
JESS?! WHERE ARE YOU?!
I'M HERE, SIMON.
THE POWER WENT OUT IS ALL.
*WHEW* I THOUGHT... I DUNNO...
THAT JAIN SWALLOWED ME UP AGAIN? NAH.

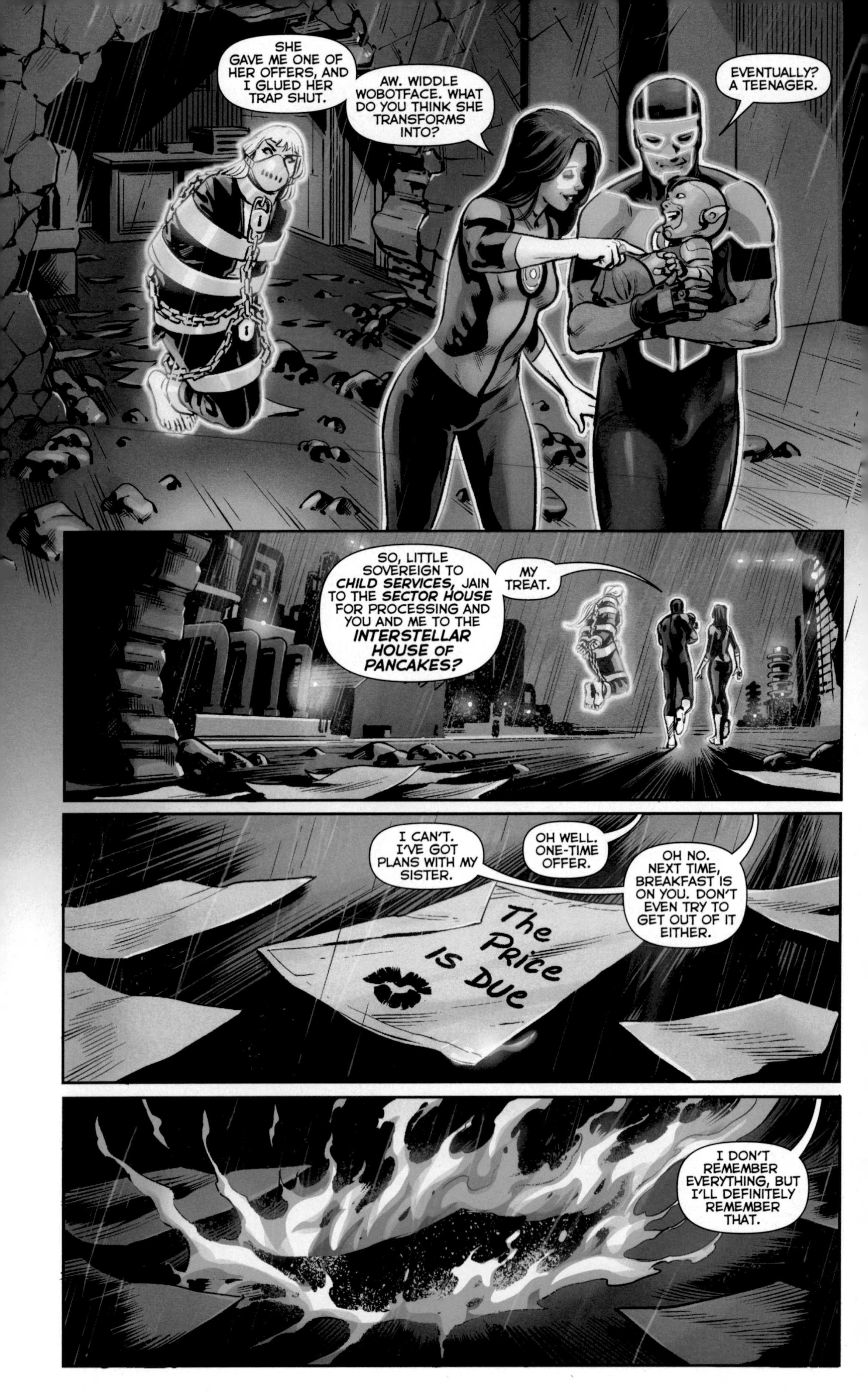
SHE GAVE ME ONE OF HER OFFERS, AND I GLUED HER TRAP SHUT.
AW. WIDDLE WOBOTFACE. WHAT DO YOU THINK SHE TRANSFORMS INTO?
EVENTUALLY? A TEENAGER.
SO, LITTLE SOVEREIGN TO CHILD SERVICES, JAIN TO THE SECTOR HOUSE FOR PROCESSING AND YOU AND ME TO THE INTERSTELLAR HOUSE OF PANCAKES?
MY TREAT.
I CAN'T. I'VE GOT PLANS WITH MY SISTER.
OH WELL. ONE-TIME OFFER.
OH NO. NEXT TIME, BREAKFAST IS ON YOU. DON'T EVEN TRY TO GET OUT OF IT EITHER.
The Price is Due
I DON'T REMEMBER EVERYTHING, BUT I'LL DEFINITELY REMEMBER THAT.

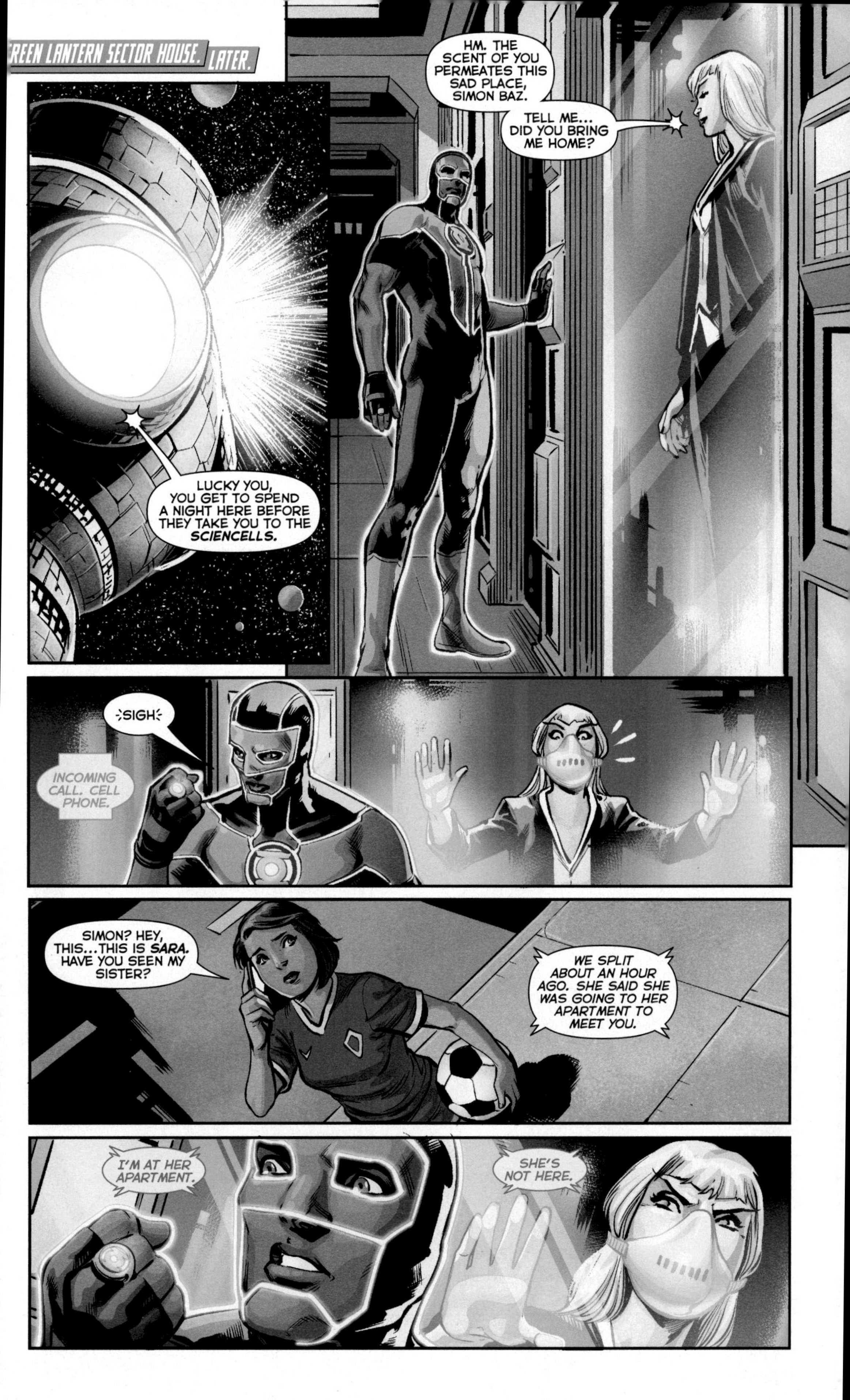
GREEN LANTERN SECTOR HOUSE. LATER.
HM. THE SCENT OF YOU PERMEATES THIS SAD PLACE, SIMON BAZ.
TELL ME... DID YOU BRING ME HOME?
LUCKY YOU, YOU GET TO SPEND A NIGHT HERE BEFORE THEY TAKE YOU TO THE SCIENCELLS.
SIGH
INCOMING CALL. CELL PHONE.
SIMON? HEY, THIS...THIS IS SARA. HAVE YOU SEEN MY SISTER?
WE SPLIT ABOUT AN HOUR AGO. SHE SAID SHE WAS GOING TO HER APARTMENT TO MEET YOU.
I'M AT HER APARTMENT.
SHE'S NOT HERE.

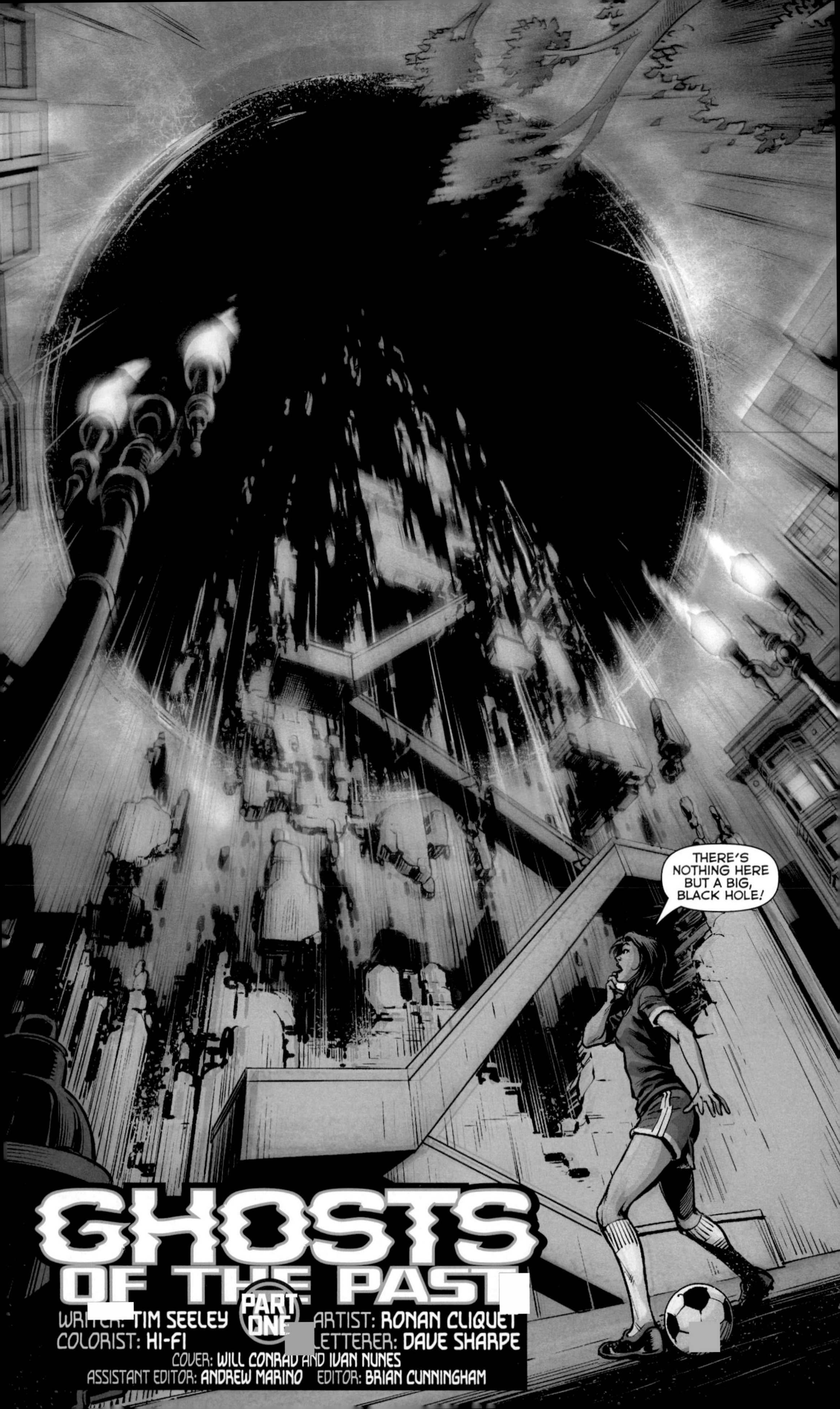
THERE'S NOTHING HERE BUT A BIG, BLACK HOLE!
GHOSTS OF THE PAST
PART ONE
WRITER: TIM SEELEY
ARTIST: RONAN CLIQUET
COLORIST: HI-FI
LETTERER: DAVE SHARPE
COVER: WILL CONRAD AND IVAN NUNES
ASSISTANT EDITOR: ANDREW MARINO
EDITOR: BRIAN CUNNINGHAM

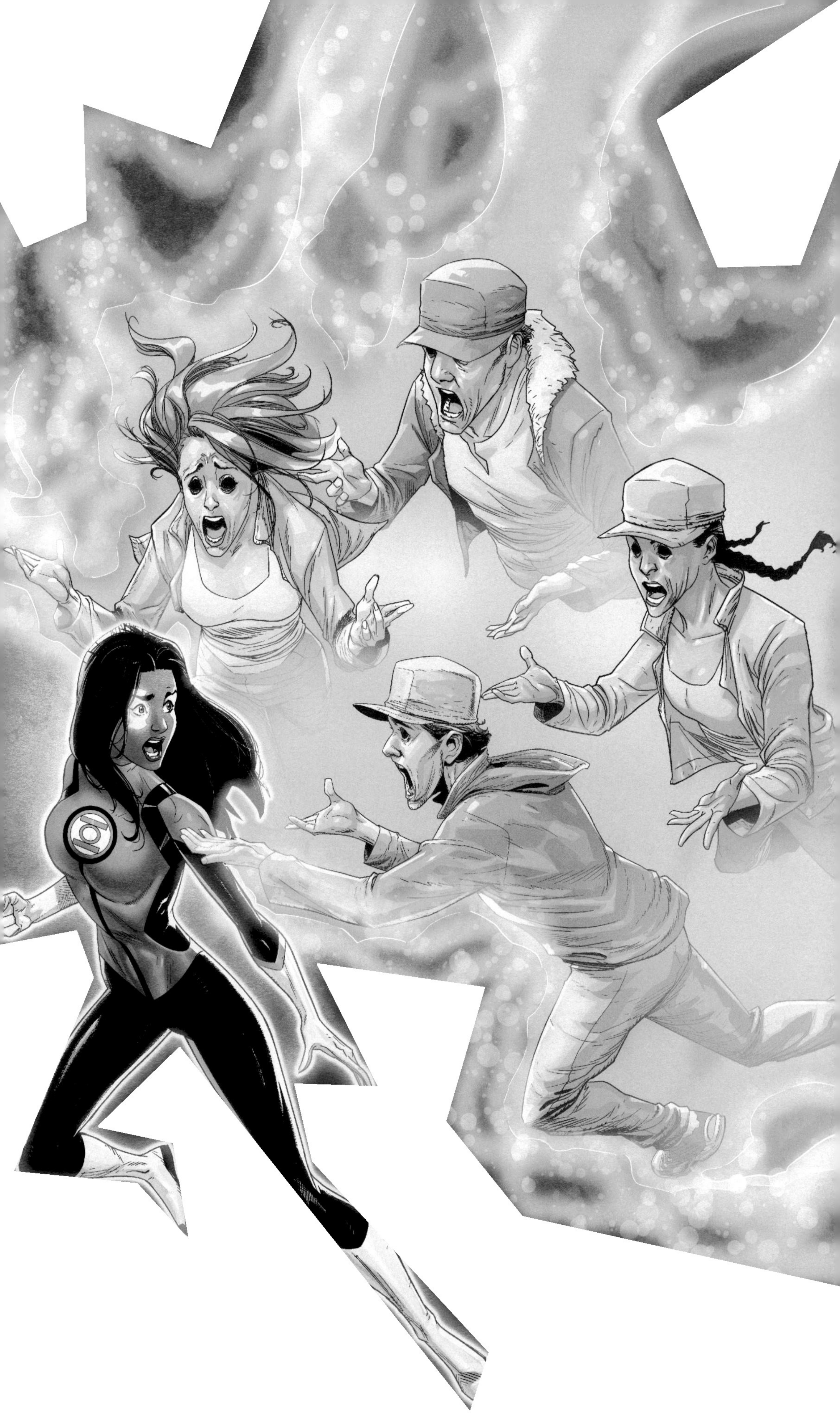

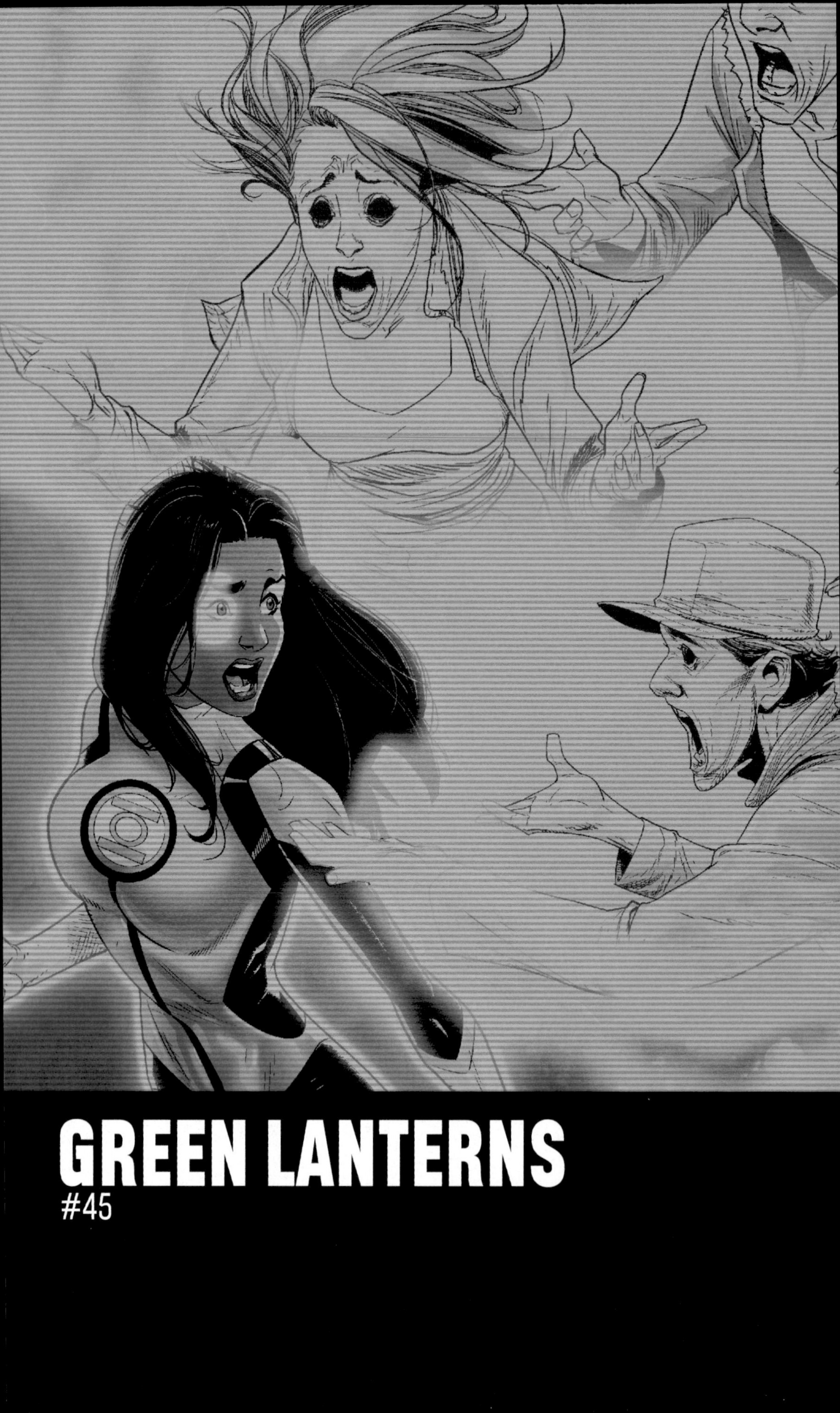

# GREEN LANTERNS
#45

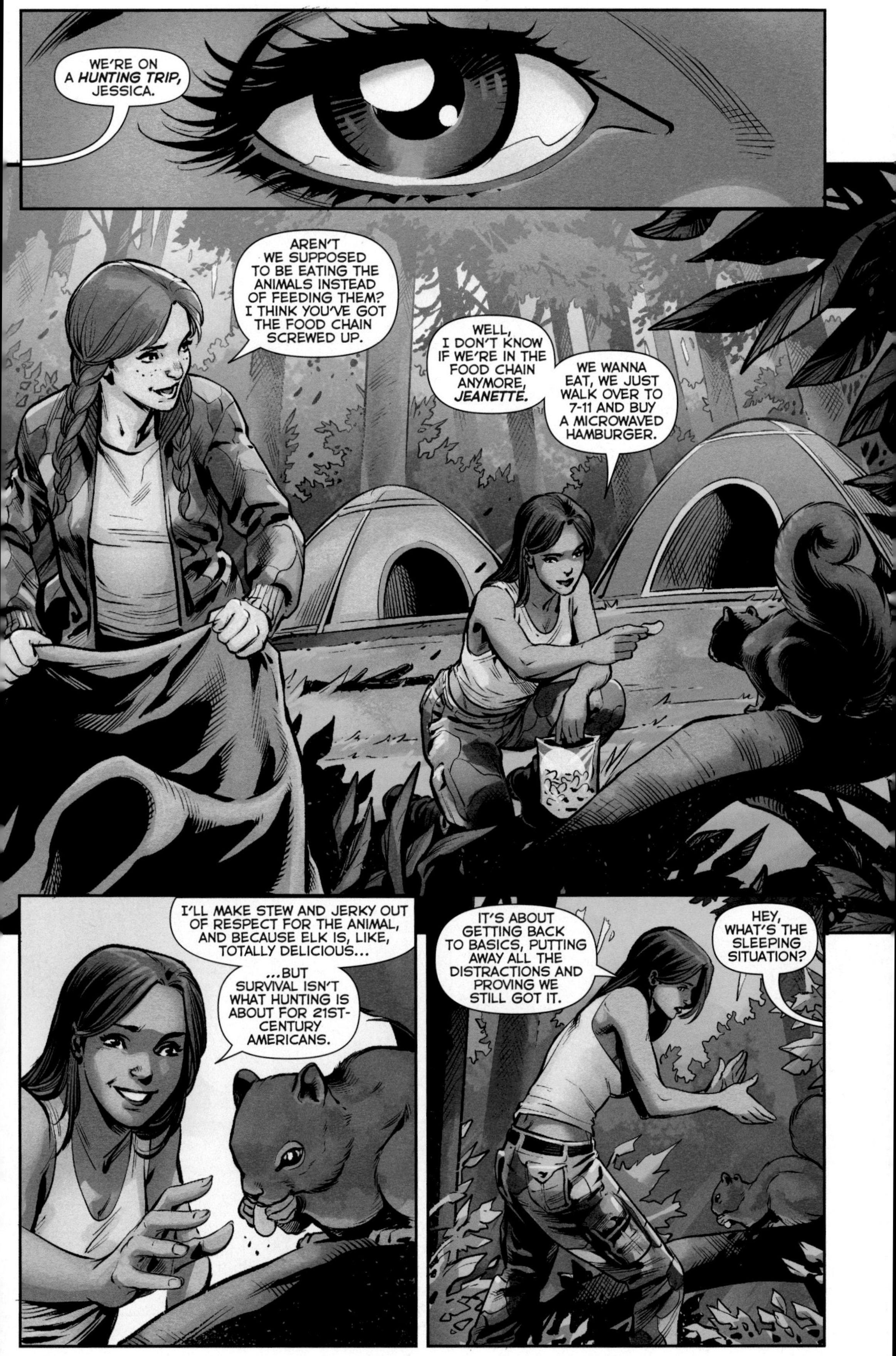
WE'RE ON A *HUNTING TRIP,* JESSICA.
AREN'T WE SUPPOSED TO BE EATING THE ANIMALS INSTEAD OF FEEDING THEM? I THINK YOU'VE GOT THE FOOD CHAIN SCREWED UP.
WELL, I DON'T KNOW IF WE'RE IN THE FOOD CHAIN ANYMORE, *JEANETTE.*
WE WANNA EAT, WE JUST WALK OVER TO 7-11 AND BUY A MICROWAVED HAMBURGER.
I'LL MAKE STEW AND JERKY OUT OF RESPECT FOR THE ANIMAL, AND BECAUSE ELK IS, LIKE, TOTALLY DELICIOUS...
...BUT SURVIVAL ISN'T WHAT HUNTING IS ABOUT FOR 21ST-CENTURY AMERICANS.
IT'S ABOUT GETTING BACK TO BASICS, PUTTING AWAY ALL THE DISTRACTIONS AND PROVING WE STILL GOT IT.
HEY, WHAT'S THE SLEEPING SITUATION?

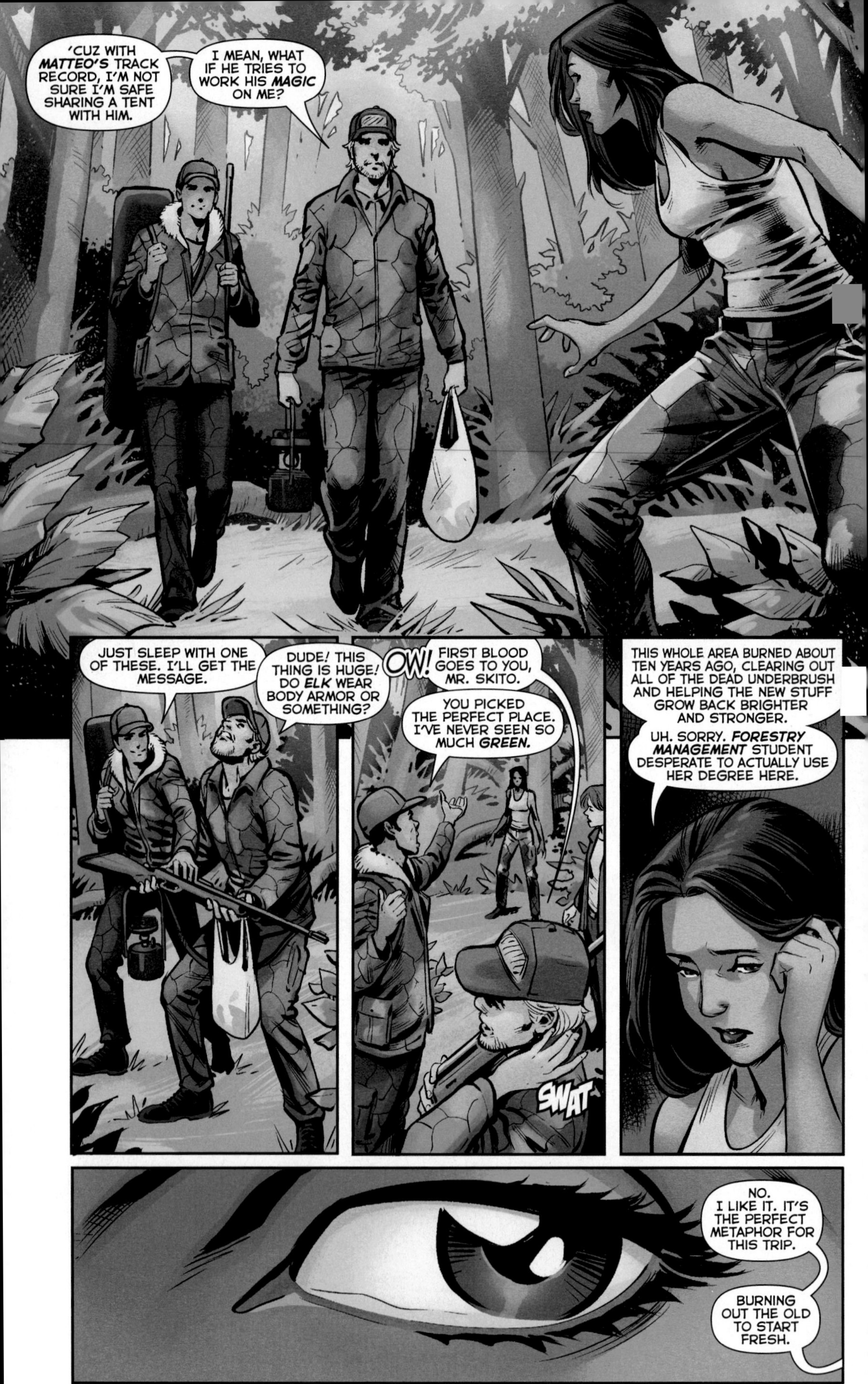
'CUZ WITH MATTEO'S TRACK RECORD, I'M NOT SURE I'M SAFE SHARING A TENT WITH HIM.
I MEAN, WHAT IF HE TRIES TO WORK HIS MAGIC ON ME?
JUST SLEEP WITH ONE OF THESE. I'LL GET THE MESSAGE.
DUDE! THIS THING IS HUGE! DO ELK WEAR BODY ARMOR OR SOMETHING?
OW!
FIRST BLOOD GOES TO YOU, MR. SKITO.
YOU PICKED THE PERFECT PLACE. I'VE NEVER SEEN SO MUCH GREEN.
SWAT
THIS WHOLE AREA BURNED ABOUT TEN YEARS AGO, CLEARING OUT ALL OF THE DEAD UNDERBRUSH AND HELPING THE NEW STUFF GROW BACK BRIGHTER AND STRONGER.
UH. SORRY. FORESTRY MANAGEMENT STUDENT DESPERATE TO ACTUALLY USE HER DEGREE HERE.
NO. I LIKE IT. IT'S THE PERFECT METAPHOR FOR THIS TRIP.
BURNING OUT THE OLD TO START FRESH.

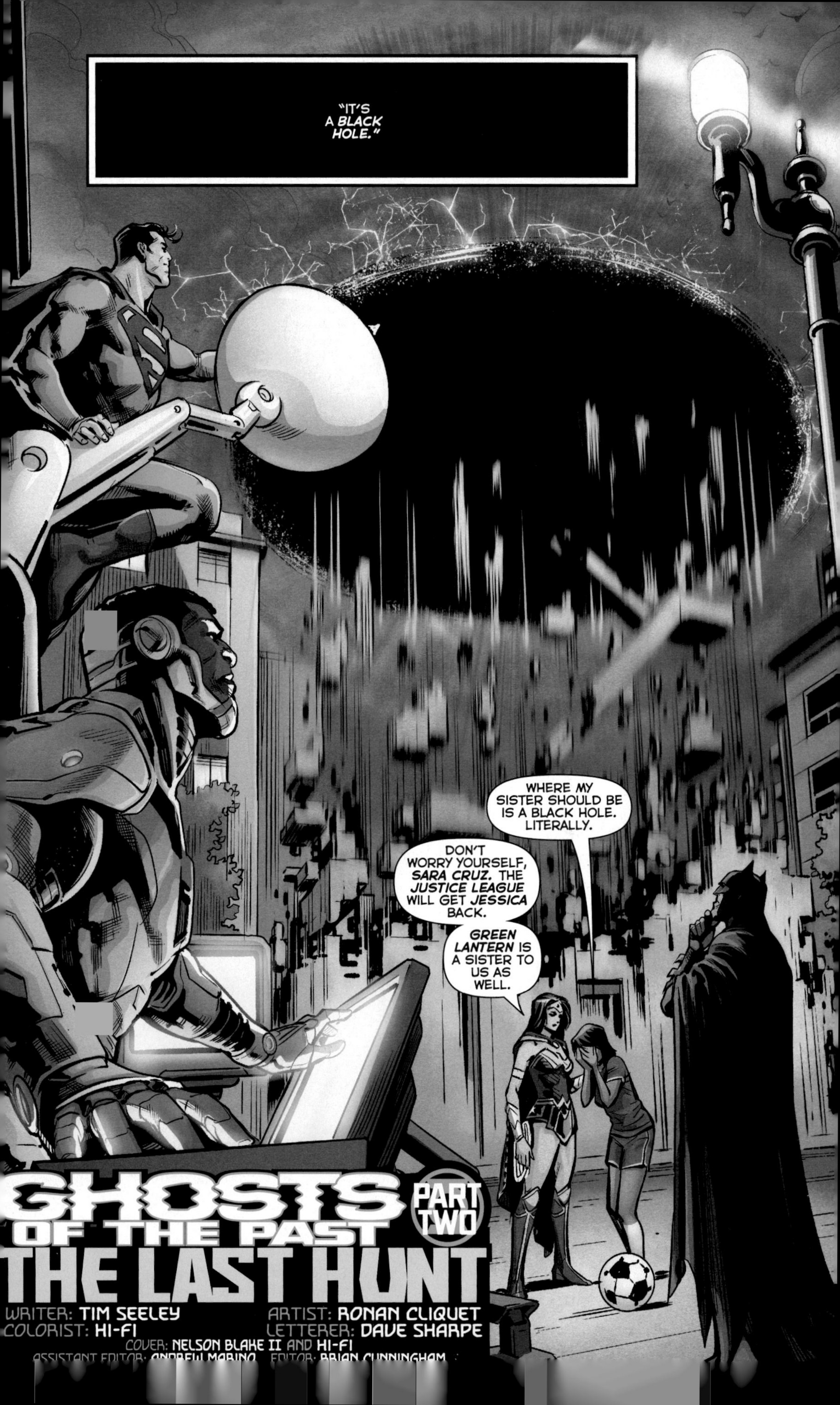
"IT'S A BLACK HOLE."
WHERE MY SISTER SHOULD BE IS A BLACK HOLE. LITERALLY.
DON'T WORRY YOURSELF, SARA CRUZ. THE JUSTICE LEAGUE WILL GET JESSICA BACK.
GREEN LANTERN IS A SISTER TO US AS WELL.
GHOSTS OF THE PAST PART TWO
THE LAST HUNT
WRITER: TIM SEELEY
ARTIST: RONAN CLIQUET
COLORIST: HI-FI
LETTERER: DAVE SHARPE
COVER: NELSON BLAKE II AND HI-FI
ASSISTANT EDITOR: ANDREW MARINO
EDITOR: BRIAN CUNNINGHAM

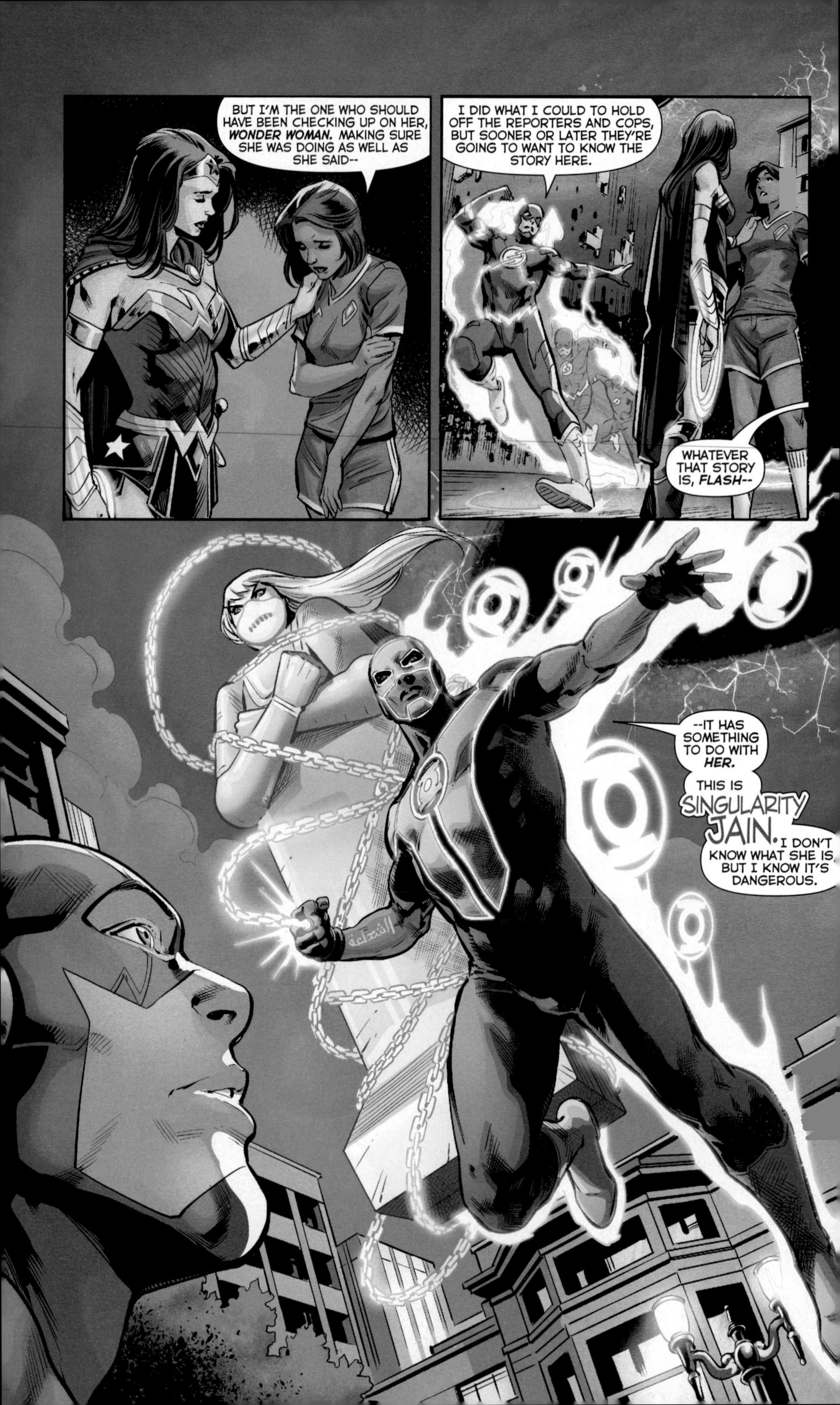

BUT I'M THE ONE WHO SHOULD HAVE BEEN CHECKING UP ON HER, *WONDER WOMAN.* MAKING SURE SHE WAS DOING AS WELL AS SHE SAID--
I DID WHAT I COULD TO HOLD OFF THE REPORTERS AND COPS, BUT SOONER OR LATER THEY'RE GOING TO WANT TO KNOW THE STORY HERE.
WHATEVER THAT STORY IS, *FLASH*--
--IT HAS SOMETHING TO DO WITH *HER.*
THIS IS SINGULARITY JAIN. I DON'T KNOW WHAT SHE IS, BUT I KNOW IT'S DANGEROUS.

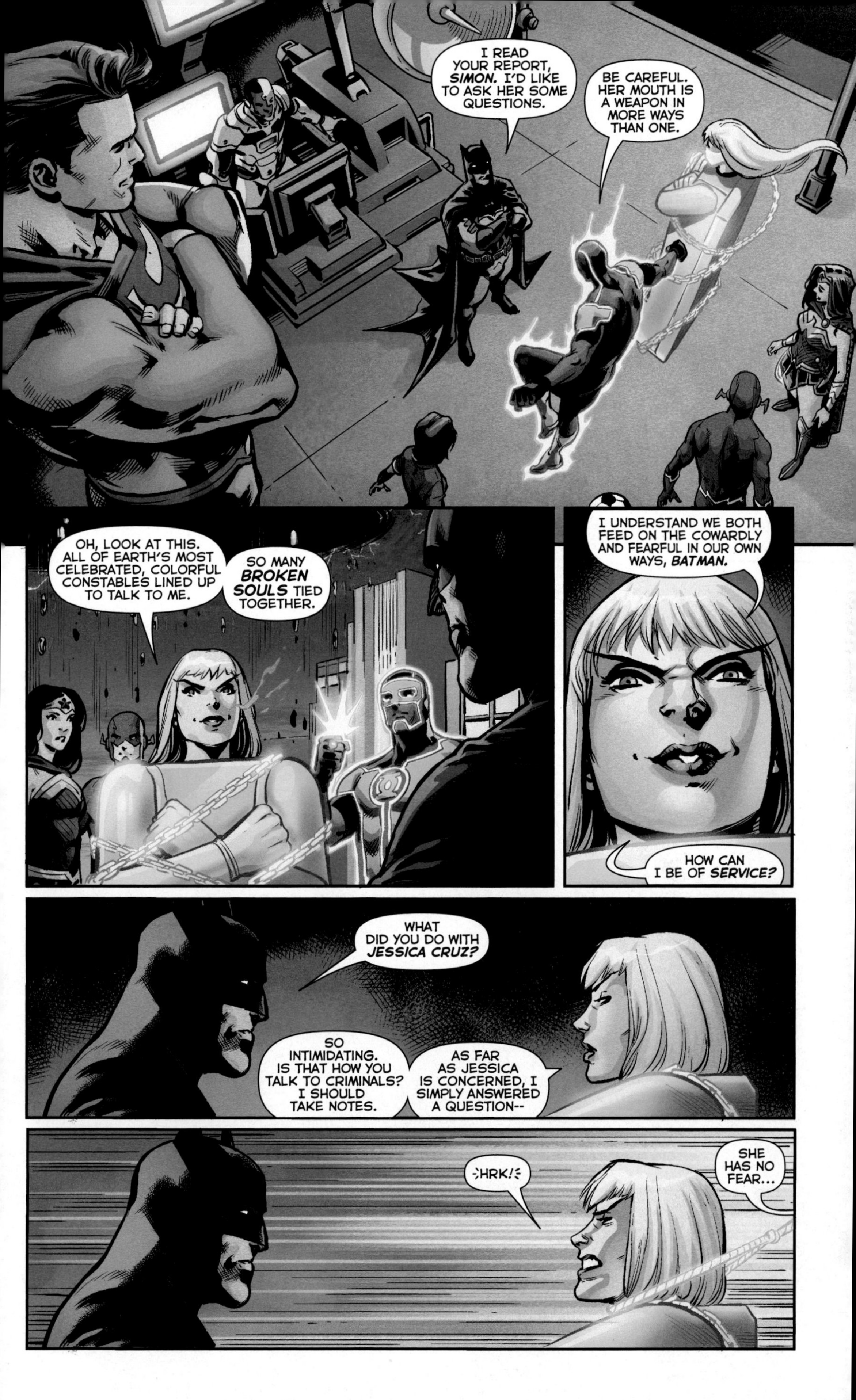
I READ YOUR REPORT, SIMON. I'D LIKE TO ASK HER SOME QUESTIONS.
BE CAREFUL. HER MOUTH IS A WEAPON IN MORE WAYS THAN ONE.
OH, LOOK AT THIS. ALL OF EARTH'S MOST CELEBRATED, COLORFUL CONSTABLES LINED UP TO TALK TO ME.
SO MANY BROKEN SOULS TIED TOGETHER.
I UNDERSTAND WE BOTH FEED ON THE COWARDLY AND FEARFUL IN OUR OWN WAYS, BATMAN.
HOW CAN I BE OF SERVICE?
WHAT DID YOU DO WITH JESSICA CRUZ?
SO INTIMIDATING. IS THAT HOW YOU TALK TO CRIMINALS? I SHOULD TAKE NOTES.
AS FAR AS JESSICA IS CONCERNED, I SIMPLY ANSWERED A QUESTION--
HRK!
SHE HAS NO FEAR...

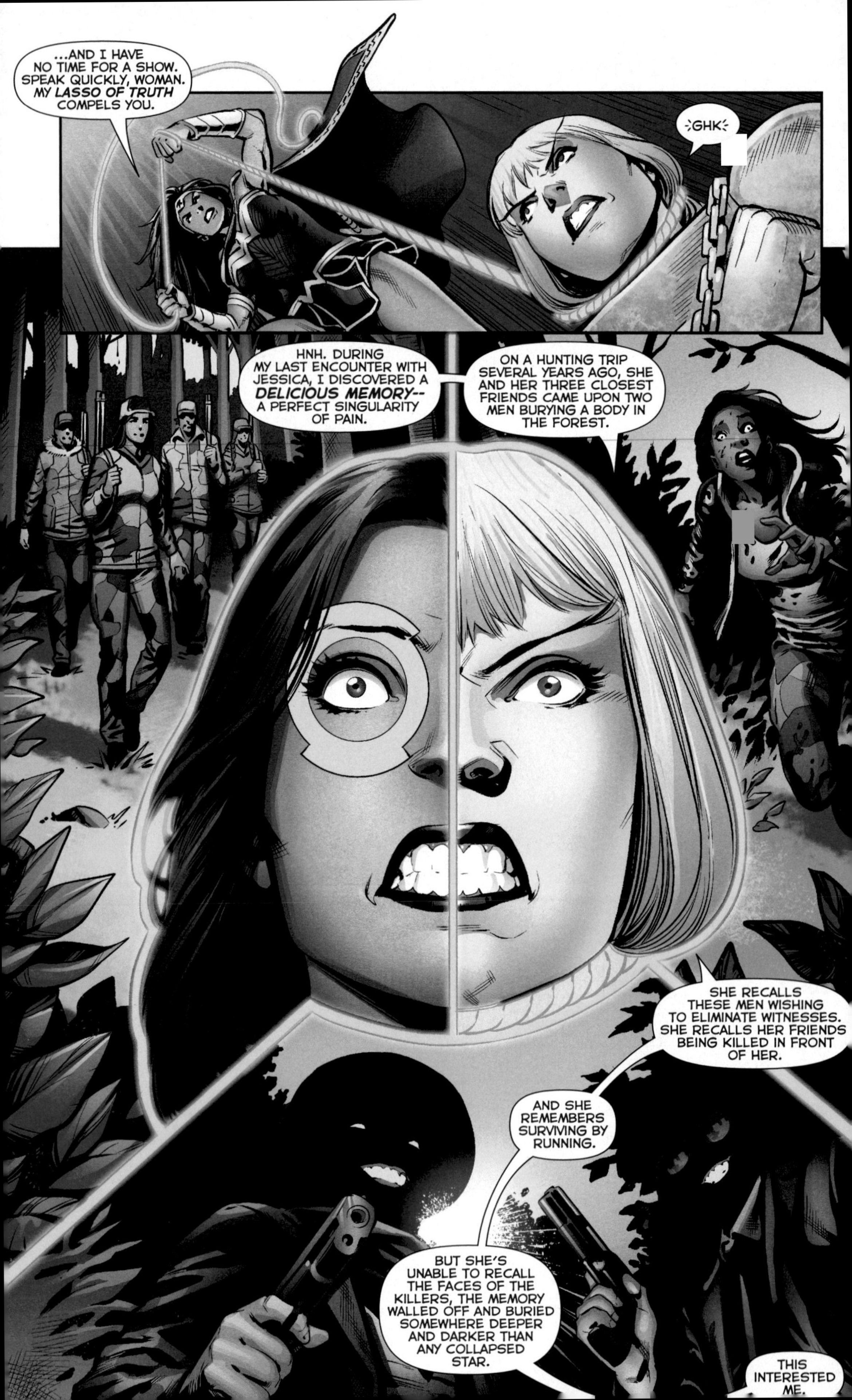
...AND I HAVE NO TIME FOR A SHOW. SPEAK QUICKLY, WOMAN. MY LASSO OF TRUTH COMPELS YOU.
GHK
HNH. DURING MY LAST ENCOUNTER WITH JESSICA, I DISCOVERED A DELICIOUS MEMORY-- A PERFECT SINGULARITY OF PAIN.
ON A HUNTING TRIP SEVERAL YEARS AGO, SHE AND HER THREE CLOSEST FRIENDS CAME UPON TWO MEN BURYING A BODY IN THE FOREST.
SHE RECALLS THESE MEN WISHING TO ELIMINATE WITNESSES. SHE RECALLS HER FRIENDS BEING KILLED IN FRONT OF HER.
AND SHE REMEMBERS SURVIVING BY RUNNING.
BUT SHE'S UNABLE TO RECALL THE FACES OF THE KILLERS, THE MEMORY WALLED OFF AND BURIED SOMEWHERE DEEPER AND DARKER THAN ANY COLLAPSED STAR.
THIS INTERESTED ME.

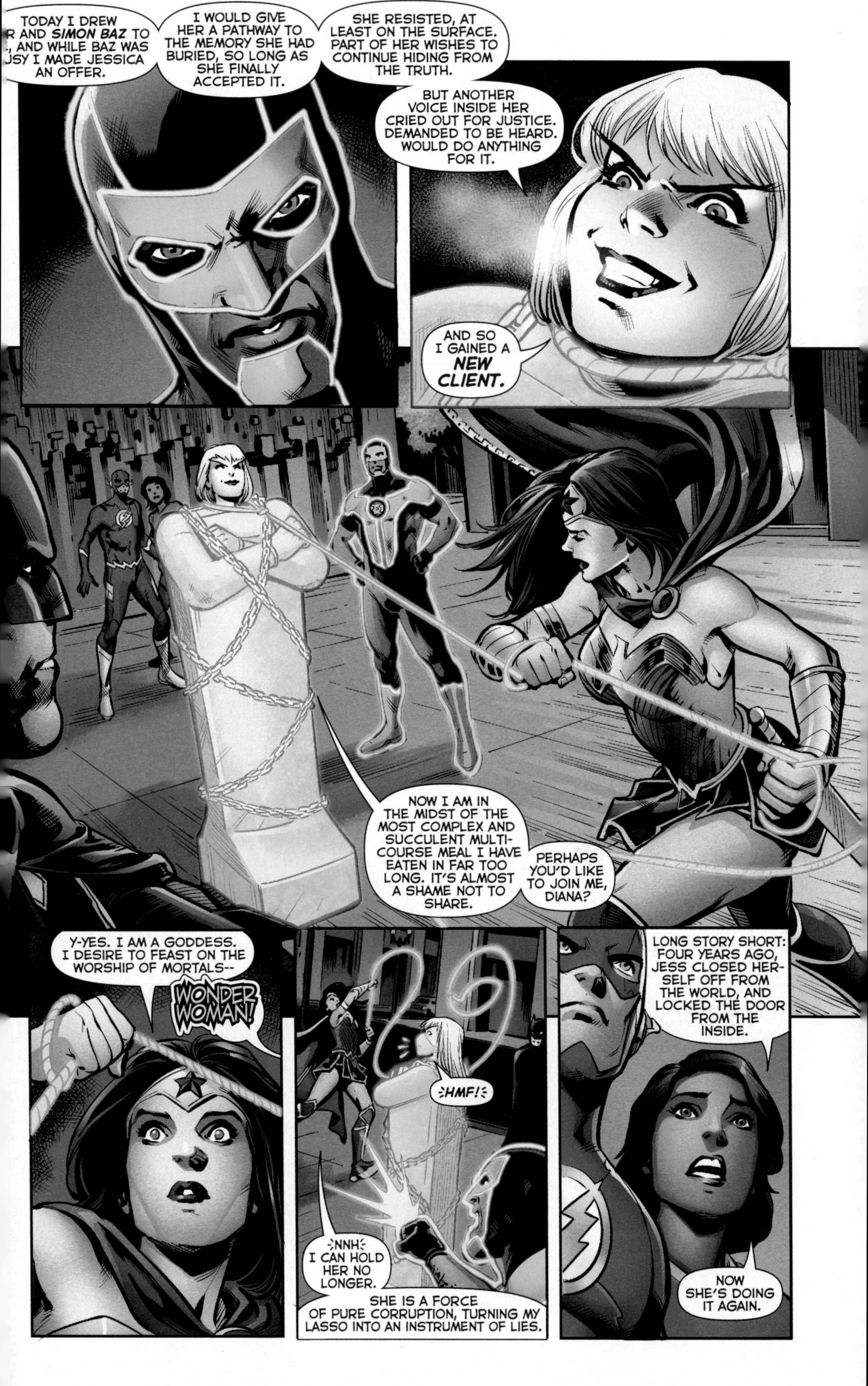
TODAY I DREW
R AND SIMON BAZ TO
E, AND WHILE BAZ WAS
USY I MADE JESSICA
AN OFFER.
I WOULD GIVE HER A PATHWAY TO THE MEMORY SHE HAD BURIED, SO LONG AS SHE FINALLY ACCEPTED IT.
SHE RESISTED, AT LEAST ON THE SURFACE. PART OF HER WISHES TO CONTINUE HIDING FROM THE TRUTH.
BUT ANOTHER VOICE INSIDE HER CRIED OUT FOR JUSTICE. DEMANDED TO BE HEARD. WOULD DO ANYTHING FOR IT.
AND SO I GAINED A NEW CLIENT.
NOW I AM IN THE MIDST OF THE MOST COMPLEX AND SUCCULENT MULTI-COURSE MEAL I HAVE EATEN IN FAR TOO LONG. IT'S ALMOST A SHAME NOT TO SHARE.
PERHAPS YOU'D LIKE TO JOIN ME, DIANA?
Y-YES. I AM A GODDESS. I DESIRE TO FEAST ON THE WORSHIP OF MORTALS--
WONDER WOMAN!
HMF!
NNH I CAN HOLD HER NO LONGER.
SHE IS A FORCE OF PURE CORRUPTION, TURNING MY LASSO INTO AN INSTRUMENT OF LIES.
LONG STORY SHORT: FOUR YEARS AGO, JESS CLOSED HERSELF OFF FROM THE WORLD, AND LOCKED THE DOOR FROM THE INSIDE.
NOW SHE'S DOING IT AGAIN.

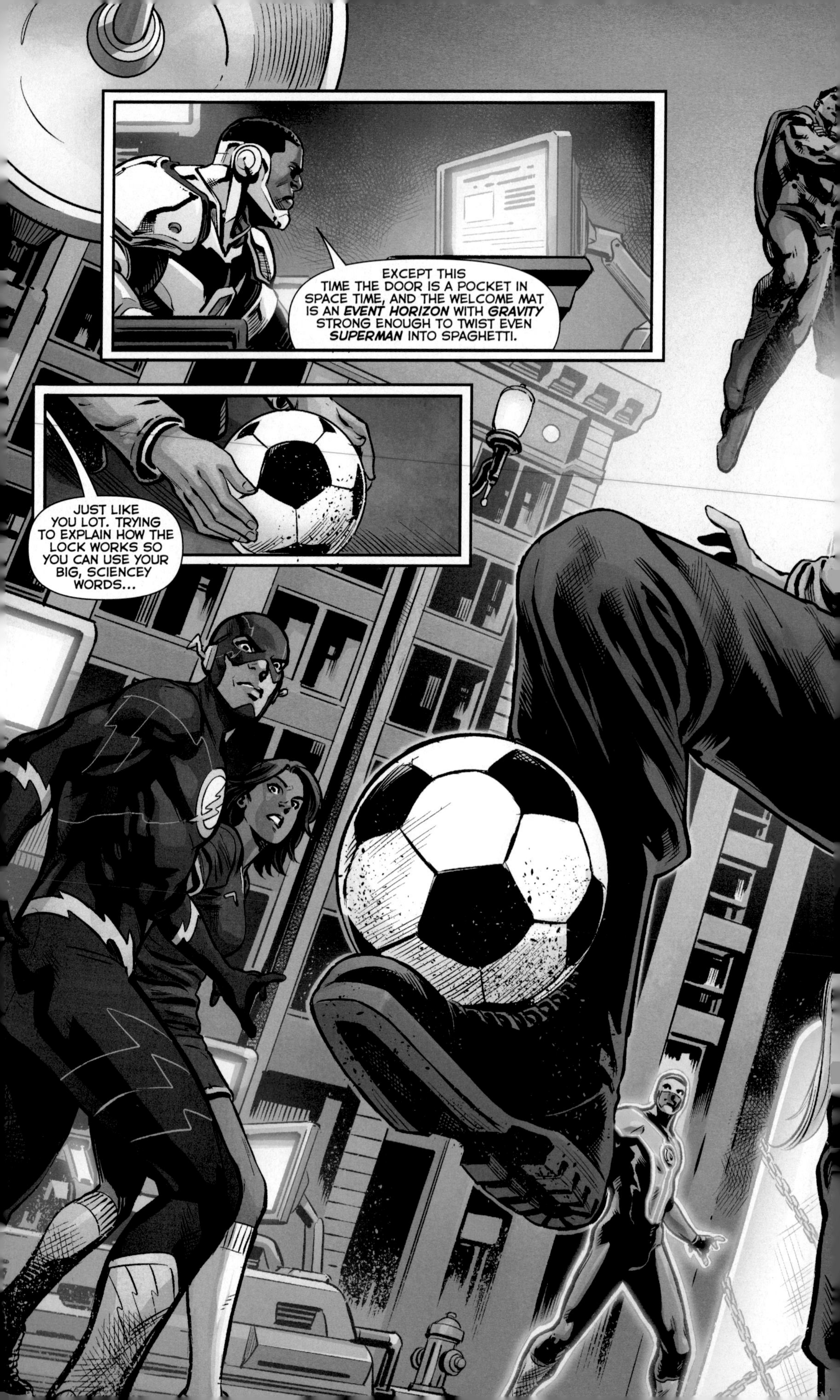
EXCEPT THIS TIME THE DOOR IS A POCKET IN SPACE TIME, AND THE WELCOME MAT IS AN *EVENT HORIZON* WITH *GRAVITY* STRONG ENOUGH TO TWIST EVEN *SUPERMAN* INTO SPAGHETTI.
JUST LIKE YOU LOT. TRYING TO EXPLAIN HOW THE LOCK WORKS SO YOU CAN USE YOUR BIG, SCIENCEY WORDS...

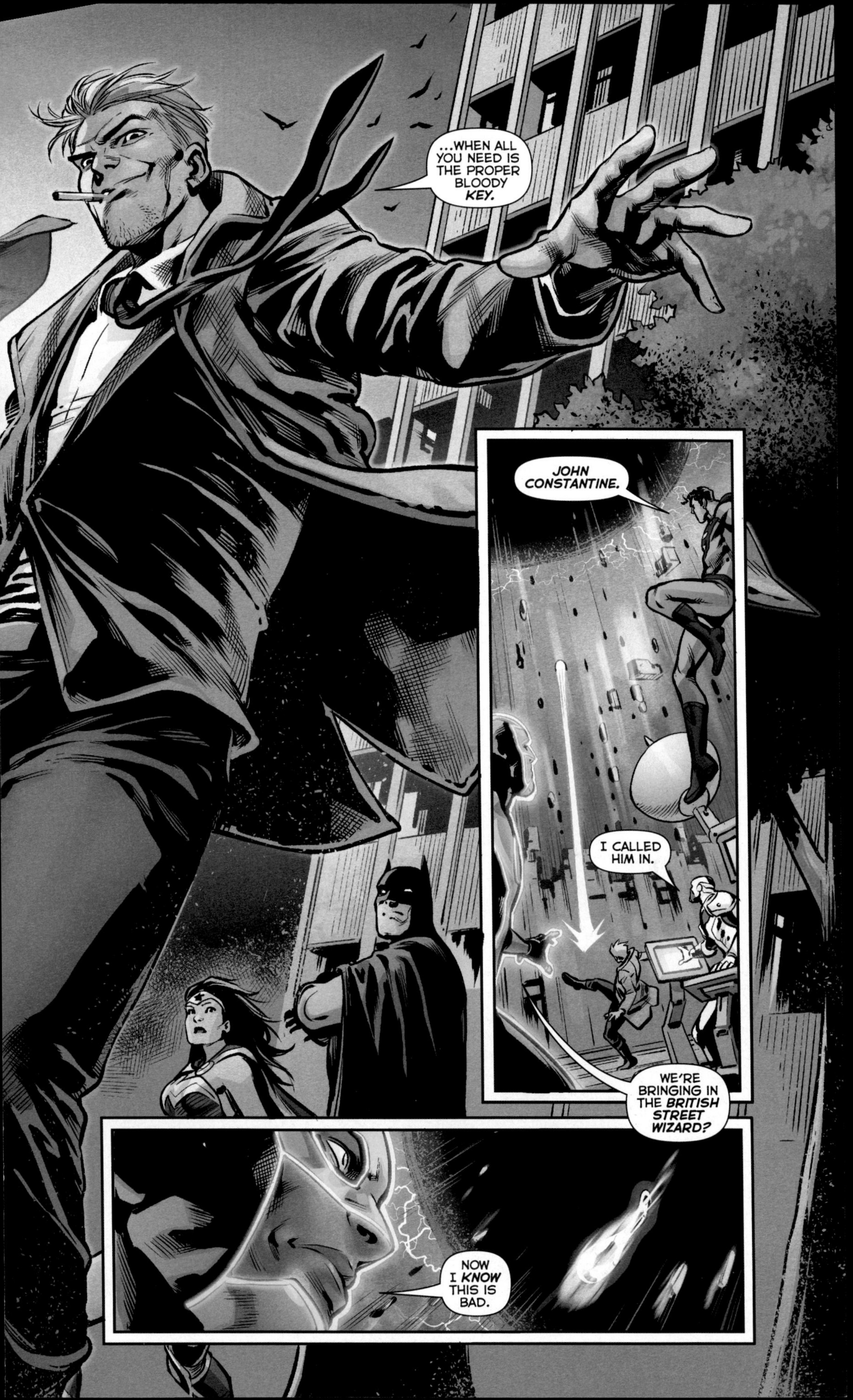
...WHEN ALL YOU NEED IS THE PROPER BLOODY *KEY.*
*JOHN CONSTANTINE.*
I CALLED HIM IN.
WE'RE BRINGING IN THE *BRITISH STREET WIZARD?*
NOW I *KNOW* THIS IS BAD.

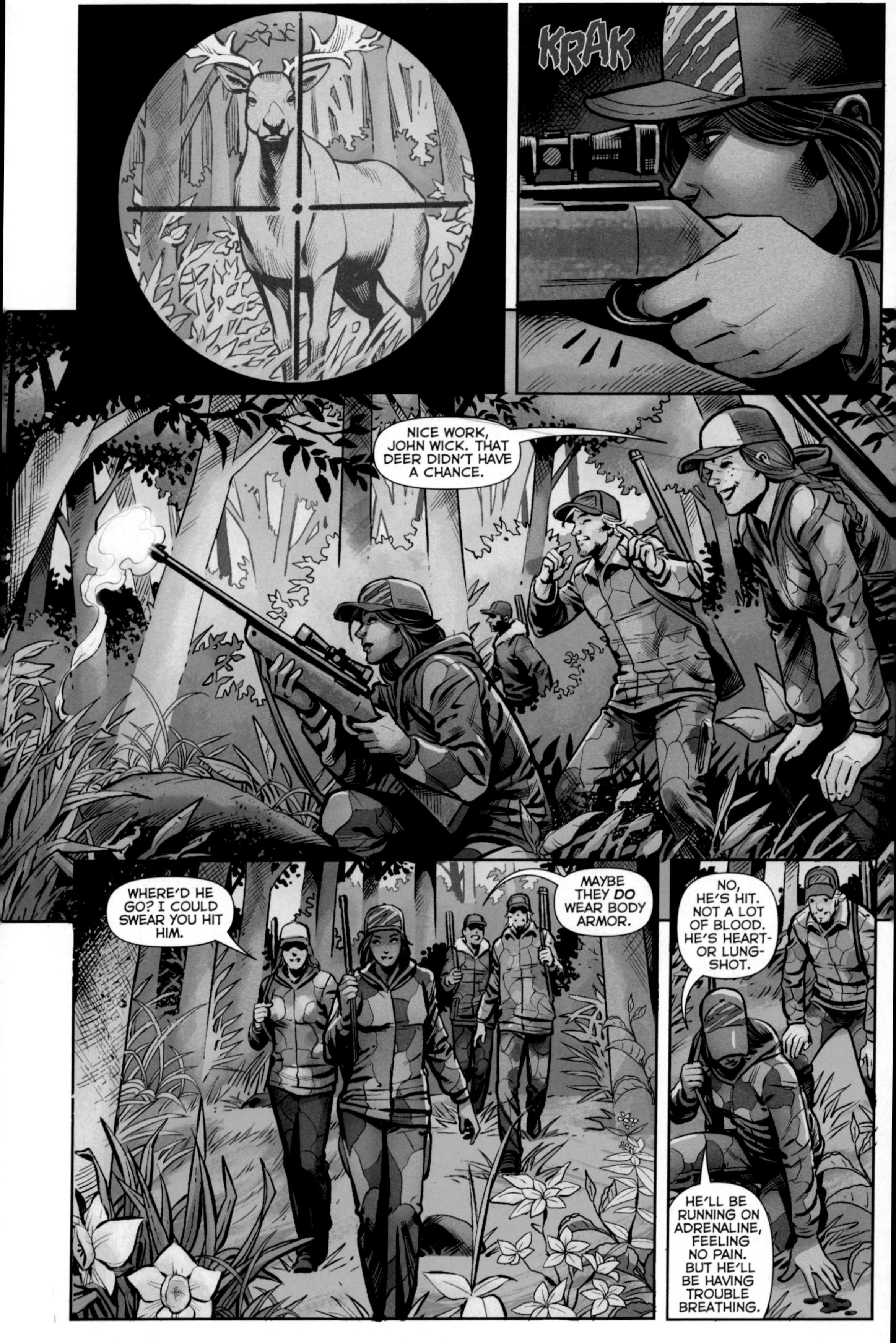
KRAK
NICE WORK, JOHN WICK. THAT DEER DIDN'T HAVE A CHANCE.
WHERE'D HE GO? I COULD SWEAR YOU HIT HIM.
MAYBE THEY *DO* WEAR BODY ARMOR.
NO, HE'S HIT. NOT A LOT OF BLOOD. HE'S HEART- OR LUNG-SHOT.
HE'LL BE RUNNING ON ADRENALINE, FEELING NO PAIN. BUT HE'LL BE HAVING TROUBLE BREATHING.

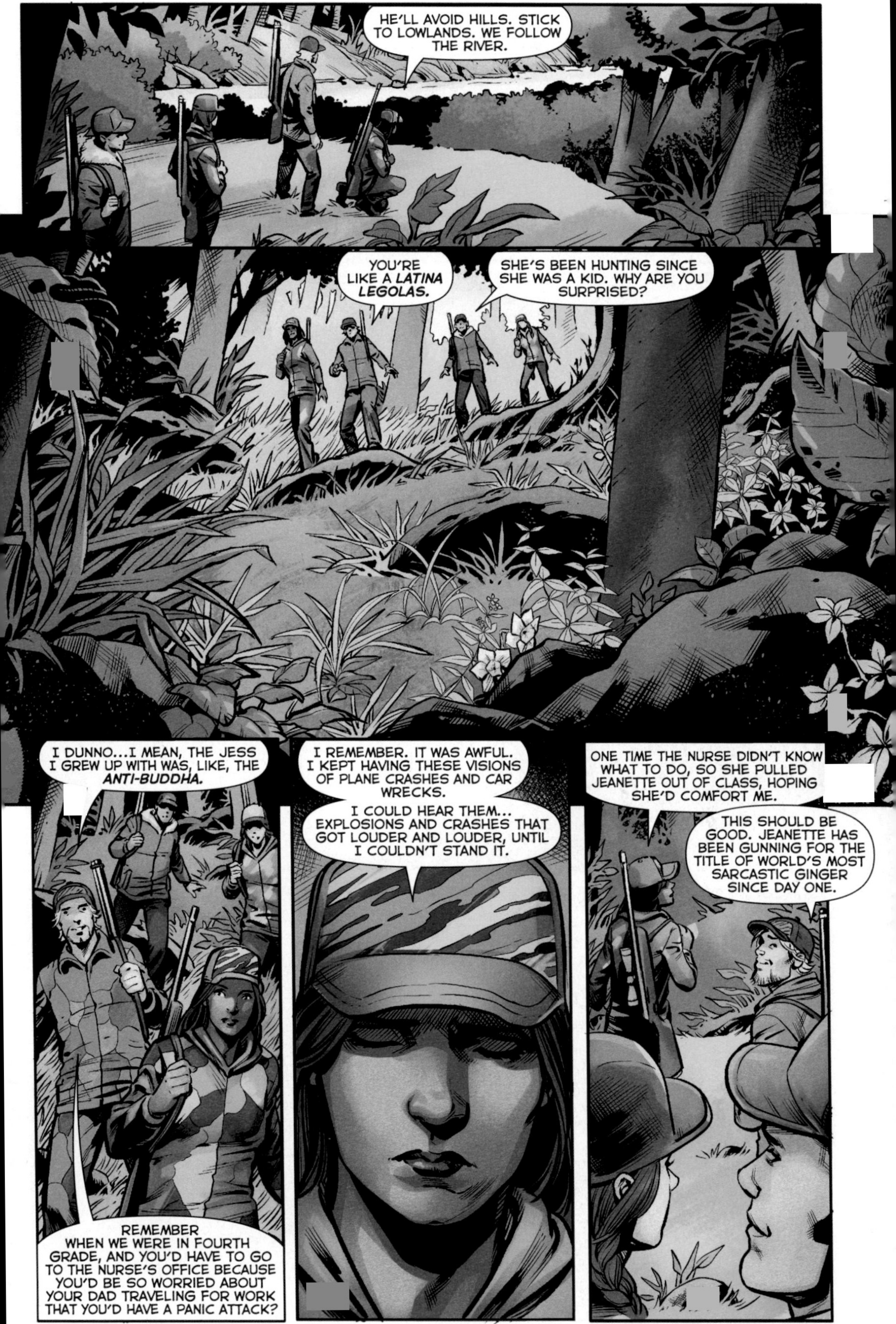
HE'LL AVOID HILLS. STICK TO LOWLANDS. WE FOLLOW THE RIVER.
YOU'RE LIKE A *LATINA LEGOLAS.*
SHE'S BEEN HUNTING SINCE SHE WAS A KID. WHY ARE YOU SURPRISED?
I DUNNO...I MEAN, THE JESS I GREW UP WITH WAS, LIKE, THE *ANTI-BUDDHA.*
REMEMBER WHEN WE WERE IN FOURTH GRADE, AND YOU'D HAVE TO GO TO THE NURSE'S OFFICE BECAUSE YOU'D BE SO WORRIED ABOUT YOUR DAD TRAVELING FOR WORK THAT YOU'D HAVE A PANIC ATTACK?
I REMEMBER. IT WAS AWFUL. I KEPT HAVING THESE VISIONS OF PLANE CRASHES AND CAR WRECKS.
I COULD HEAR THEM... EXPLOSIONS AND CRASHES THAT GOT LOUDER AND LOUDER, UNTIL I COULDN'T STAND IT.
ONE TIME THE NURSE DIDN'T KNOW WHAT TO DO, SO SHE PULLED JEANETTE OUT OF CLASS, HOPING SHE'D COMFORT ME.
THIS SHOULD BE GOOD. JEANETTE HAS BEEN GUNNING FOR THE TITLE OF WORLD'S MOST SARCASTIC GINGER SINCE DAY ONE.

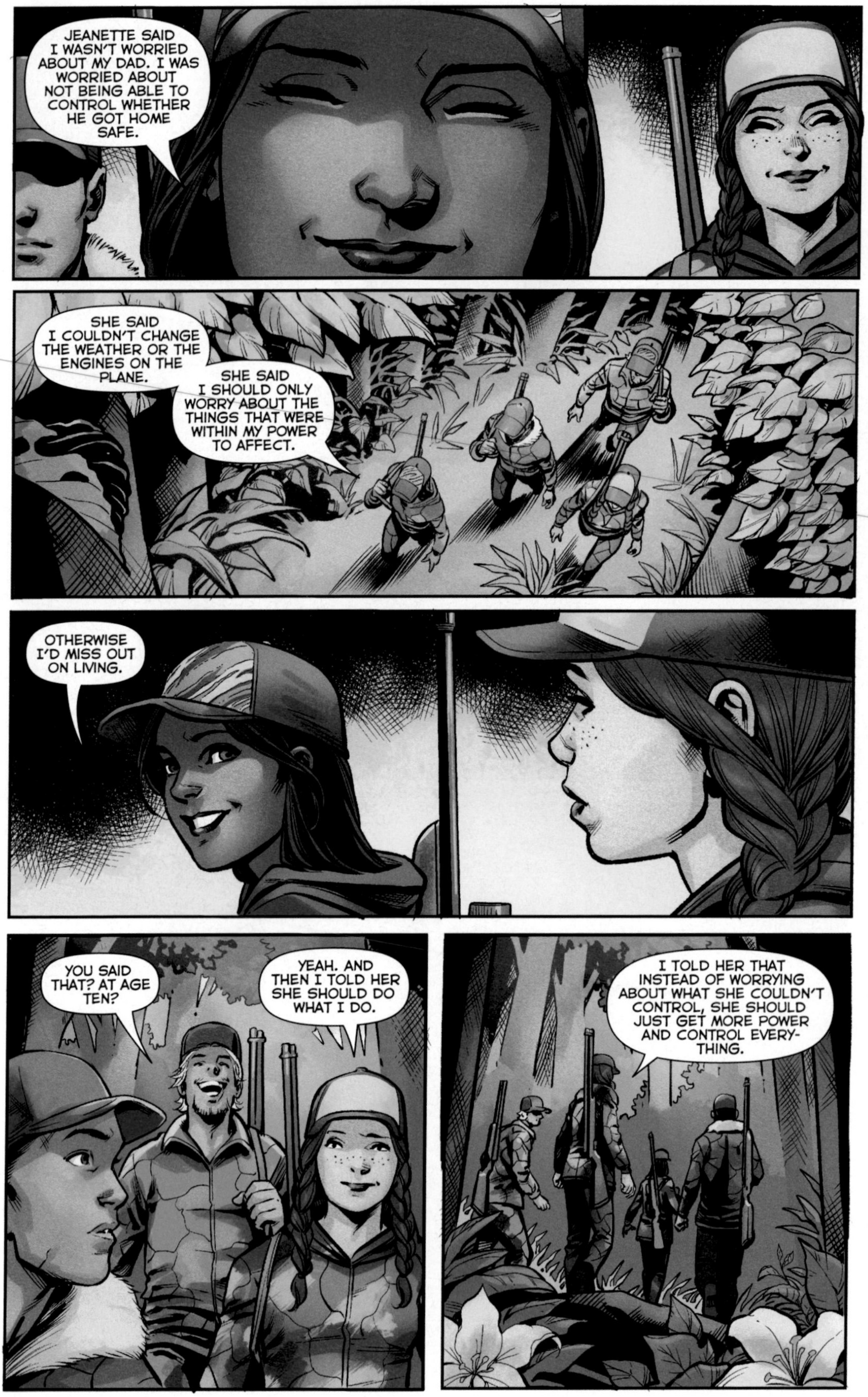
JEANETTE SAID I WASN'T WORRIED ABOUT MY DAD. I WAS WORRIED ABOUT NOT BEING ABLE TO CONTROL WHETHER HE GOT HOME SAFE.
SHE SAID I COULDN'T CHANGE THE WEATHER OR THE ENGINES ON THE PLANE.
SHE SAID I SHOULD ONLY WORRY ABOUT THE THINGS THAT WERE WITHIN MY POWER TO AFFECT.
OTHERWISE I'D MISS OUT ON LIVING.
YOU SAID THAT? AT AGE TEN?
YEAH. AND THEN I TOLD HER SHE SHOULD DO WHAT I DO.
I TOLD HER THAT INSTEAD OF WORRYING ABOUT WHAT SHE COULDN'T CONTROL, SHE SHOULD JUST GET MORE POWER AND CONTROL EVERY-THING.

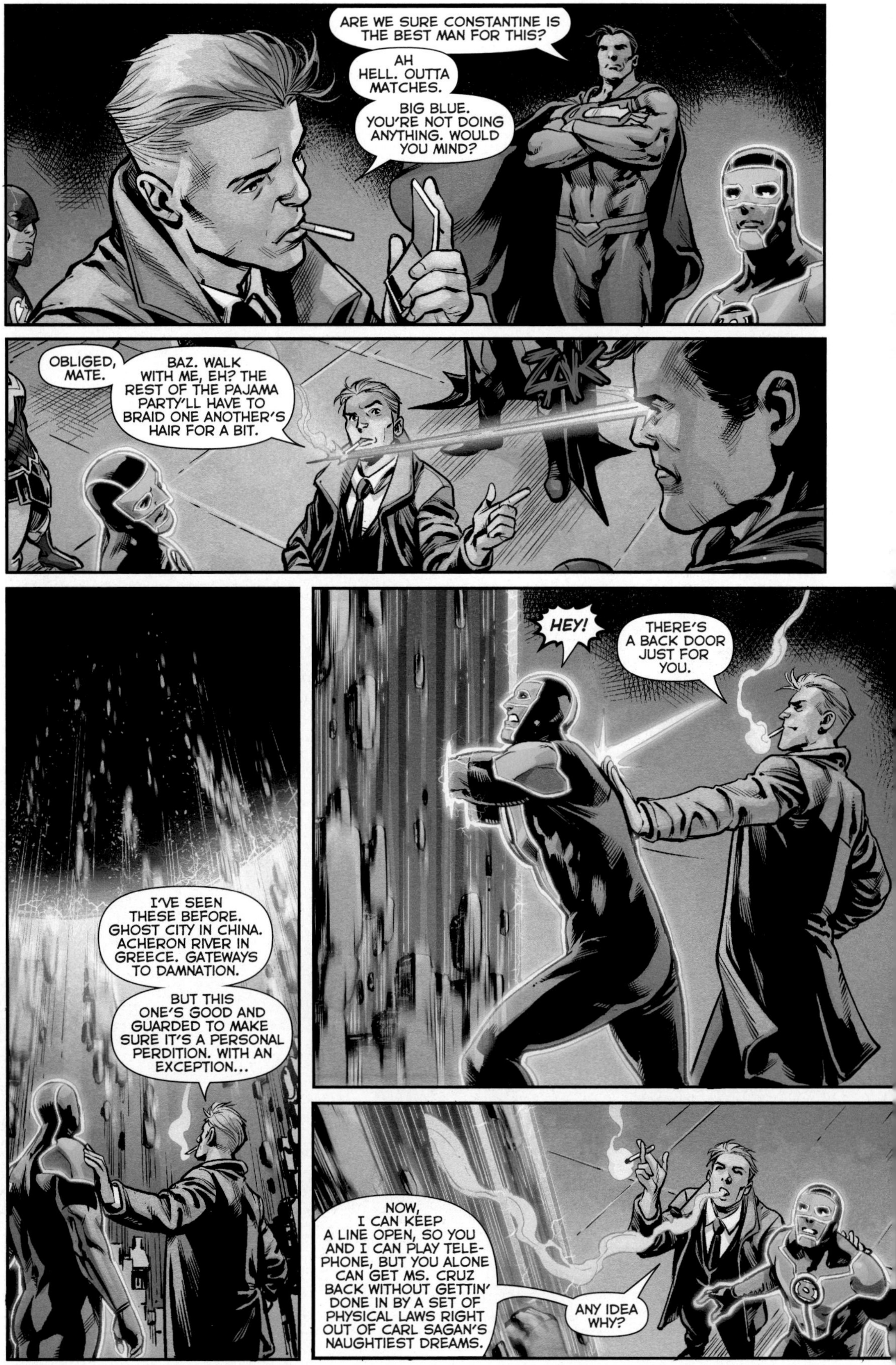
ARE WE SURE CONSTANTINE IS THE BEST MAN FOR THIS?
AH HELL. OUTTA MATCHES.
BIG BLUE. YOU'RE NOT DOING ANYTHING. WOULD YOU MIND?
ZAK
OBLIGED, MATE.
BAZ. WALK WITH ME, EH? THE REST OF THE PAJAMA PARTY'LL HAVE TO BRAID ONE ANOTHER'S HAIR FOR A BIT.
I'VE SEEN THESE BEFORE. GHOST CITY IN CHINA. ACHERON RIVER IN GREECE. GATEWAYS TO DAMNATION.
BUT THIS ONE'S GOOD AND GUARDED TO MAKE SURE IT'S A PERSONAL PERDITION. WITH AN EXCEPTION...
HEY!
THERE'S A BACK DOOR JUST FOR YOU.
NOW, I CAN KEEP A LINE OPEN, SO YOU AND I CAN PLAY TELE-PHONE, BUT YOU ALONE CAN GET MS. CRUZ BACK WITHOUT GETTIN' DONE IN BY A SET OF PHYSICAL LAWS RIGHT OUT OF CARL SAGAN'S NAUGHTIEST DREAMS.
ANY IDEA WHY?

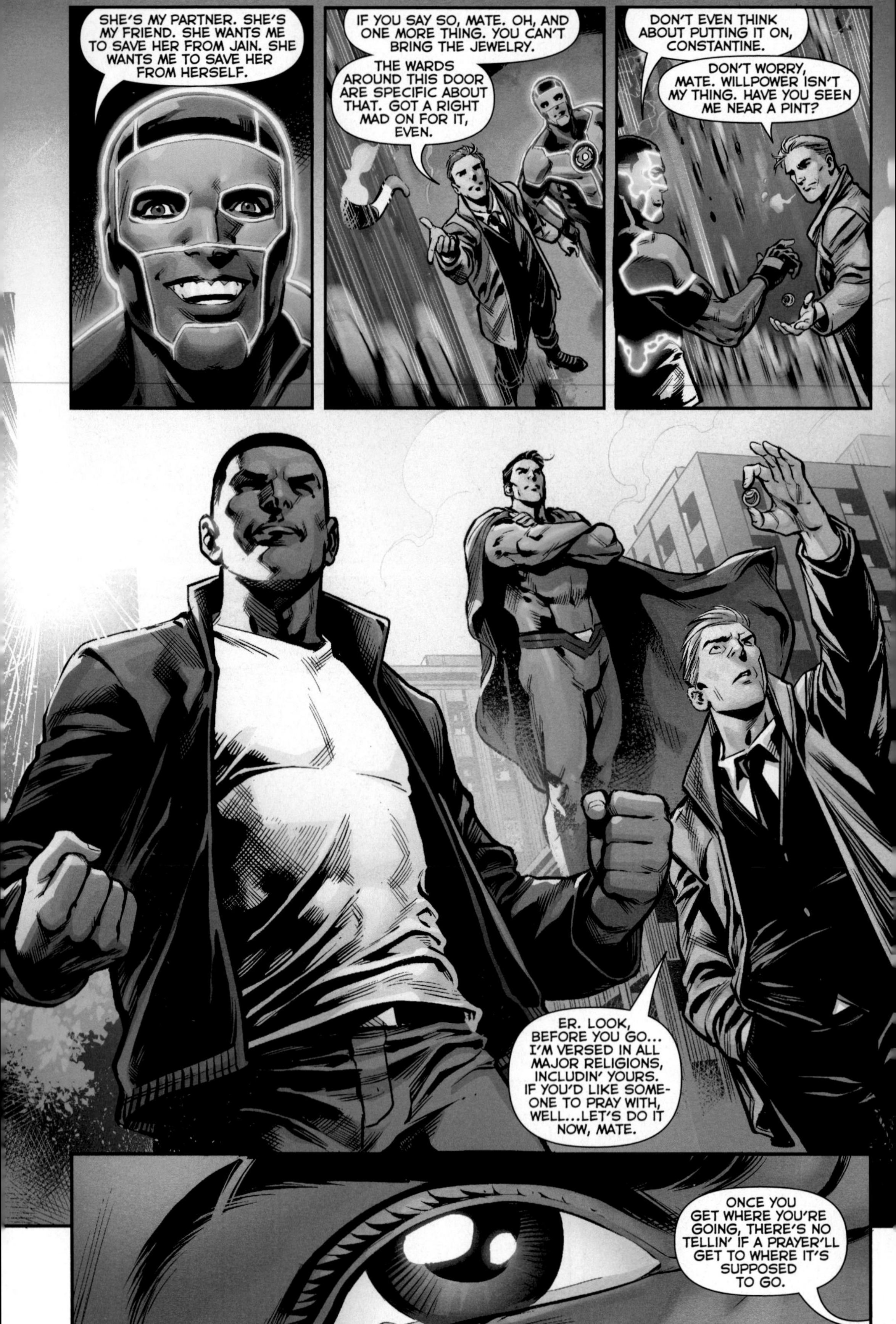
SHE'S MY PARTNER. SHE'S MY FRIEND. SHE WANTS ME TO SAVE HER FROM JAIN. SHE WANTS ME TO SAVE HER FROM HERSELF.
IF YOU SAY SO, MATE. OH, AND ONE MORE THING. YOU CAN'T BRING THE JEWELRY.
THE WARDS AROUND THIS DOOR ARE SPECIFIC ABOUT THAT. GOT A RIGHT MAD ON FOR IT, EVEN.
DON'T EVEN THINK ABOUT PUTTING IT ON, CONSTANTINE.
DON'T WORRY, MATE. WILLPOWER ISN'T MY THING. HAVE YOU SEEN ME NEAR A PINT?
ER. LOOK, BEFORE YOU GO... I'M VERSED IN ALL MAJOR RELIGIONS, INCLUDIN' YOURS. IF YOU'D LIKE SOME-ONE TO PRAY WITH, WELL...LET'S DO IT NOW, MATE.
ONCE YOU GET WHERE YOU'RE GOING, THERE'S NO TELLIN' IF A PRAYER'LL GET TO WHERE IT'S SUPPOSED TO GO.

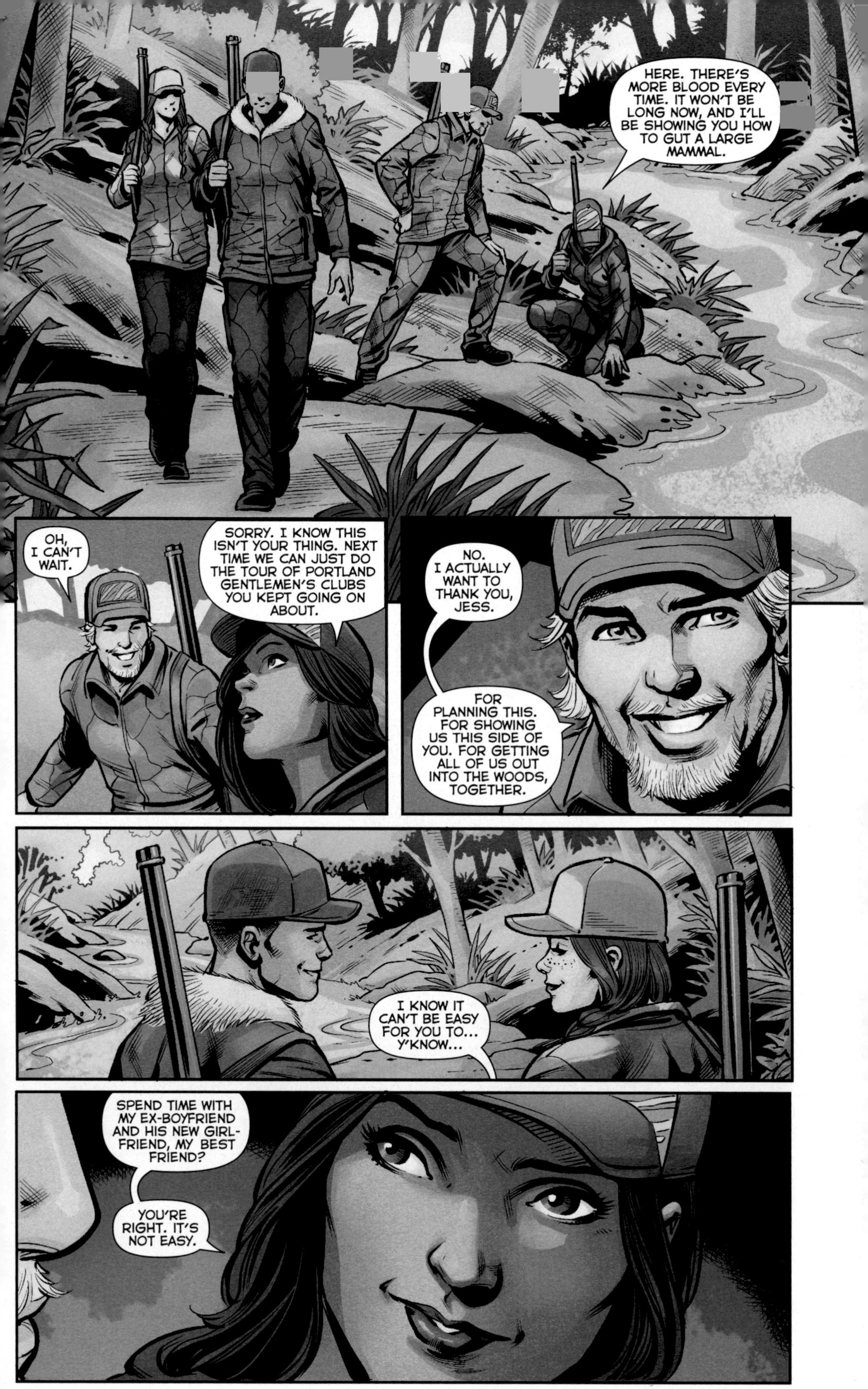
HERE. THERE'S MORE BLOOD EVERY TIME. IT WON'T BE LONG NOW, AND I'LL BE SHOWING YOU HOW TO GUT A LARGE MAMMAL.
OH, I CAN'T WAIT.
SORRY. I KNOW THIS ISN'T YOUR THING. NEXT TIME WE CAN JUST DO THE TOUR OF PORTLAND GENTLEMEN'S CLUBS YOU KEPT GOING ON ABOUT.
NO. I ACTUALLY WANT TO THANK YOU, JESS.
FOR PLANNING THIS. FOR SHOWING US THIS SIDE OF YOU. FOR GETTING ALL OF US OUT INTO THE WOODS, TOGETHER.
I KNOW IT CAN'T BE EASY FOR YOU TO... Y'KNOW...
SPEND TIME WITH MY EX-BOYFRIEND AND HIS NEW GIRL-FRIEND, MY BEST FRIEND?
YOU'RE RIGHT. IT'S NOT EASY.

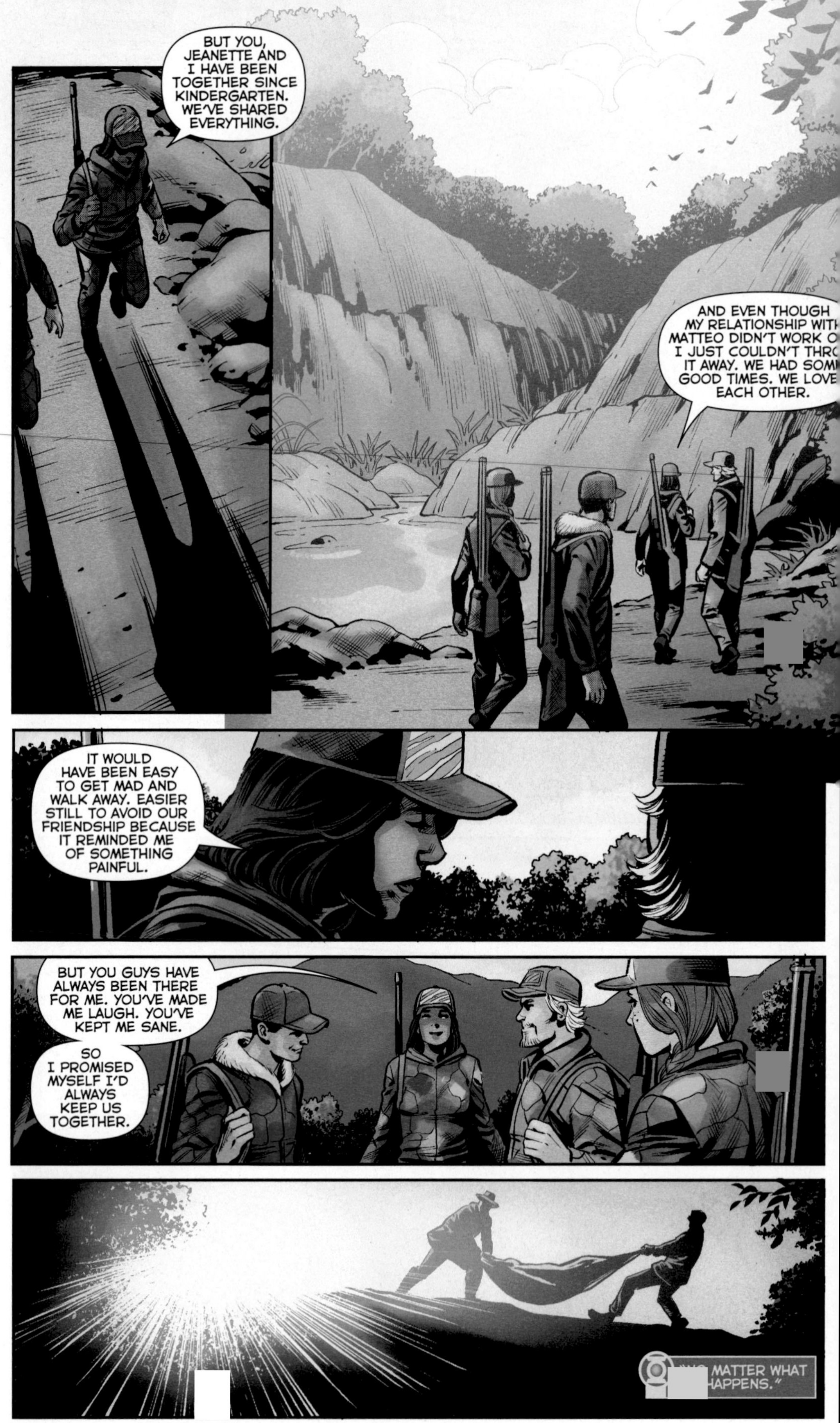
BUT YOU, JEANETTE AND I HAVE BEEN TOGETHER SINCE KINDERGARTEN. WE'VE SHARED EVERYTHING.
AND EVEN THOUGH MY RELATIONSHIP WIT MATTEO DIDN'T WORK O I JUST COULDN'T THRO IT AWAY. WE HAD SOM GOOD TIMES. WE LOVE EACH OTHER.
IT WOULD HAVE BEEN EASY TO GET MAD AND WALK AWAY. EASIER STILL TO AVOID OUR FRIENDSHIP BECAUSE IT REMINDED ME OF SOMETHING PAINFUL.
BUT YOU GUYS HAVE ALWAYS BEEN THERE FOR ME. YOU'VE MADE ME LAUGH. YOU'VE KEPT ME SANE.
SO I PROMISED MYSELF I'D ALWAYS KEEP US TOGETHER.
MATTER WHAT HAPPENS.”

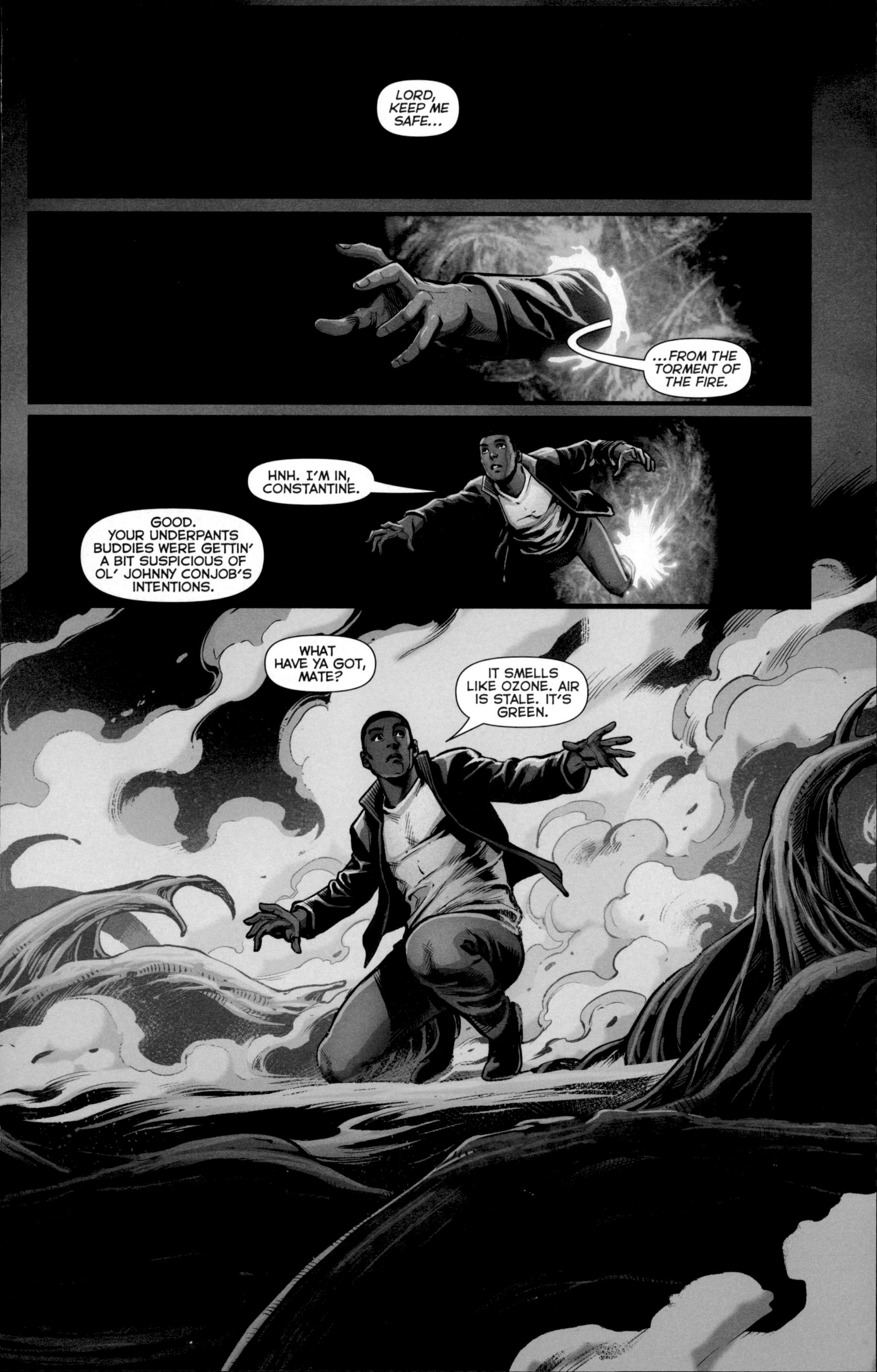

LORD, KEEP ME SAFE...
...FROM THE TORMENT OF THE FIRE.
HNH. I'M IN, CONSTANTINE.
GOOD. YOUR UNDERPANTS BUDDIES WERE GETTIN' A BIT SUSPICIOUS OF OL' JOHNNY CONJOB'S INTENTIONS.
WHAT HAVE YA GOT, MATE?
IT SMELLS LIKE OZONE. AIR IS STALE. IT'S GREEN.

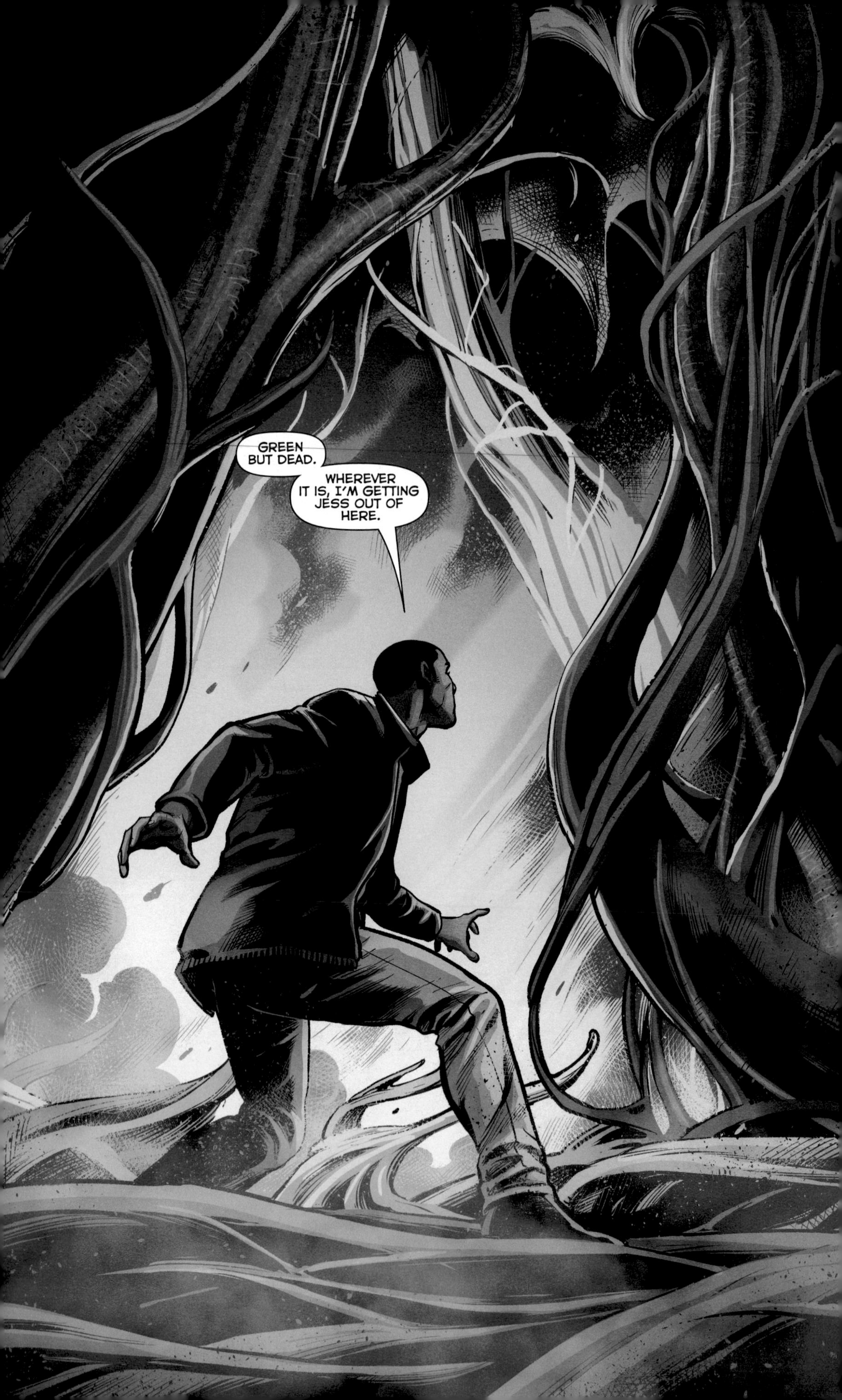
GREEN BUT DEAD.
WHEREVER IT IS, I'M GETTING JESS OUT OF HERE.

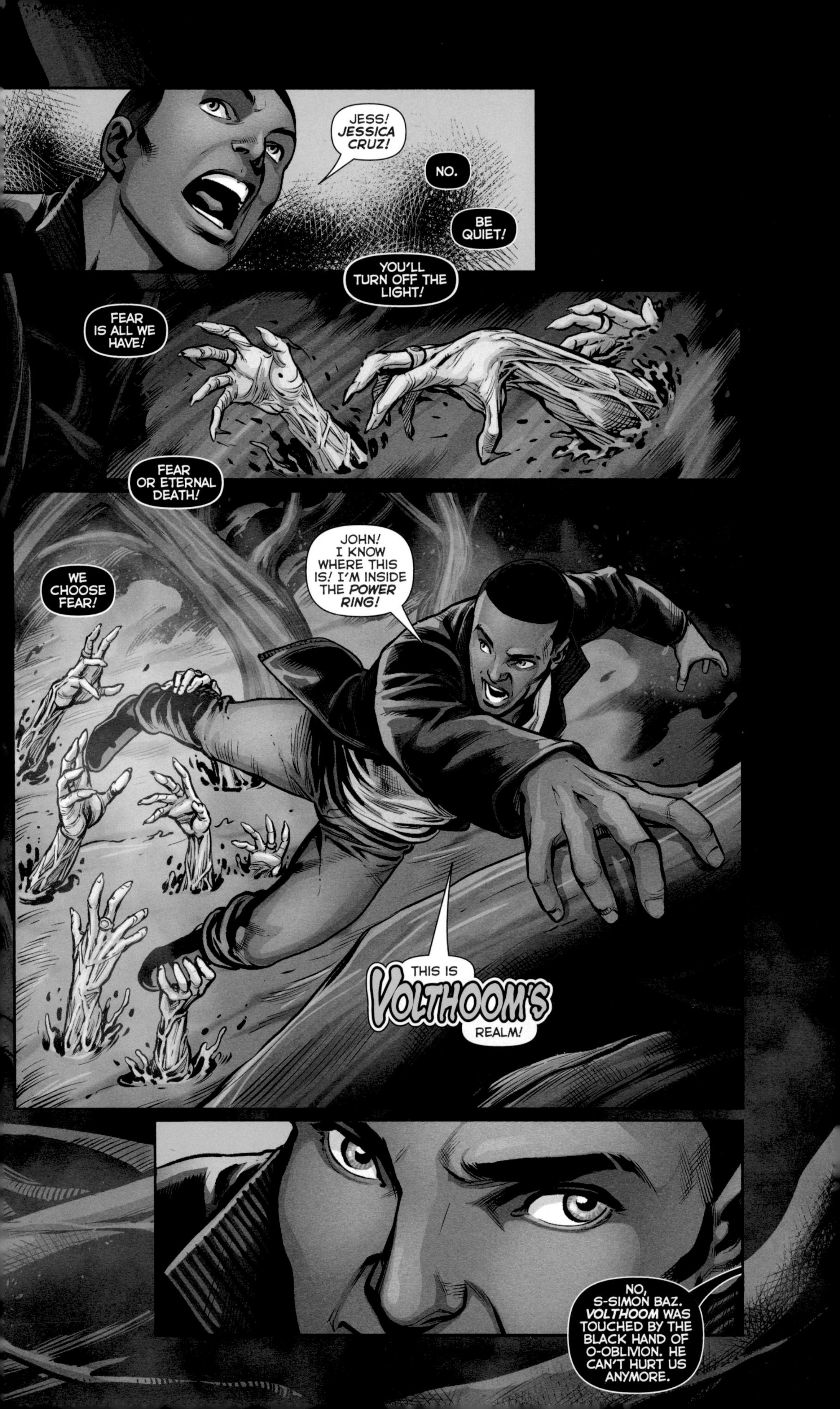

JESS! JESSICA CRUZ!
NO.
BE QUIET!
YOU'LL TURN OFF THE LIGHT!
FEAR IS ALL WE HAVE!
FEAR OR ETERNAL DEATH!
WE CHOOSE FEAR!
JOHN! I KNOW WHERE THIS IS! I'M INSIDE THE POWER RING!
THIS IS VOLTHOOM'S REALM!
NO, S-SIMON BAZ. VOLTHOOM WAS TOUCHED BY THE BLACK HAND OF O-OBLIVION. HE CAN'T HURT US ANYMORE.

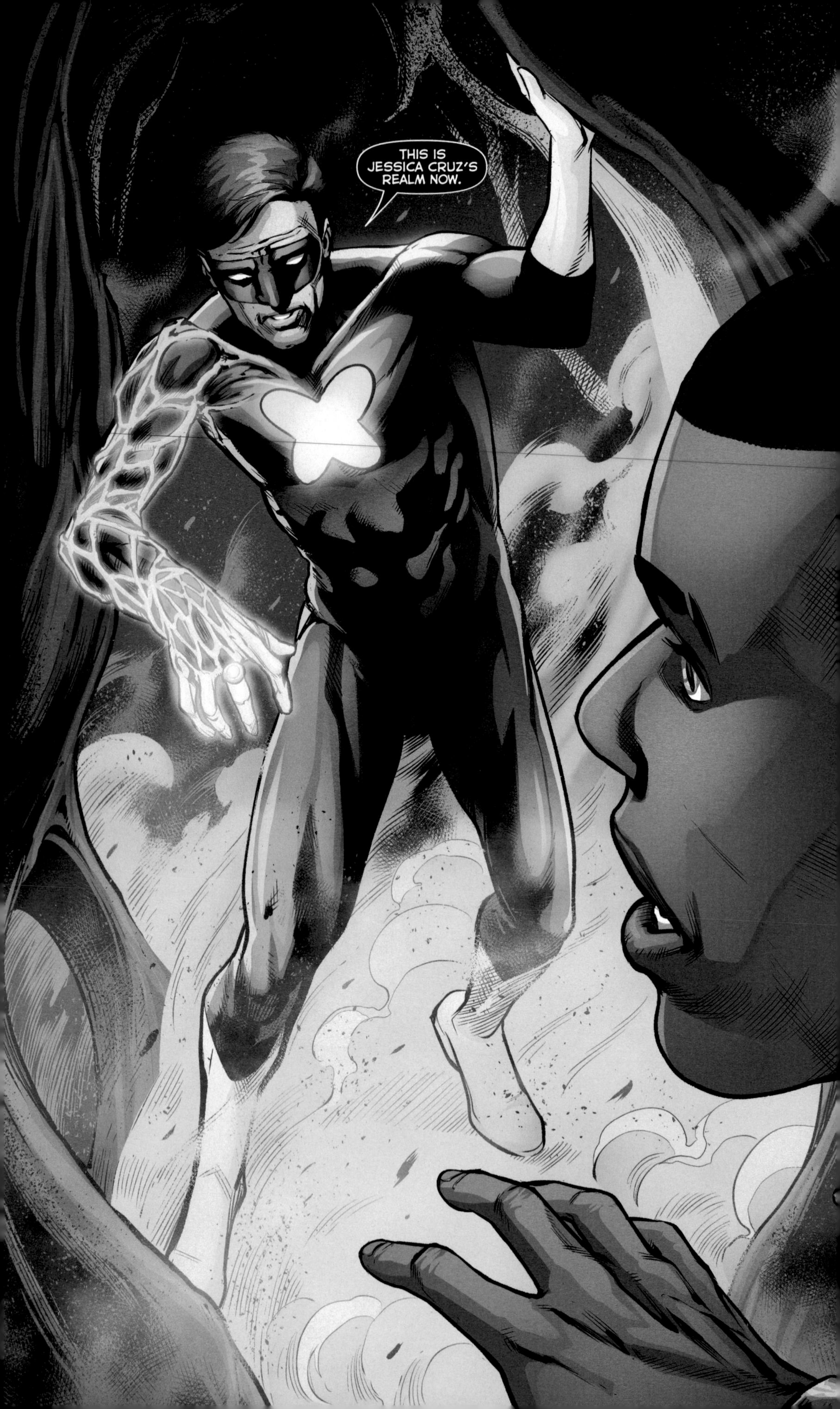
THIS IS JESSICA CRUZ'S REALM NOW.

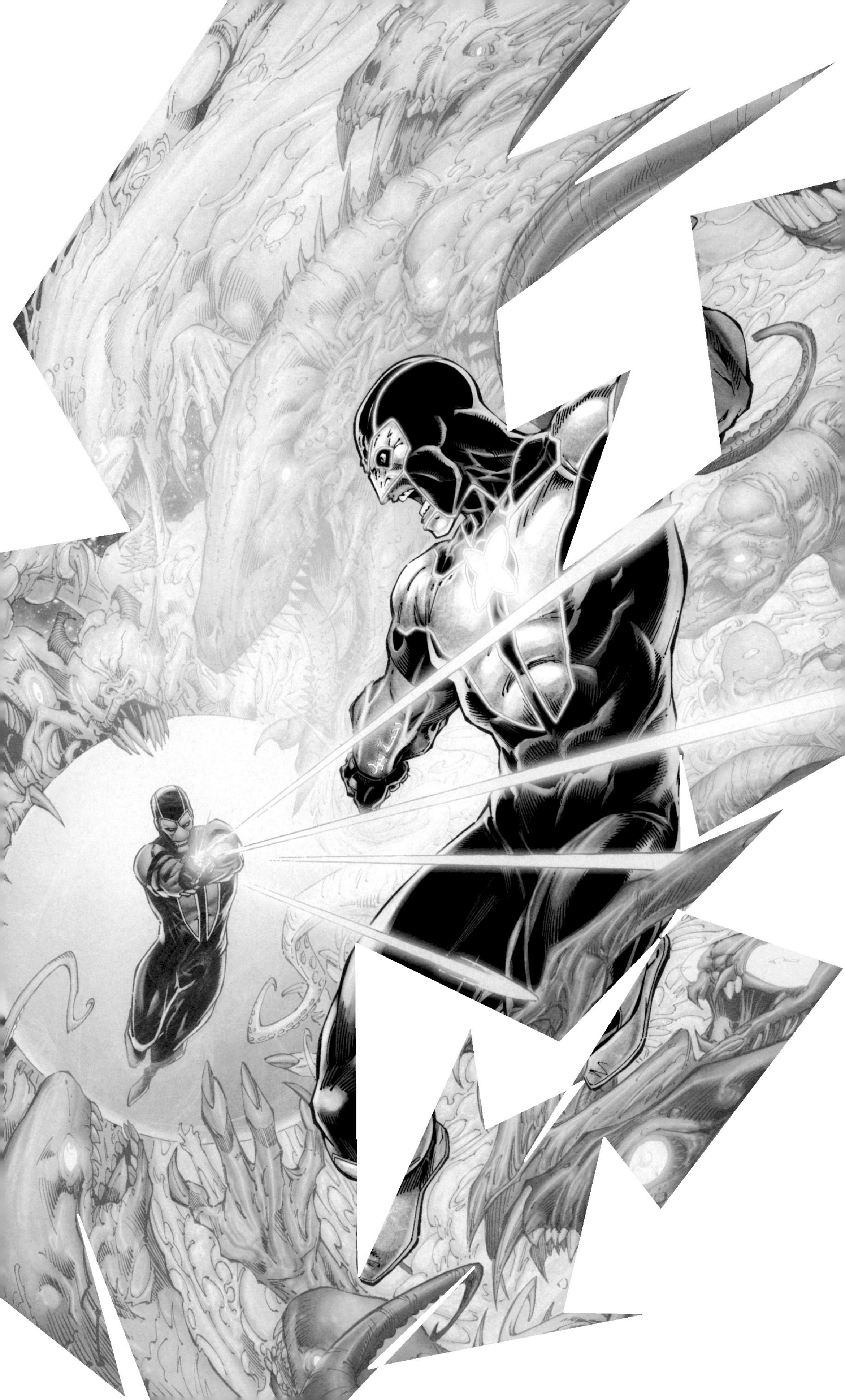

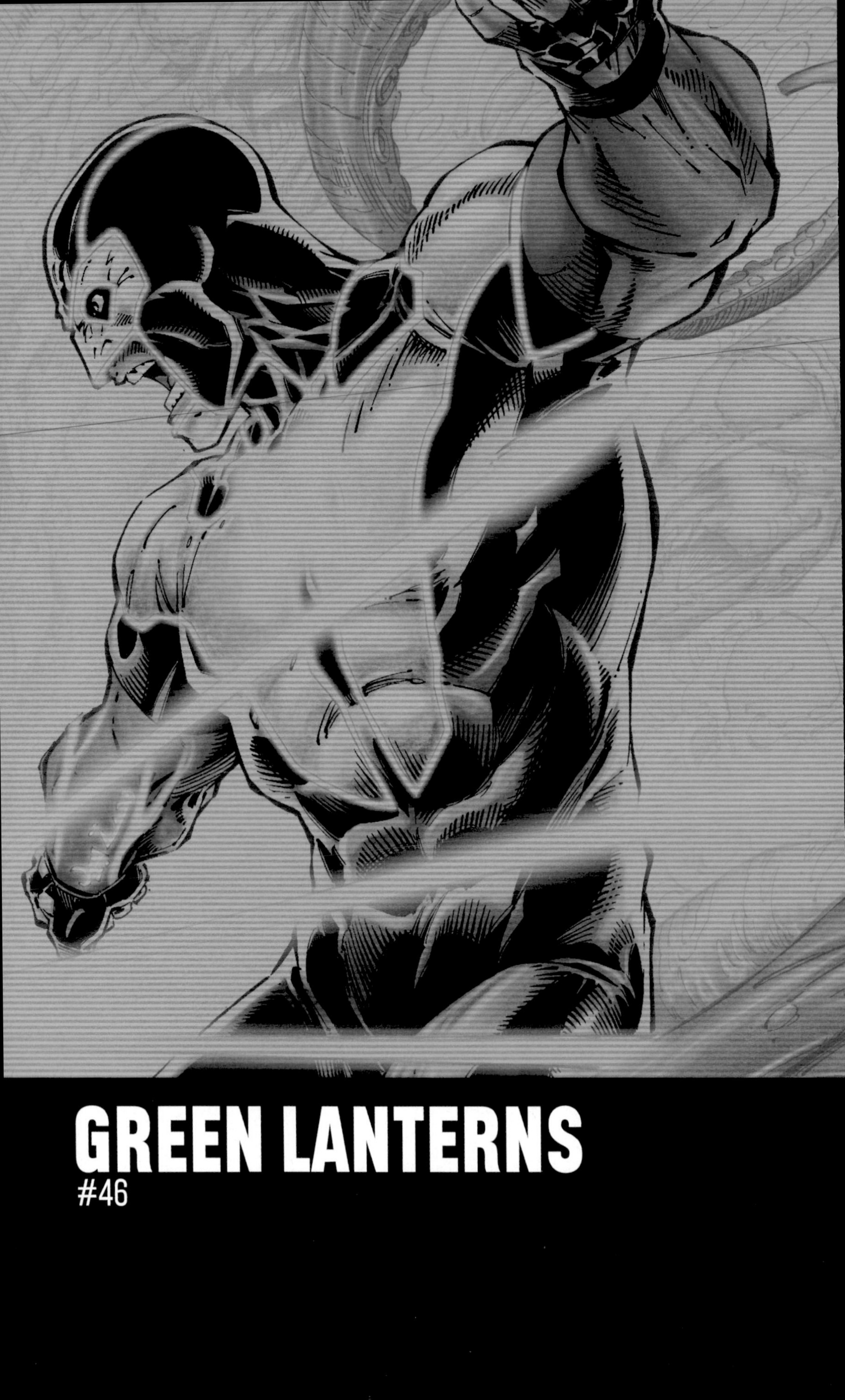

# GREEN LANTERNS
#46

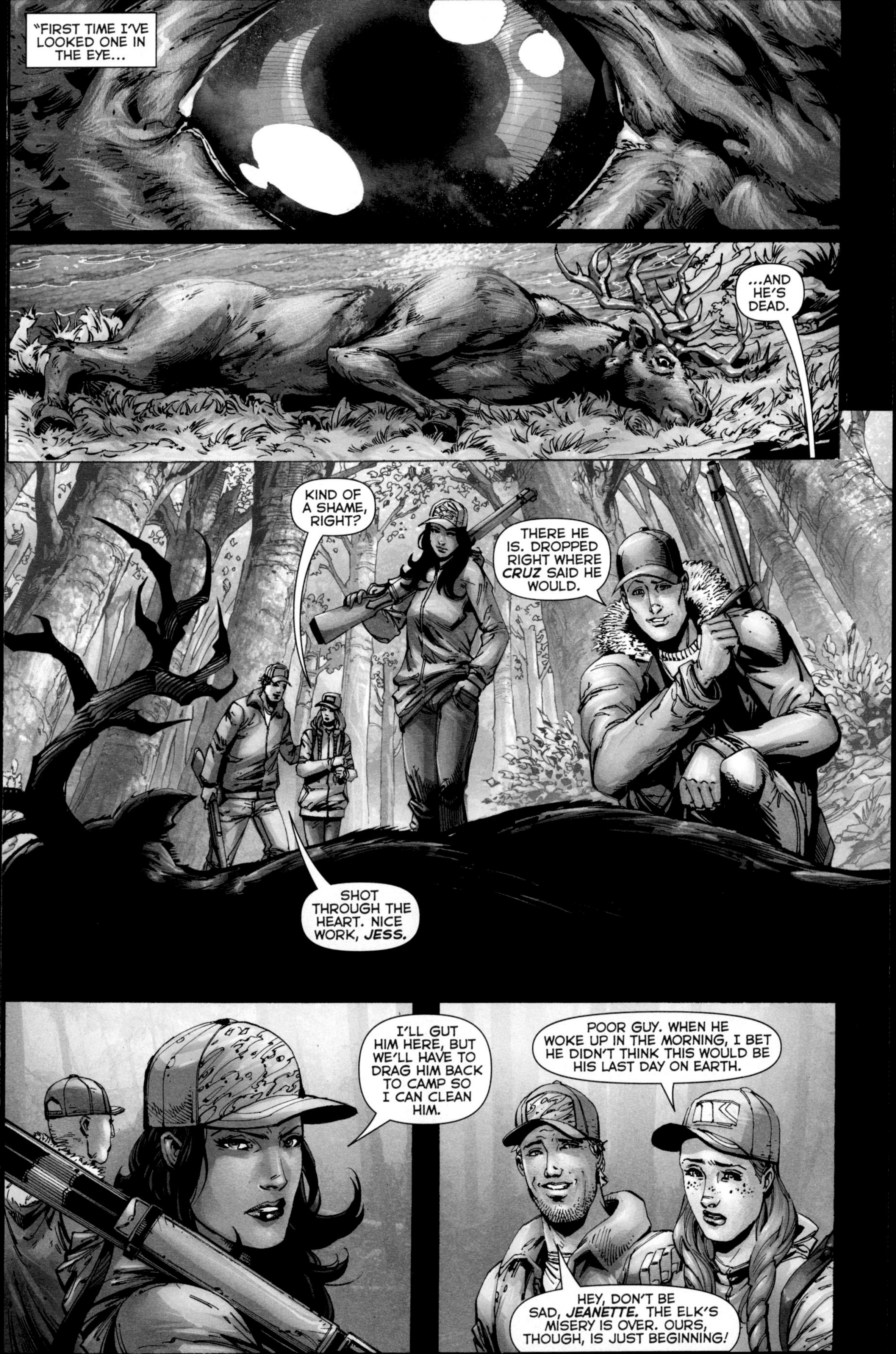
"FIRST TIME I'VE LOOKED ONE IN THE EYE...
...AND HE'S DEAD.
KIND OF A SHAME, RIGHT?
THERE HE IS. DROPPED RIGHT WHERE CRUZ SAID HE WOULD.
SHOT THROUGH THE HEART. NICE WORK, JESS.
I'LL GUT HIM HERE, BUT WE'LL HAVE TO DRAG HIM BACK TO CAMP SO I CAN CLEAN HIM.
POOR GUY. WHEN HE WOKE UP IN THE MORNING, I BET HE DIDN'T THINK THIS WOULD BE HIS LAST DAY ON EARTH.
HEY, DON'T BE SAD, JEANETTE. THE ELK'S MISERY IS OVER. OURS, THOUGH, IS JUST BEGINNING!

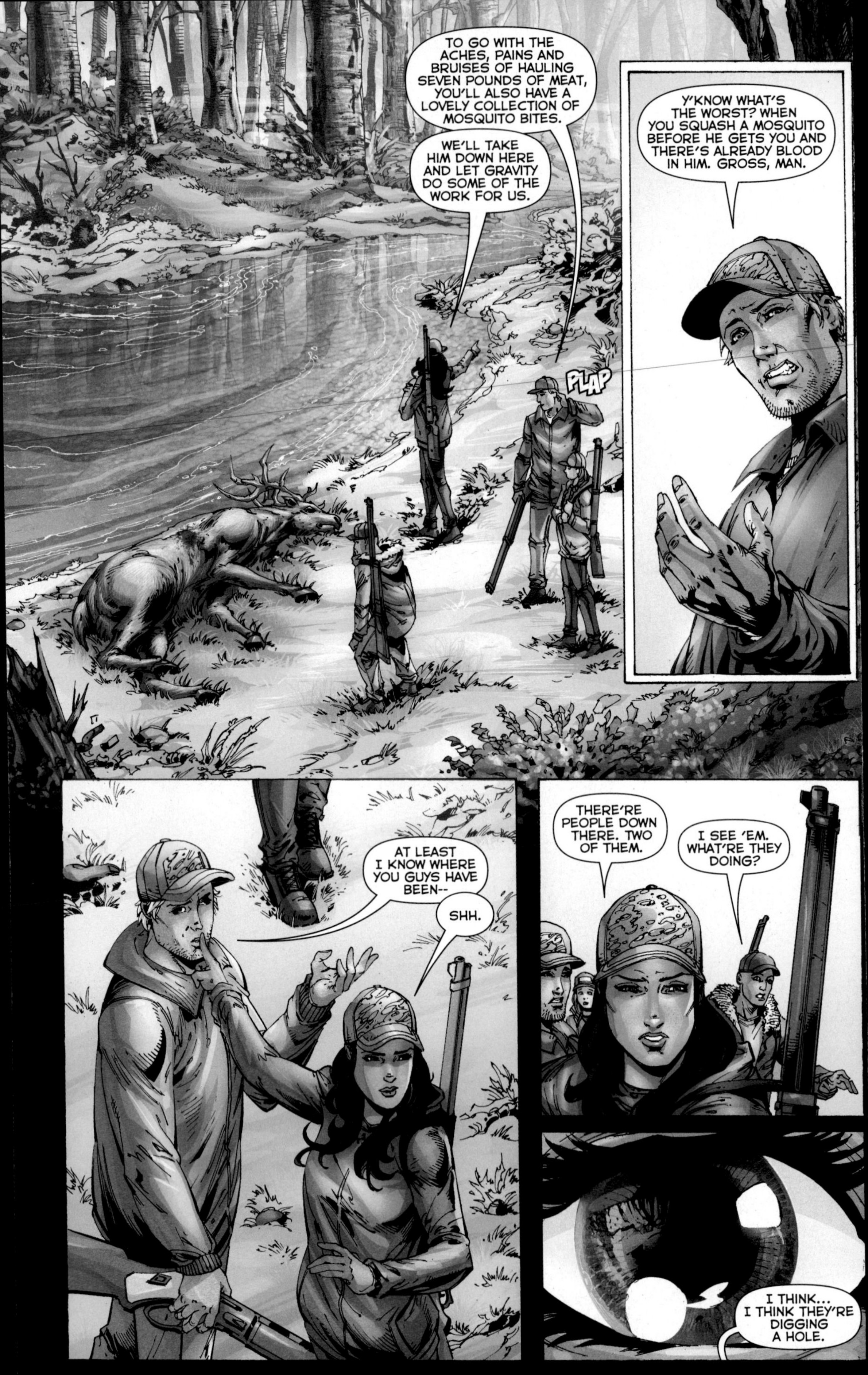
TO GO WITH THE ACHES, PAINS AND BRUISES OF HAULING SEVEN POUNDS OF MEAT, YOU'LL ALSO HAVE A LOVELY COLLECTION OF MOSQUITO BITES.
WE'LL TAKE HIM DOWN HERE AND LET GRAVITY DO SOME OF THE WORK FOR US.
PLAP
Y'KNOW WHAT'S THE WORST? WHEN YOU SQUASH A MOSQUITO BEFORE HE GETS YOU AND THERE'S ALREADY BLOOD IN HIM. GROSS, MAN.
AT LEAST I KNOW WHERE YOU GUYS HAVE BEEN--
SHH.
THERE'RE PEOPLE DOWN THERE. TWO OF THEM.
I SEE 'EM. WHAT'RE THEY DOING?
I THINK... I THINK THEY'RE DIGGING A HOLE.

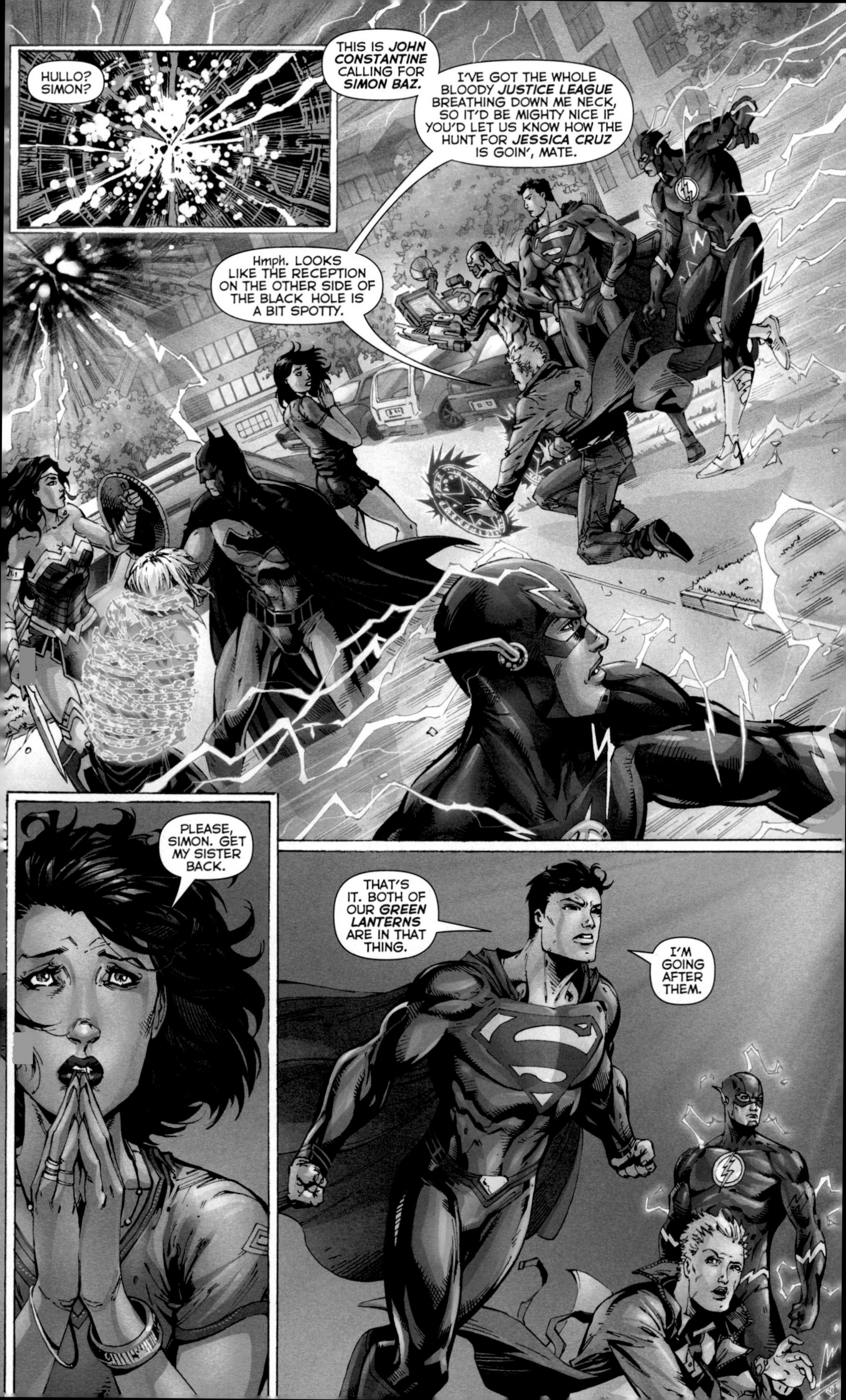
HULLO? SIMON?
THIS IS JOHN CONSTANTINE CALLING FOR SIMON BAZ.
I'VE GOT THE WHOLE BLOODY JUSTICE LEAGUE BREATHING DOWN ME NECK, SO IT'D BE MIGHTY NICE IF YOU'D LET US KNOW HOW THE HUNT FOR JESSICA CRUZ IS GOIN', MATE.
Hmph. LOOKS LIKE THE RECEPTION ON THE OTHER SIDE OF THE BLACK HOLE IS A BIT SPOTTY.
PLEASE, SIMON. GET MY SISTER BACK.
THAT'S IT. BOTH OF OUR GREEN LANTERNS ARE IN THAT THING.
I'M GOING AFTER THEM.

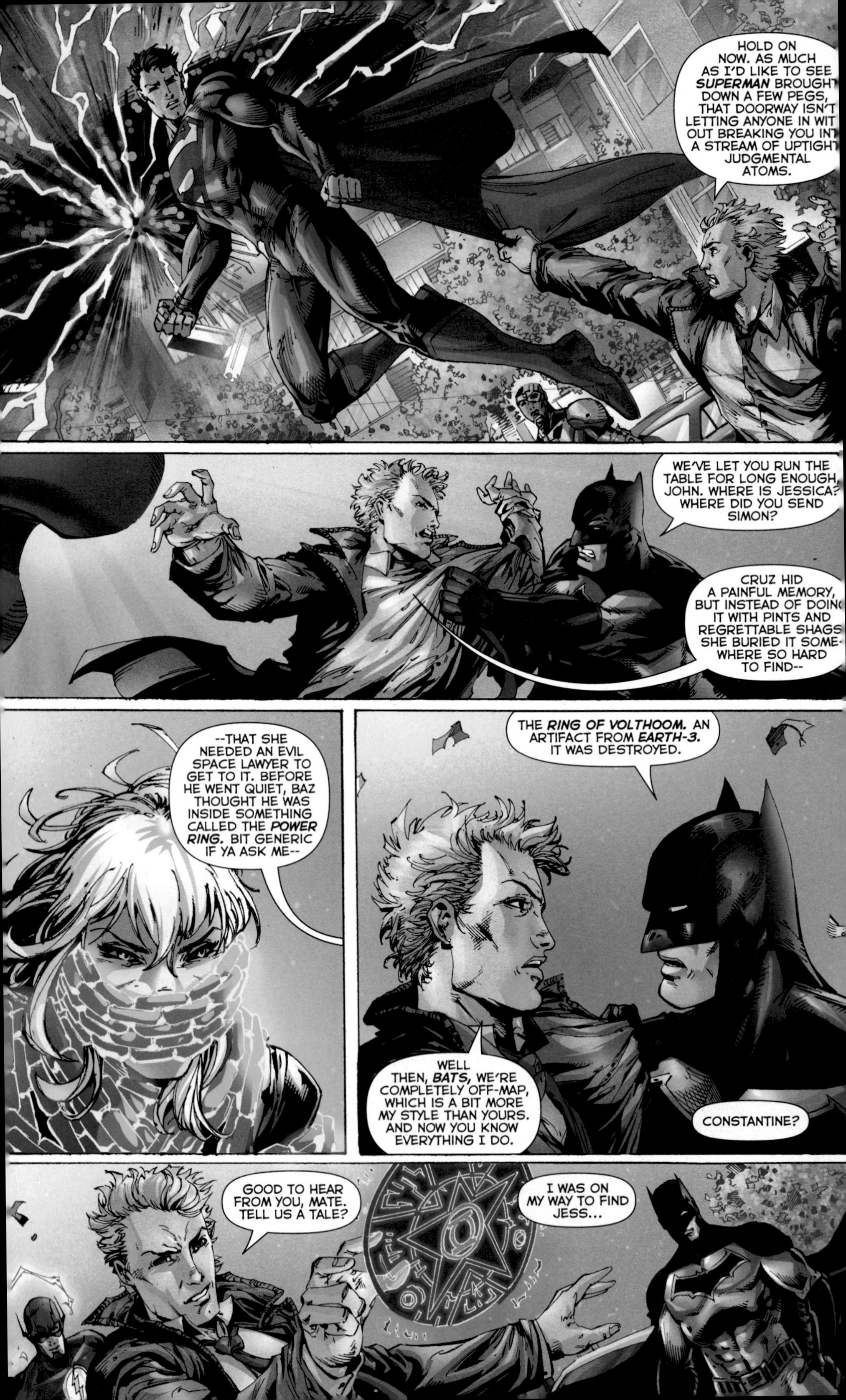
HOLD ON NOW. AS MUCH AS I'D LIKE TO SEE SUPERMAN BROUGHT DOWN A FEW PEGS, THAT DOORWAY ISN'T LETTING ANYONE IN WIT OUT BREAKING YOU INT A STREAM OF UPTIGHT JUDGMENTAL ATOMS.
WE'VE LET YOU RUN THE TABLE FOR LONG ENOUGH, JOHN. WHERE IS JESSICA? WHERE DID YOU SEND SIMON?
CRUZ HID A PAINFUL MEMORY, BUT INSTEAD OF DOIN IT WITH PINTS AND REGRETTABLE SHAGS SHE BURIED IT SOME-WHERE SO HARD TO FIND--
--THAT SHE NEEDED AN EVIL SPACE LAWYER TO GET TO IT. BEFORE HE WENT QUIET, BAZ THOUGHT HE WAS INSIDE SOMETHING CALLED THE POWER RING. BIT GENERIC IF YA ASK ME--
THE RING OF VOLTHOOM. AN ARTIFACT FROM EARTH-3. IT WAS DESTROYED.
WELL THEN, BATS, WE'RE COMPLETELY OFF-MAP, WHICH IS A BIT MORE MY STYLE THAN YOURS. AND NOW YOU KNOW EVERYTHING I DO.
CONSTANTINE?
GOOD TO HEAR FROM YOU, MATE. TELL US A TALE?
I WAS ON MY WAY TO FIND JESS...

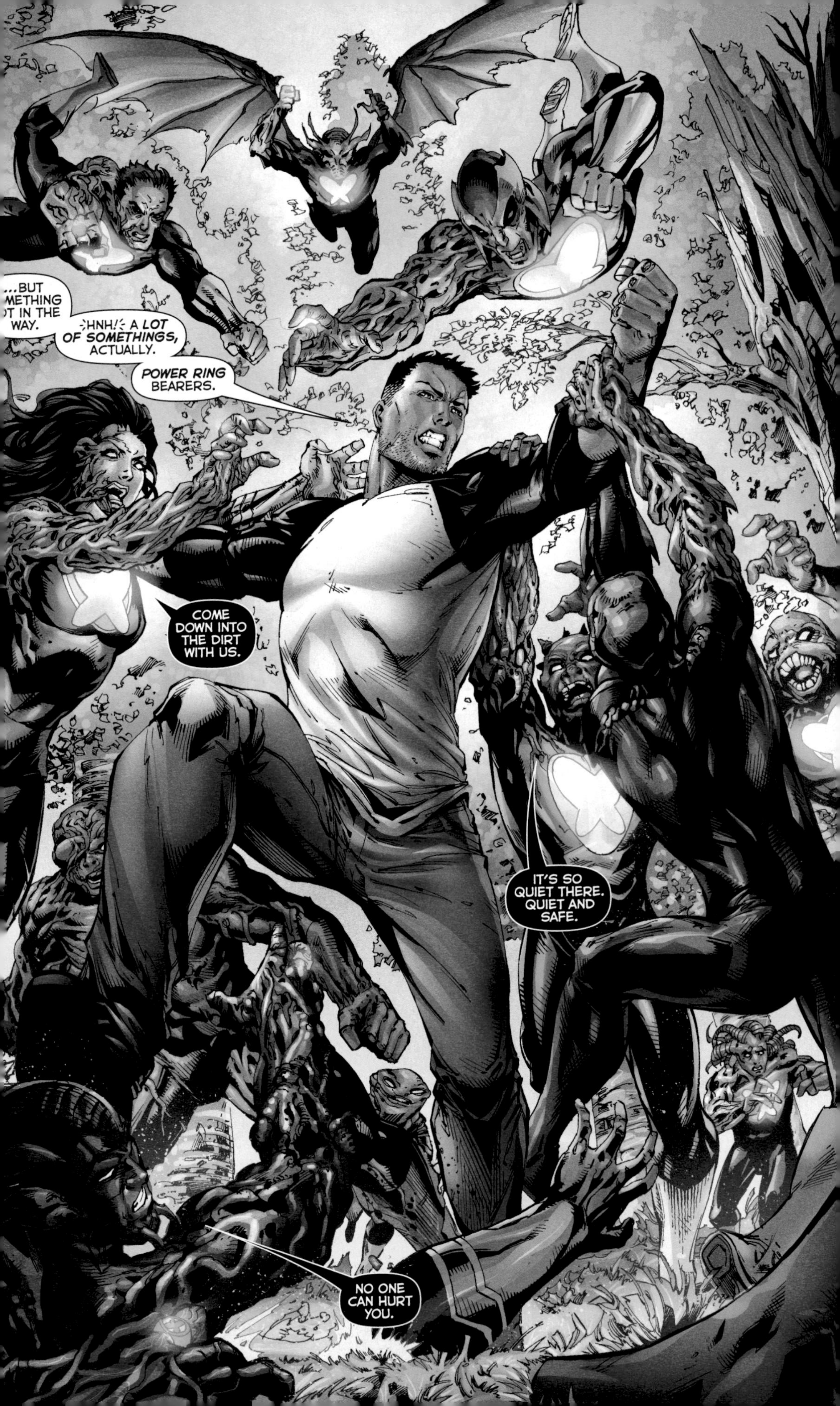
...BUT
METHING
T IN THE
WAY.
HNH! A LOT OF SOMETHINGS, ACTUALLY.
POWER RING BEARERS.
COME DOWN INTO THE DIRT WITH US.
IT'S SO QUIET THERE. QUIET AND SAFE.
NO ONE CAN HURT YOU.

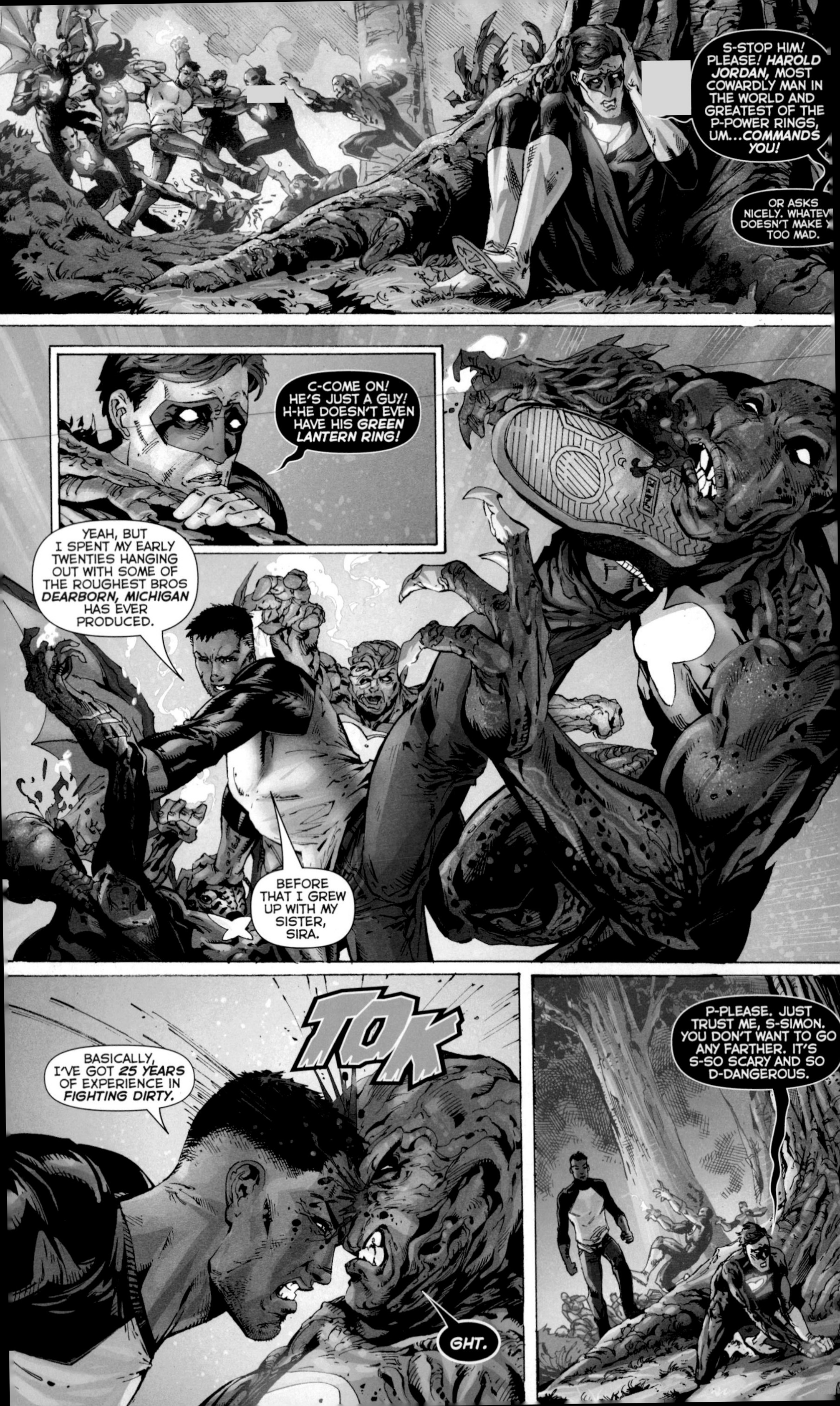

S-STOP HIM! PLEASE! HAROLD JORDAN, MOST COWARDLY MAN IN THE WORLD AND GREATEST OF THE P-POWER RINGS, UM...COMMANDS YOU!
OR ASKS NICELY. WHATEV DOESN'T MAKE TOO MAD.
C-COME ON! HE'S JUST A GUY! H-HE DOESN'T EVEN HAVE HIS GREEN LANTERN RING!
YEAH, BUT I SPENT MY EARLY TWENTIES HANGING OUT WITH SOME OF THE ROUGHEST BROS DEARBORN, MICHIGAN HAS EVER PRODUCED.
BEFORE THAT I GREW UP WITH MY SISTER, SIRA.
TOK
BASICALLY, I'VE GOT 25 YEARS OF EXPERIENCE IN FIGHTING DIRTY.
GHT.
P-PLEASE. JUST TRUST ME, S-SIMON. YOU DON'T WANT TO GO ANY FARTHER. IT'S S-SO SCARY AND SO D-DANGEROUS.

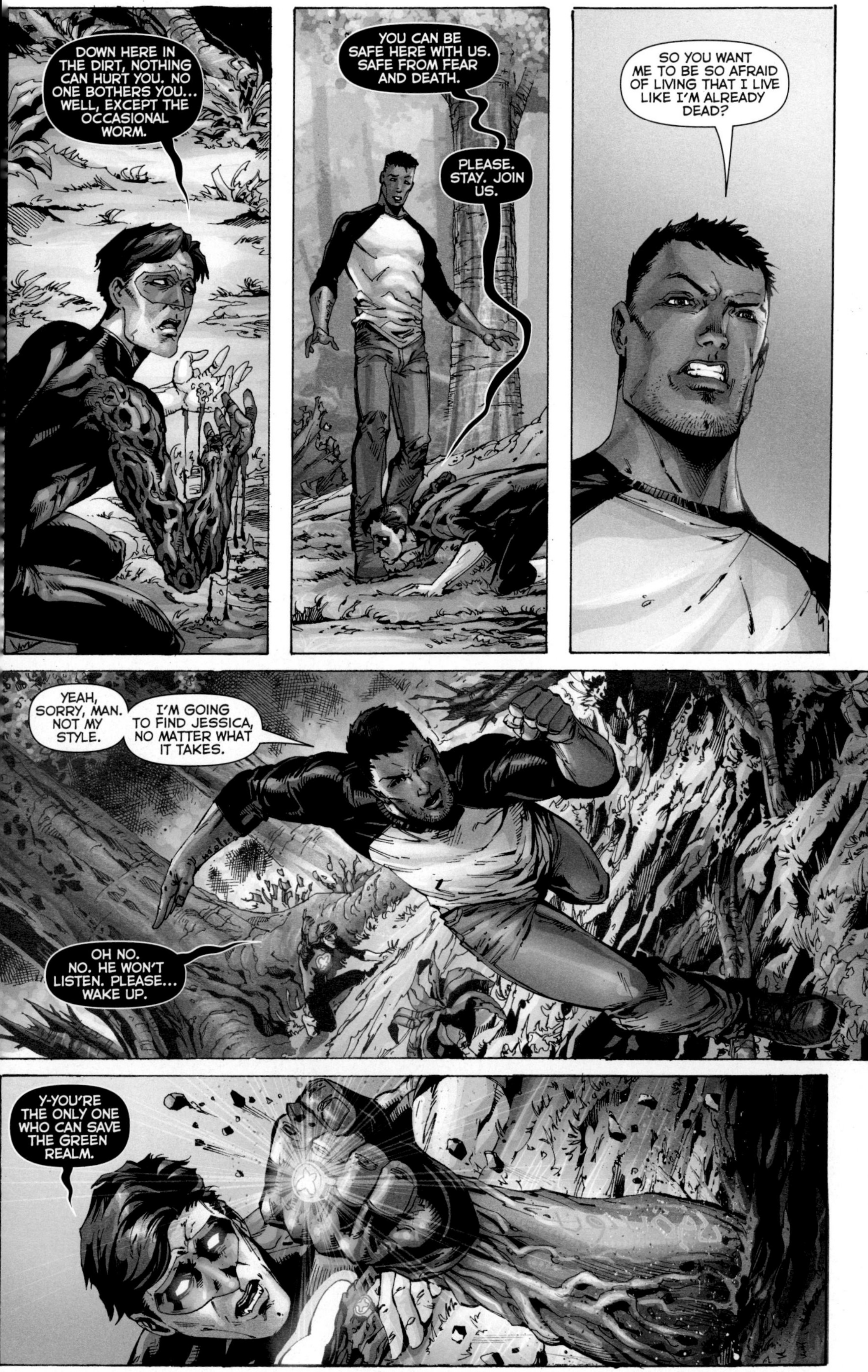
DOWN HERE IN THE DIRT, NOTHING CAN HURT YOU. NO ONE BOTHERS YOU... WELL, EXCEPT THE OCCASIONAL WORM.
YOU CAN BE SAFE HERE WITH US. SAFE FROM FEAR AND DEATH.
PLEASE. STAY. JOIN US.
SO YOU WANT ME TO BE SO AFRAID OF LIVING THAT I LIVE LIKE I'M ALREADY DEAD?
YEAH, SORRY, MAN. NOT MY STYLE.
I'M GOING TO FIND JESSICA, NO MATTER WHAT IT TAKES.
OH NO. NO. HE WON'T LISTEN. PLEASE... WAKE UP.
Y-YOU'RE THE ONLY ONE WHO CAN SAVE THE GREEN REALM.

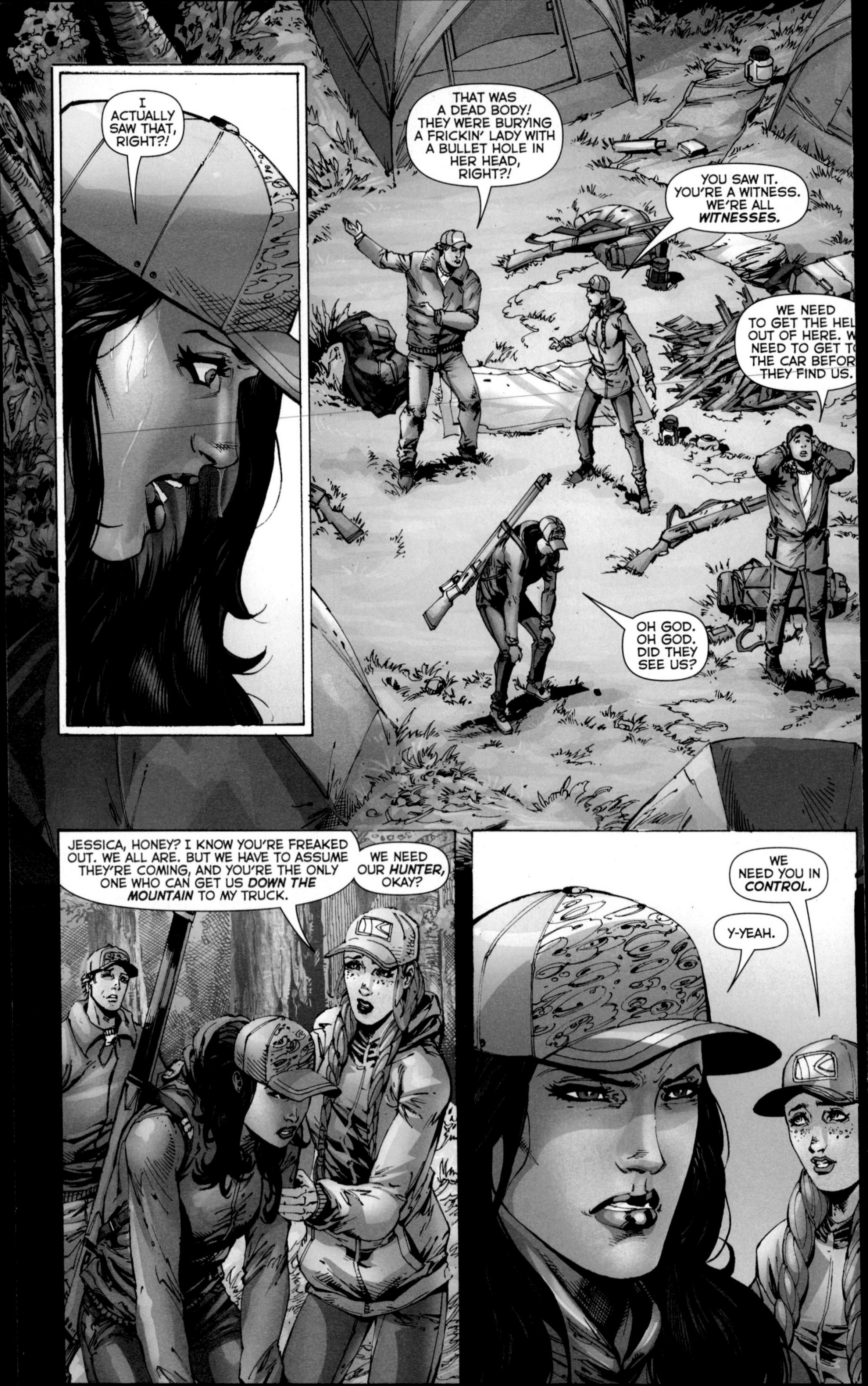
I ACTUALLY SAW THAT, RIGHT?!
THAT WAS A DEAD BODY! THEY WERE BURYING A FRICKIN' LADY WITH A BULLET HOLE IN HER HEAD, RIGHT?!
YOU SAW IT. YOU'RE A WITNESS. WE'RE ALL *WITNESSES.*
WE NEED TO GET THE HEL OUT OF HERE. W NEED TO GET TO THE CAR BEFOR THEY FIND US.
OH GOD. OH GOD. DID THEY SEE US?
JESSICA, HONEY? I KNOW YOU'RE FREAKED OUT. WE ALL ARE. BUT WE HAVE TO ASSUME THEY'RE COMING, AND YOU'RE THE ONLY ONE WHO CAN GET US *DOWN THE MOUNTAIN* TO MY TRUCK.
WE NEED OUR *HUNTER,* OKAY?
WE NEED YOU IN *CONTROL.*
Y-YEAH.

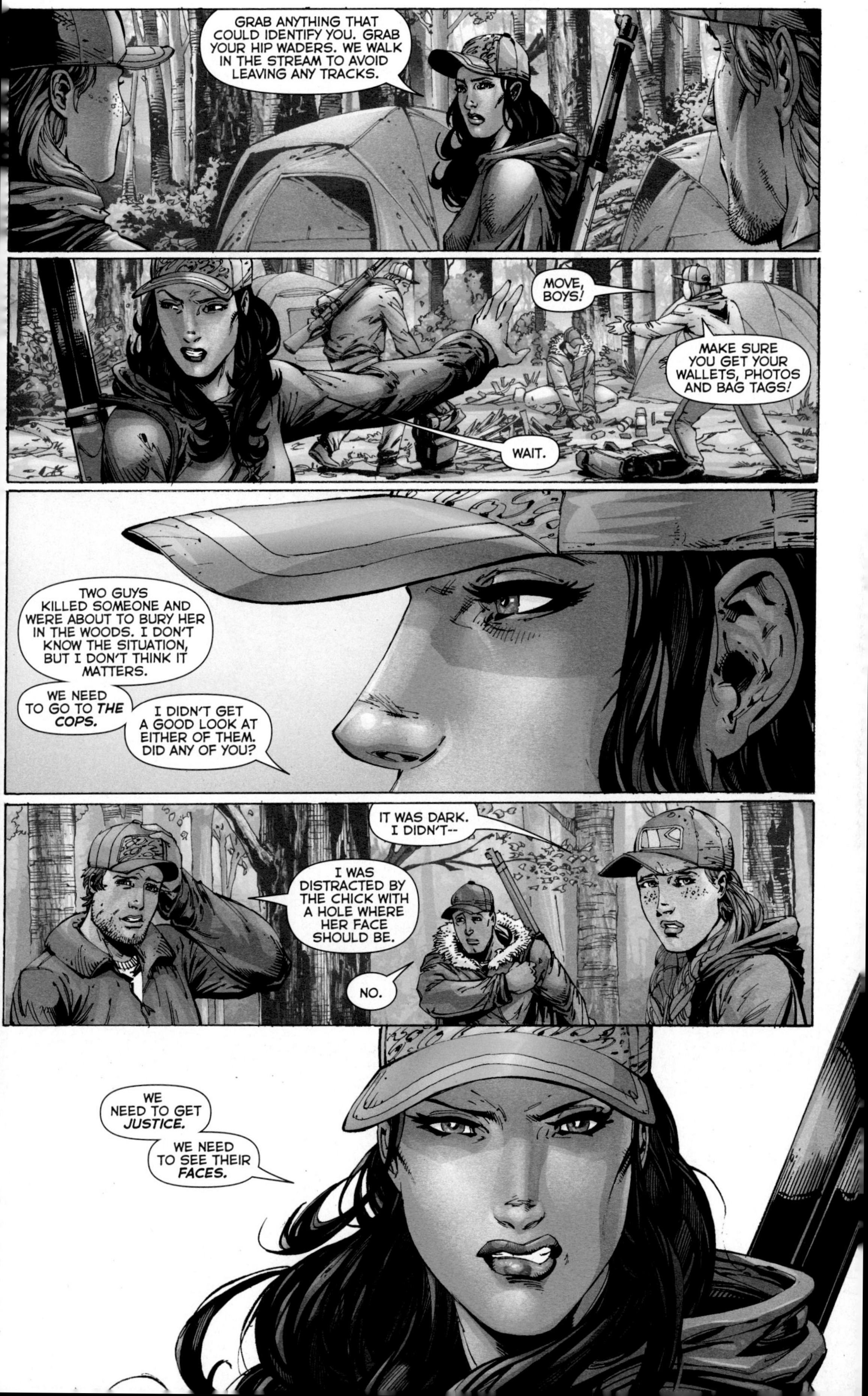
GRAB ANYTHING THAT COULD IDENTIFY YOU. GRAB YOUR HIP WADERS. WE WALK IN THE STREAM TO AVOID LEAVING ANY TRACKS.
MOVE, BOYS!
MAKE SURE YOU GET YOUR WALLETS, PHOTOS AND BAG TAGS!
WAIT.
TWO GUYS KILLED SOMEONE AND WERE ABOUT TO BURY HER IN THE WOODS. I DON'T KNOW THE SITUATION, BUT I DON'T THINK IT MATTERS.
WE NEED TO GO TO *THE COPS.*
I DIDN'T GET A GOOD LOOK AT EITHER OF THEM. DID ANY OF YOU?
IT WAS DARK. I DIDN'T--
I WAS DISTRACTED BY THE CHICK WITH A HOLE WHERE HER FACE SHOULD BE.
NO.
WE NEED TO GET *JUSTICE.*
WE NEED TO SEE THEIR *FACES.*

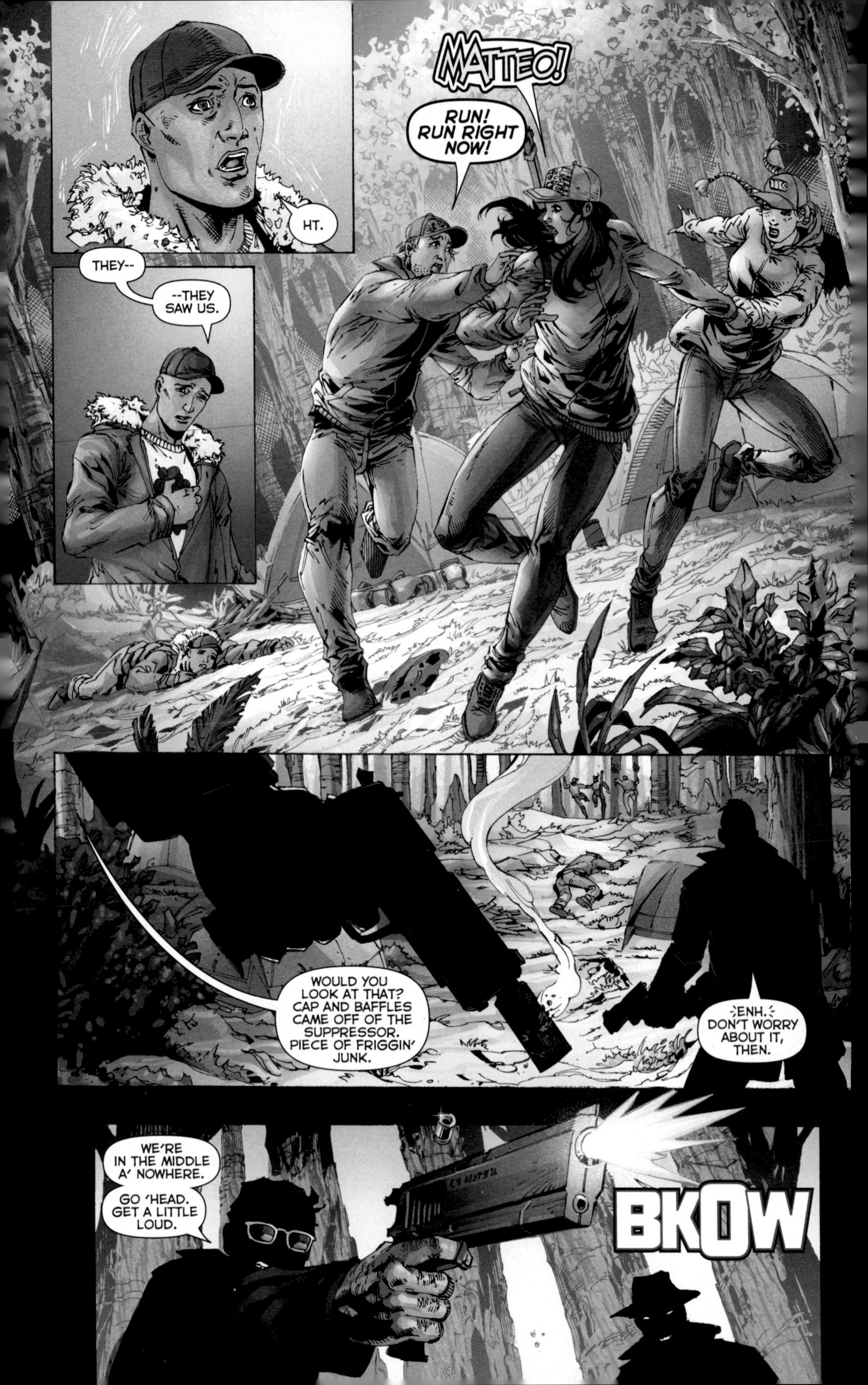
HT.
THEY--
--THEY SAW US.
MATTEO!
RUN! RUN RIGHT NOW!
WOULD YOU LOOK AT THAT? CAP AND BAFFLES CAME OFF OF THE SUPPRESSOR. PIECE OF FRIGGIN' JUNK.
ENH. DON'T WORRY ABOUT IT, THEN.
WE'RE IN THE MIDDLE A' NOWHERE.
GO 'HEAD. GET A LITTLE LOUD.
BKOW

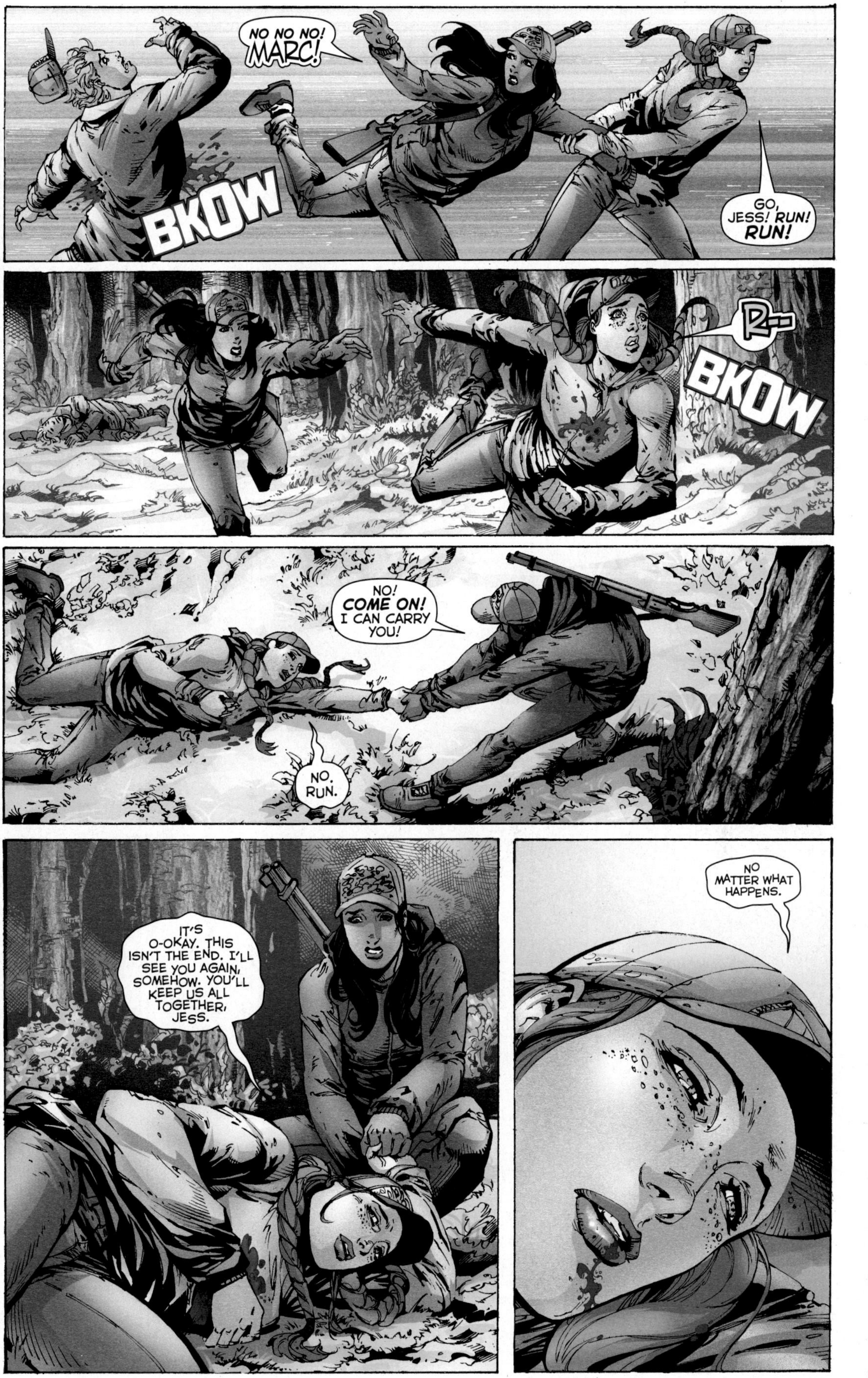
NO NO NO! MARC!
BKOW
GO, JESS! RUN! RUN!
R--
BKOW
NO! COME ON! I CAN CARRY YOU!
NO. RUN.
IT'S O-OKAY. THIS ISN'T THE END. I'LL SEE YOU AGAIN, SOMEHOW. YOU'LL KEEP US ALL TOGETHER, JESS.
NO MATTER WHAT HAPPENS.

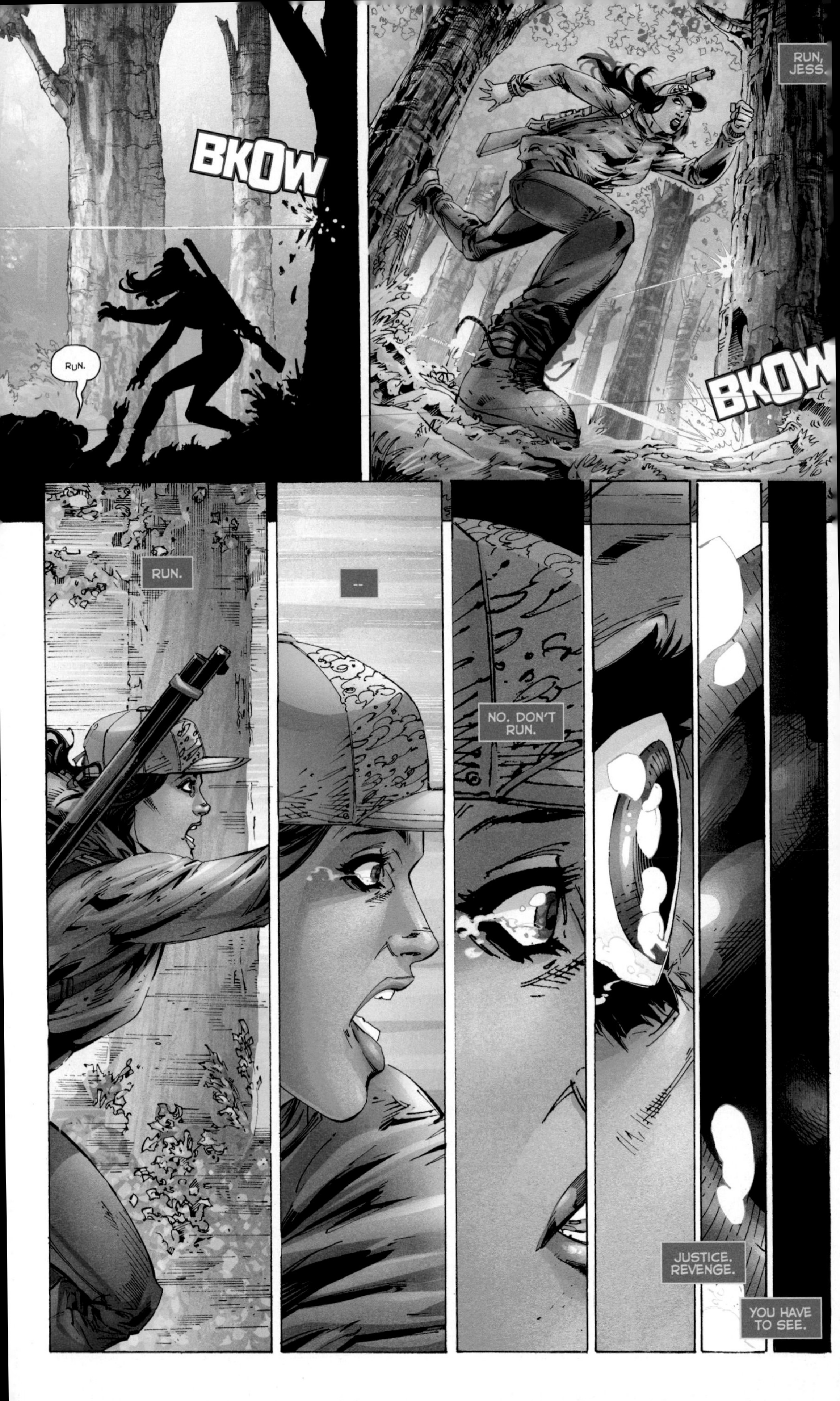
BKOW
RUN.
RUN, JESS.
BKOW
RUN.
--
NO. DON'T RUN.
JUSTICE. REVENGE.
YOU HAVE TO SEE.

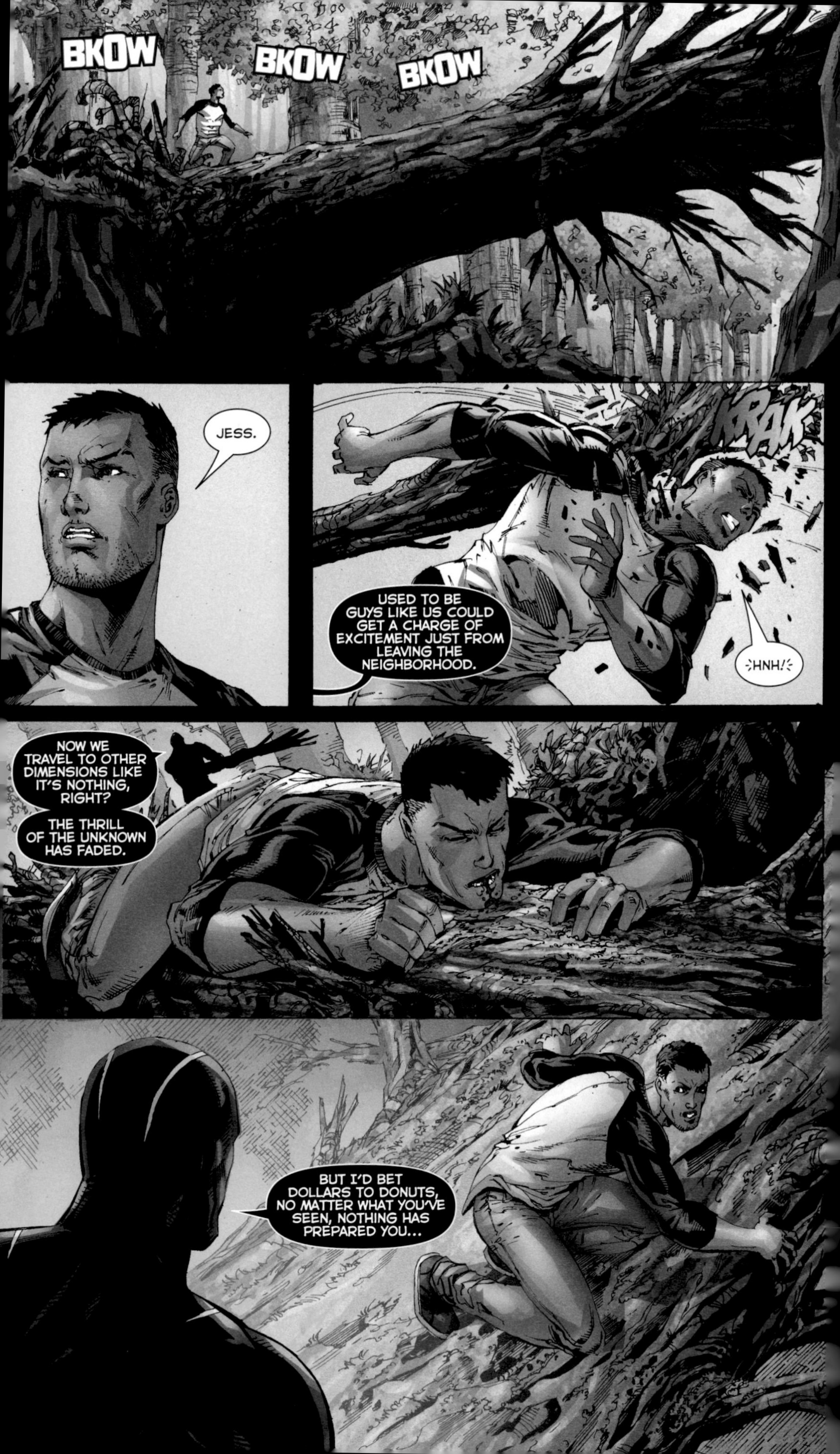
BKOW
BKOW
BKOW
JESS.
KRAK
USED TO BE GUYS LIKE US COULD GET A CHARGE OF EXCITEMENT JUST FROM LEAVING THE NEIGHBORHOOD.
HNH!
NOW WE TRAVEL TO OTHER DIMENSIONS LIKE IT'S NOTHING, RIGHT?
THE THRILL OF THE UNKNOWN HAS FADED.
BUT I'D BET DOLLARS TO DONUTS, NO MATTER WHAT YOU'VE SEEN, NOTHING HAS PREPARED YOU...

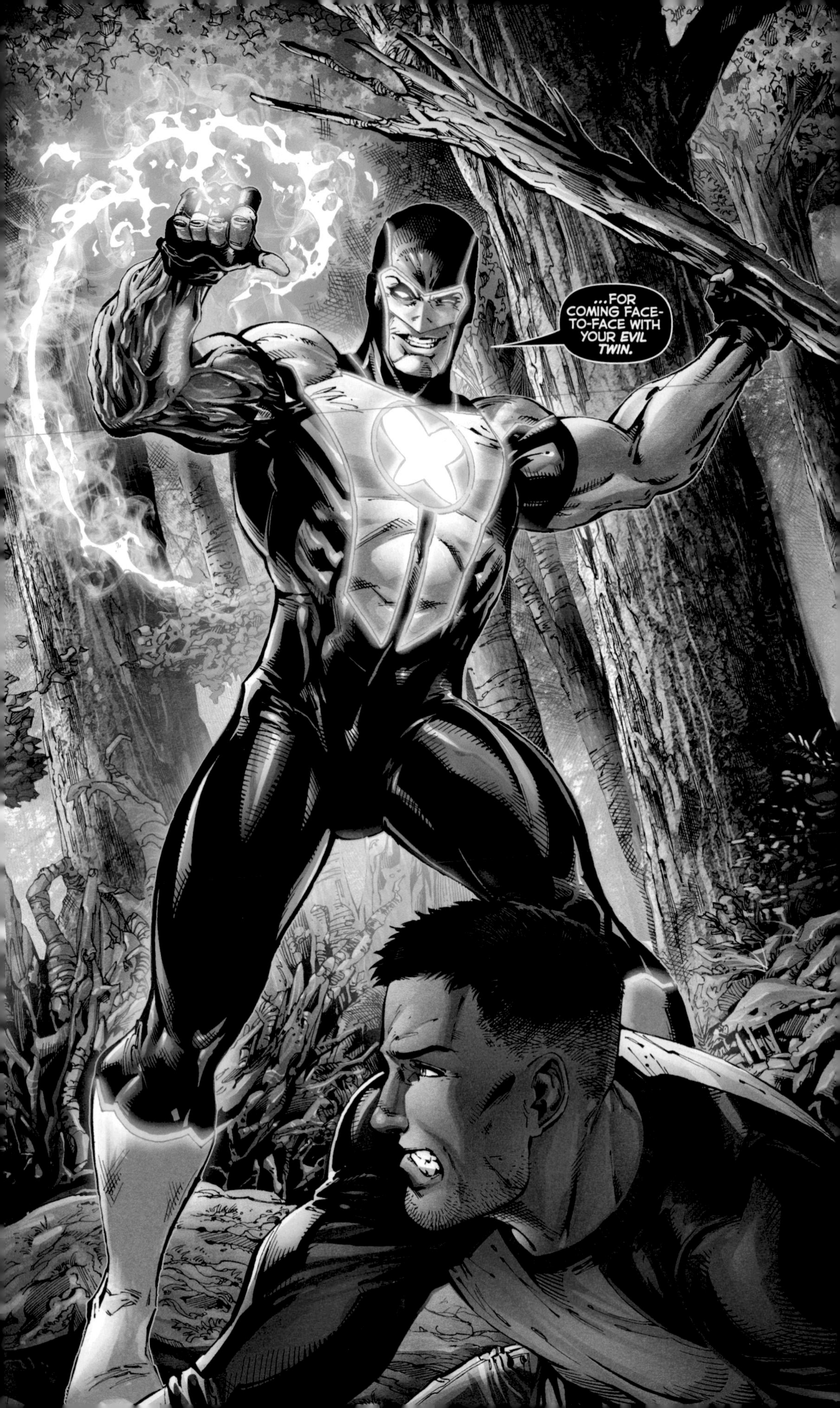
...FOR COMING FACE-TO-FACE WITH YOUR EVIL TWIN.

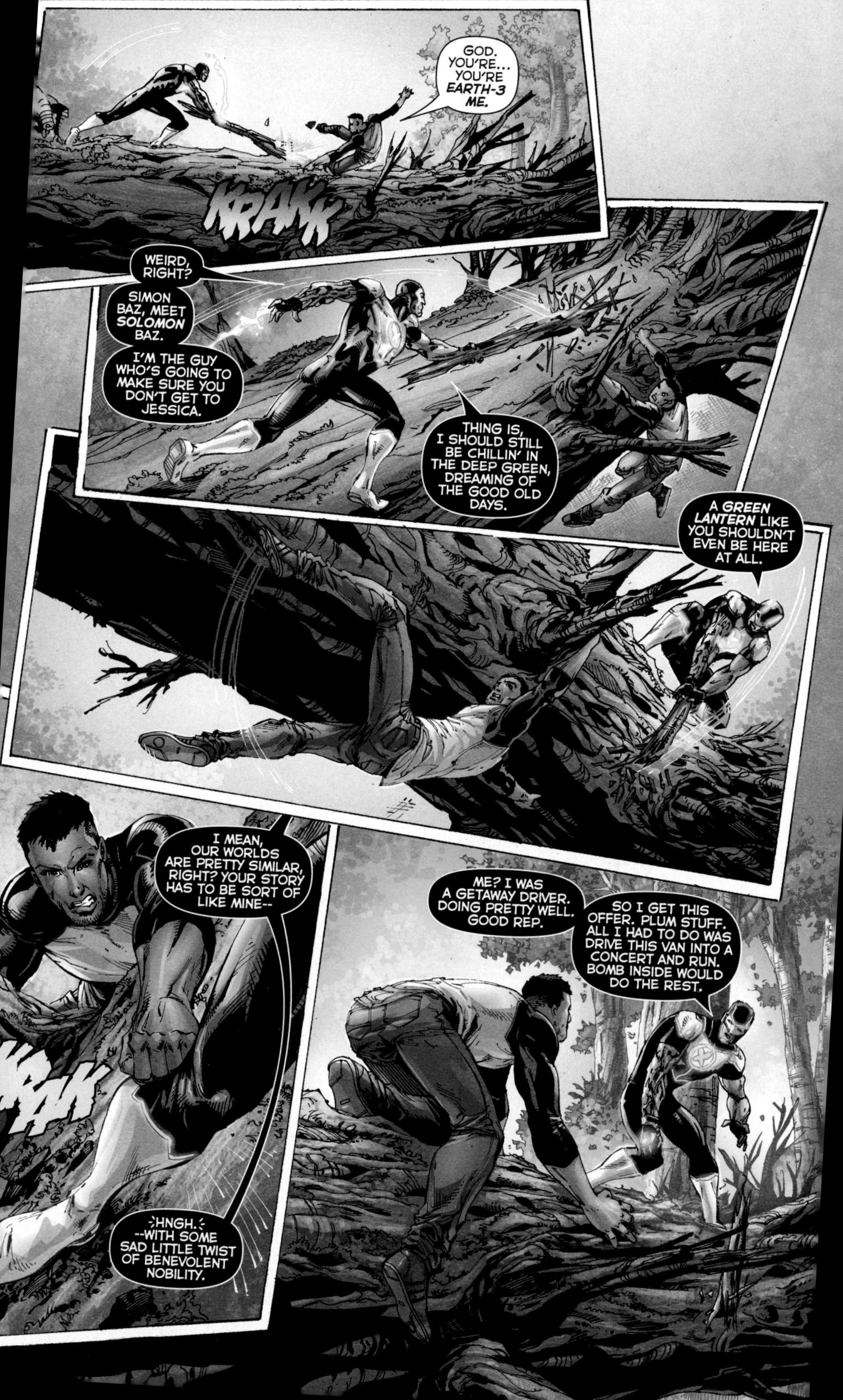
GOD. YOU'RE... YOU'RE EARTH-3 ME.
KRAKK
WEIRD, RIGHT?
SIMON BAZ, MEET SOLOMON BAZ.
I'M THE GUY WHO'S GOING TO MAKE SURE YOU DON'T GET TO JESSICA.
THING IS, I SHOULD STILL BE CHILLIN' IN THE DEEP GREEN, DREAMING OF THE GOOD OLD DAYS.
A GREEN LANTERN LIKE YOU SHOULDN'T EVEN BE HERE AT ALL.
I MEAN, OUR WORLDS ARE PRETTY SIMILAR, RIGHT? YOUR STORY HAS TO BE SORT OF LIKE MINE--
HNGH.
--WITH SOME SAD LITTLE TWIST OF BENEVOLENT NOBILITY.
ME? I WAS A GETAWAY DRIVER. DOING PRETTY WELL. GOOD REP.
SO I GET THIS OFFER. PLUM STUFF. ALL I HAD TO DO WAS DRIVE THIS VAN INTO A CONCERT AND RUN. BOMB INSIDE WOULD DO THE REST.

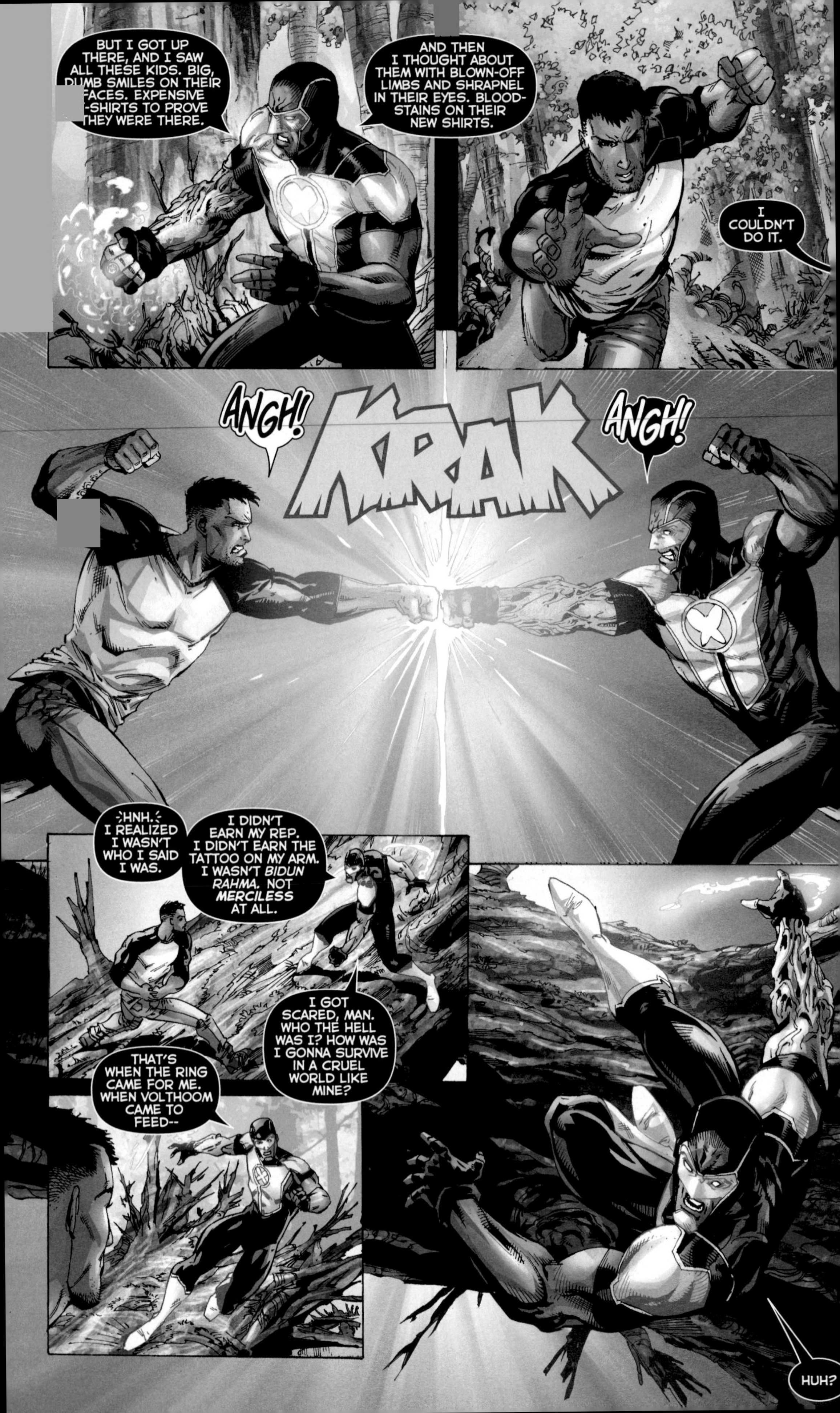

BUT I GOT UP THERE, AND I SAW ALL THESE KIDS. BIG, DUMB SMILES ON THEIR FACES. EXPENSIVE -SHIRTS TO PROVE THEY WERE THERE.
AND THEN I THOUGHT ABOUT THEM WITH BLOWN-OFF LIMBS AND SHRAPNEL IN THEIR EYES. BLOOD-STAINS ON THEIR NEW SHIRTS.
I COULDN'T DO IT.
ANGH!
KRAK
ANGH!
HNH. I REALIZED I WASN'T WHO I SAID I WAS.
I DIDN'T EARN MY REP. I DIDN'T EARN THE TATTOO ON MY ARM. I WASN'T *BIDUN RAHMA*. NOT *MERCILESS* AT ALL.
I GOT SCARED, MAN. WHO THE HELL WAS I? HOW WAS I GONNA SURVIVE IN A CRUEL WORLD LIKE MINE?
THAT'S WHEN THE RING CAME FOR ME. WHEN VOLTHOOM CAME TO FEED--
HUH?

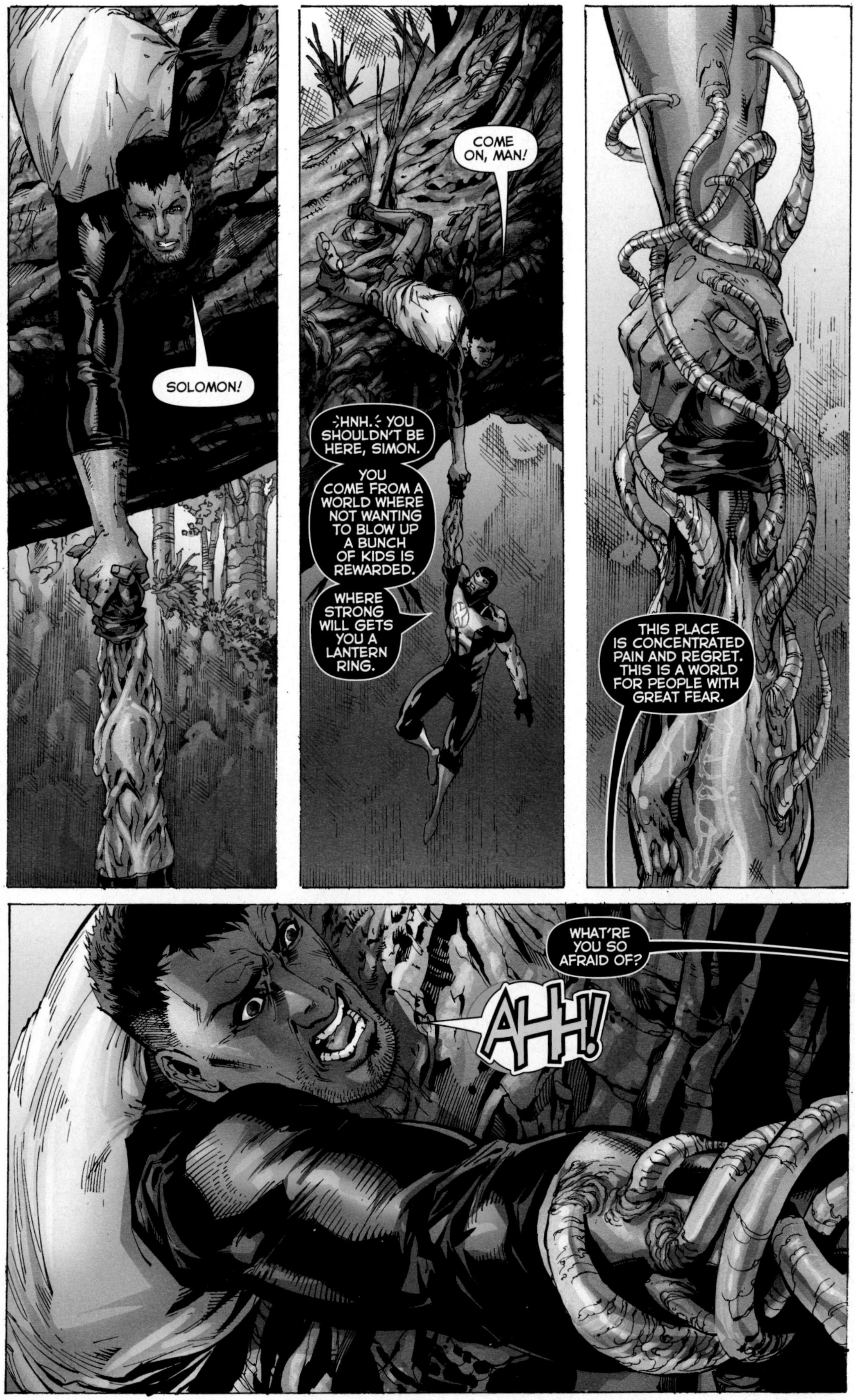
SOLOMON!
COME ON, MAN!
HNH. YOU SHOULDN'T BE HERE, SIMON.
YOU COME FROM A WORLD WHERE NOT WANTING TO BLOW UP A BUNCH OF KIDS IS REWARDED.
WHERE STRONG WILL GETS YOU A LANTERN RING.
THIS PLACE IS CONCENTRATED PAIN AND REGRET. THIS IS A WORLD FOR PEOPLE WITH GREAT FEAR.
WHAT'RE YOU SO AFRAID OF?
AHH!

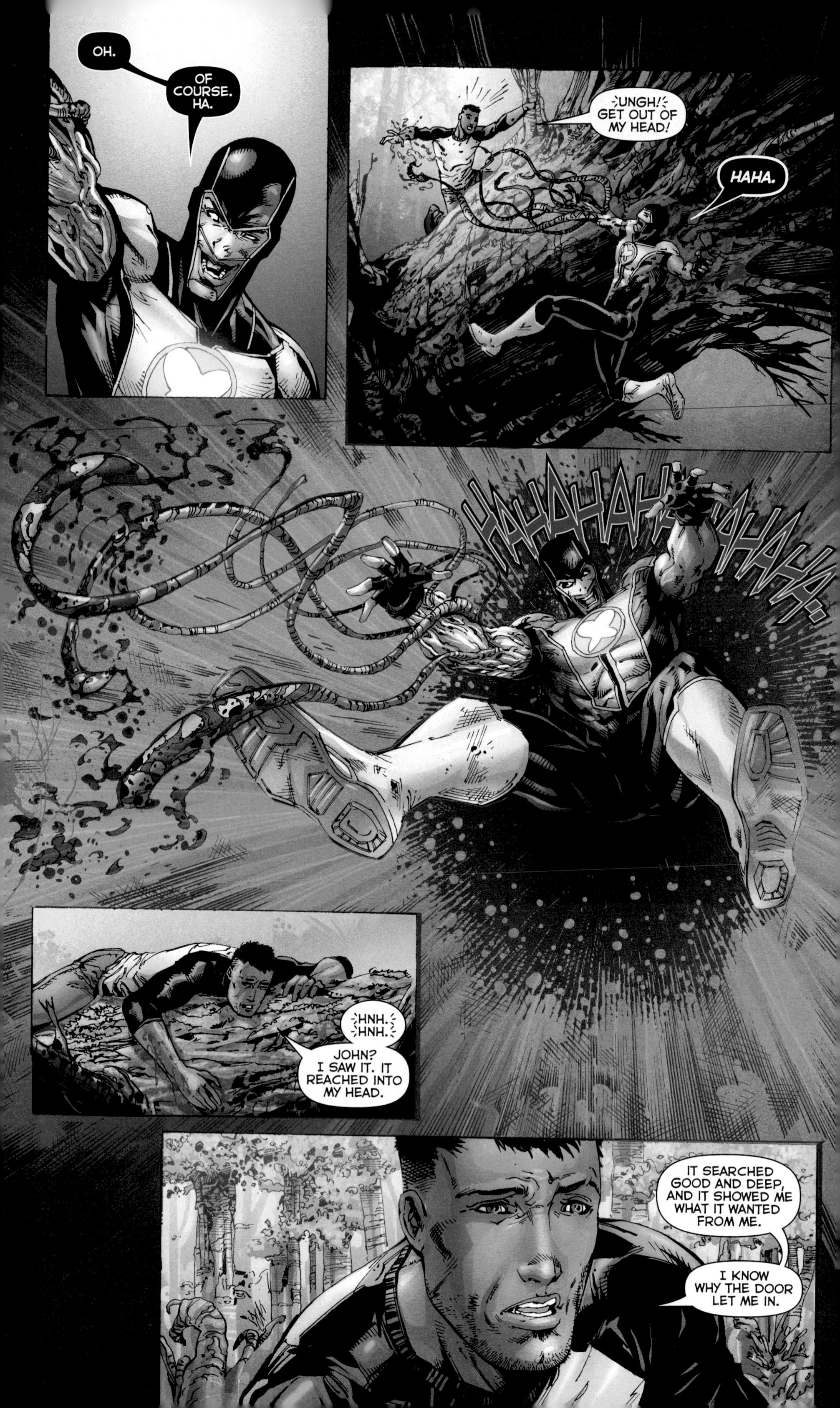
OH.
OF COURSE. HA.
UNGH! GET OUT OF MY HEAD!
HAHA.
HAHAHAHAHAHAHAHA!
HNH. HNH.
JOHN? I SAW IT. IT REACHED INTO MY HEAD.
IT SEARCHED GOOD AND DEEP, AND IT SHOWED ME WHAT IT WANTED FROM ME.
I KNOW WHY THE DOOR LET ME IN.

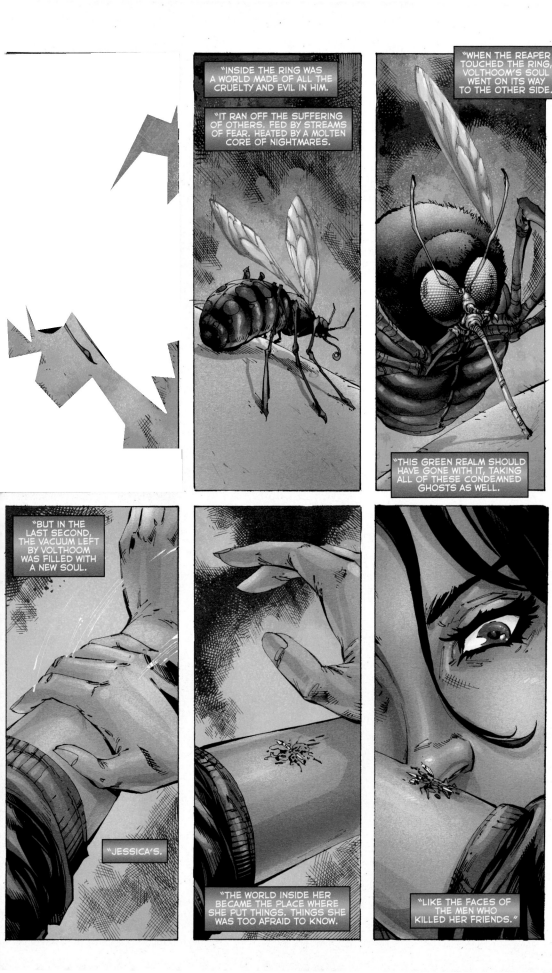

"INSIDE THE RING WAS A WORLD MADE OF ALL THE CRUELTY AND EVIL IN HIM.

"IT RAN OFF THE SUFFERING OF OTHERS. FED BY STREAMS OF FEAR. HEATED BY A MOLTEN CORE OF NIGHTMARES.

"WHEN THE REAPER TOUCHED THE RING, VOLTHOOM'S SOUL WENT ON ITS WAY TO THE OTHER SIDE.

"THIS GREEN REALM SHOULD HAVE GONE WITH IT, TAKING ALL OF THESE CONDEMNED GHOSTS AS WELL.

"BUT IN THE LAST SECOND, THE VACUUM LEFT BY VOLTHOOM WAS FILLED WITH A NEW SOUL.

"JESSICA'S.

"THE WORLD INSIDE HER BECAME THE PLACE WHERE SHE PUT THINGS. THINGS SHE WAS TOO AFRAID TO KNOW.

"LIKE THE FACES OF THE MEN WHO KILLED HER FRIENDS."

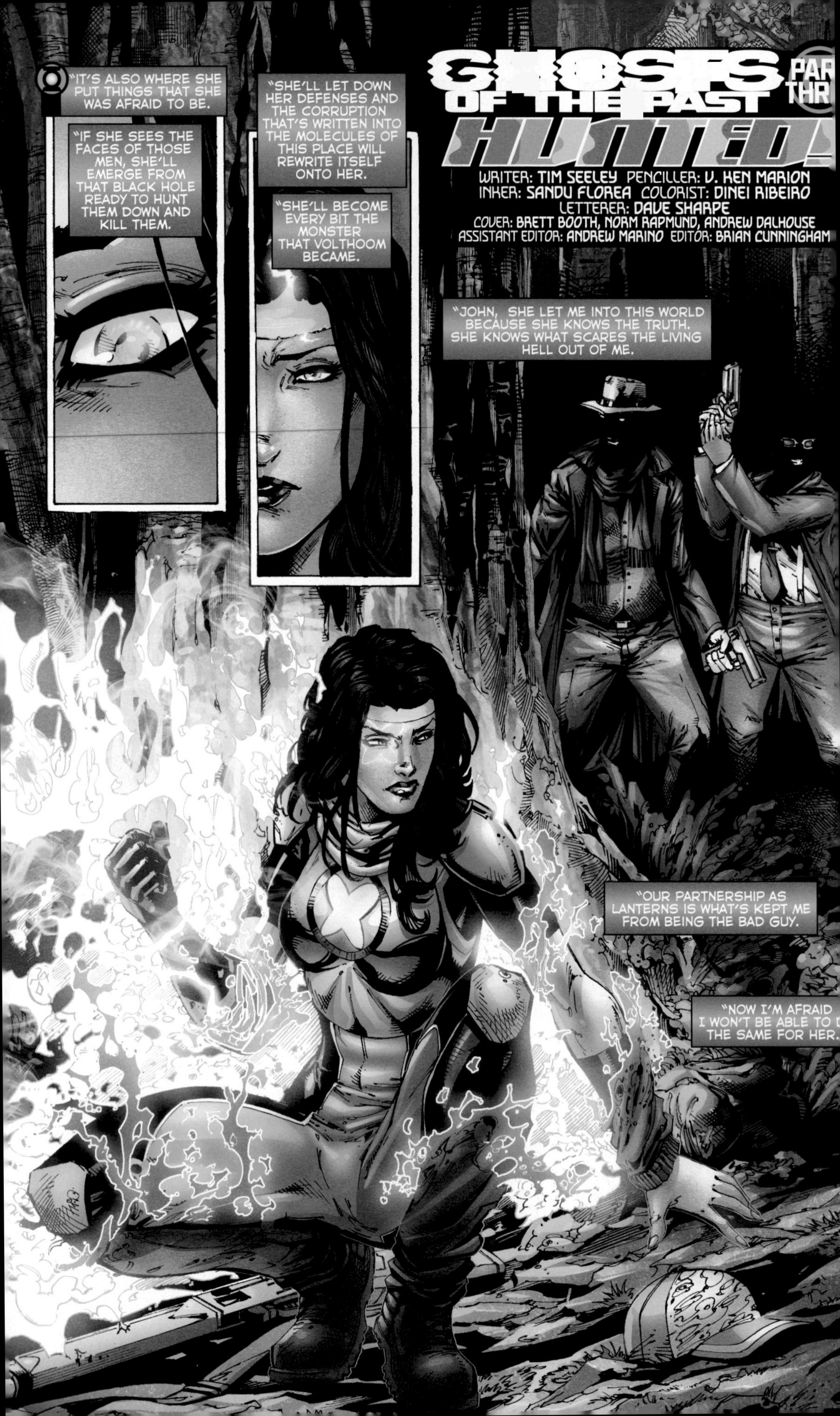
"IT'S ALSO WHERE SHE PUT THINGS THAT SHE WAS AFRAID TO BE.
"IF SHE SEES THE FACES OF THOSE MEN, SHE'LL EMERGE FROM THAT BLACK HOLE READY TO HUNT THEM DOWN AND KILL THEM.
"SHE'LL LET DOWN HER DEFENSES AND THE CORRUPTION THAT'S WRITTEN INTO THE MOLECULES OF THIS PLACE WILL REWRITE ITSELF ONTO HER.
"SHE'LL BECOME EVERY BIT THE MONSTER THAT VOLTHOOM BECAME.
GHOSTS OF THE PAST
PAR
THR
HUNTED!
WRITER: TIM SEELEY PENCILLER: V. KEN MARION
INKER: SANDU FLOREA COLORIST: DINEI RIBEIRO
LETTERER: DAVE SHARPE
COVER: BRETT BOOTH, NORM RAPMUND, ANDREW DALHOUSE
ASSISTANT EDITOR: ANDREW MARINO EDITOR: BRIAN CUNNINGHAM
"JOHN, SHE LET ME INTO THIS WORLD BECAUSE SHE KNOWS THE TRUTH. SHE KNOWS WHAT SCARES THE LIVING HELL OUT OF ME.
"OUR PARTNERSHIP AS LANTERNS IS WHAT'S KEPT ME FROM BEING THE BAD GUY.
"NOW I'M AFRAID I WON'T BE ABLE TO
THE SAME FOR HER.

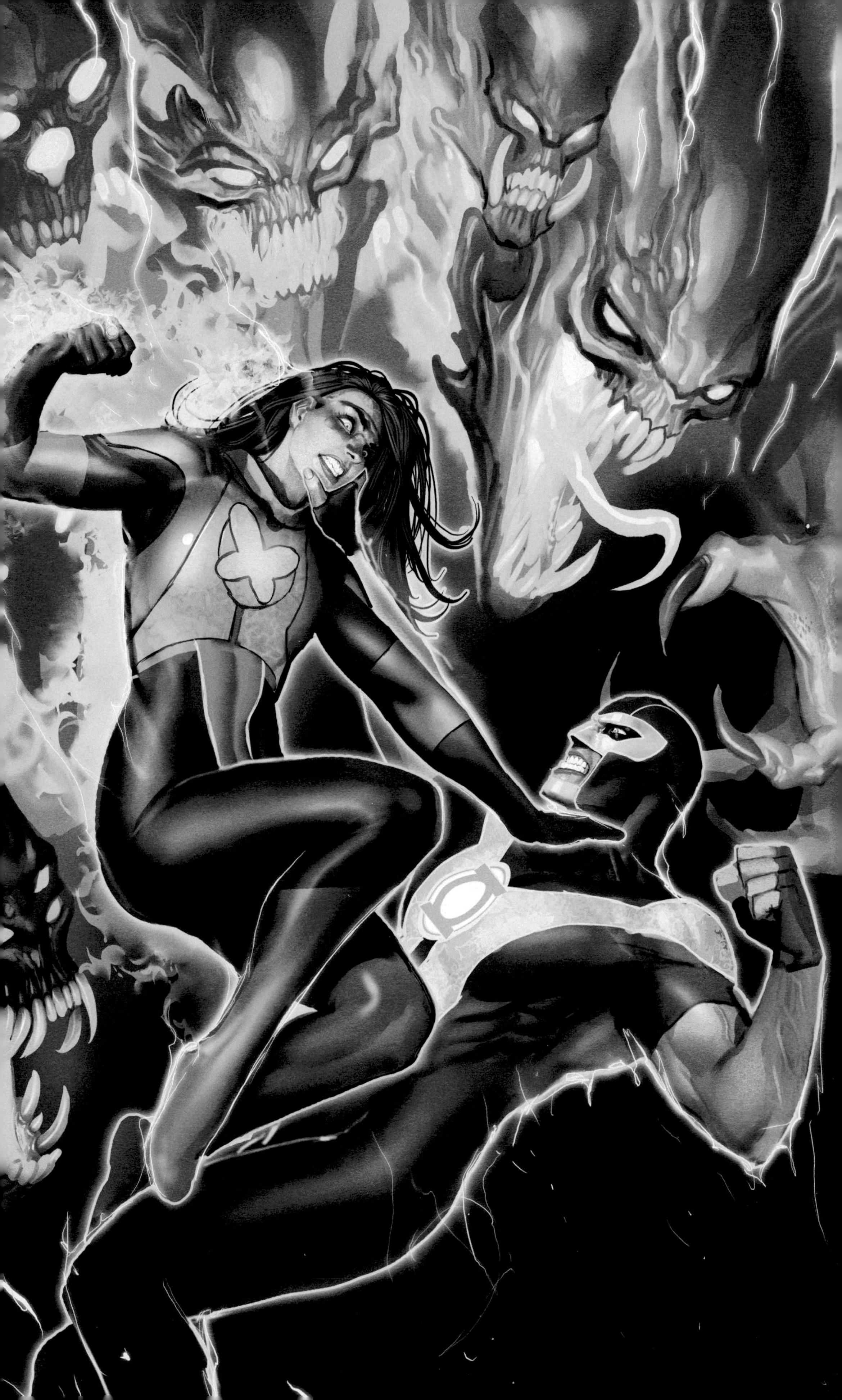

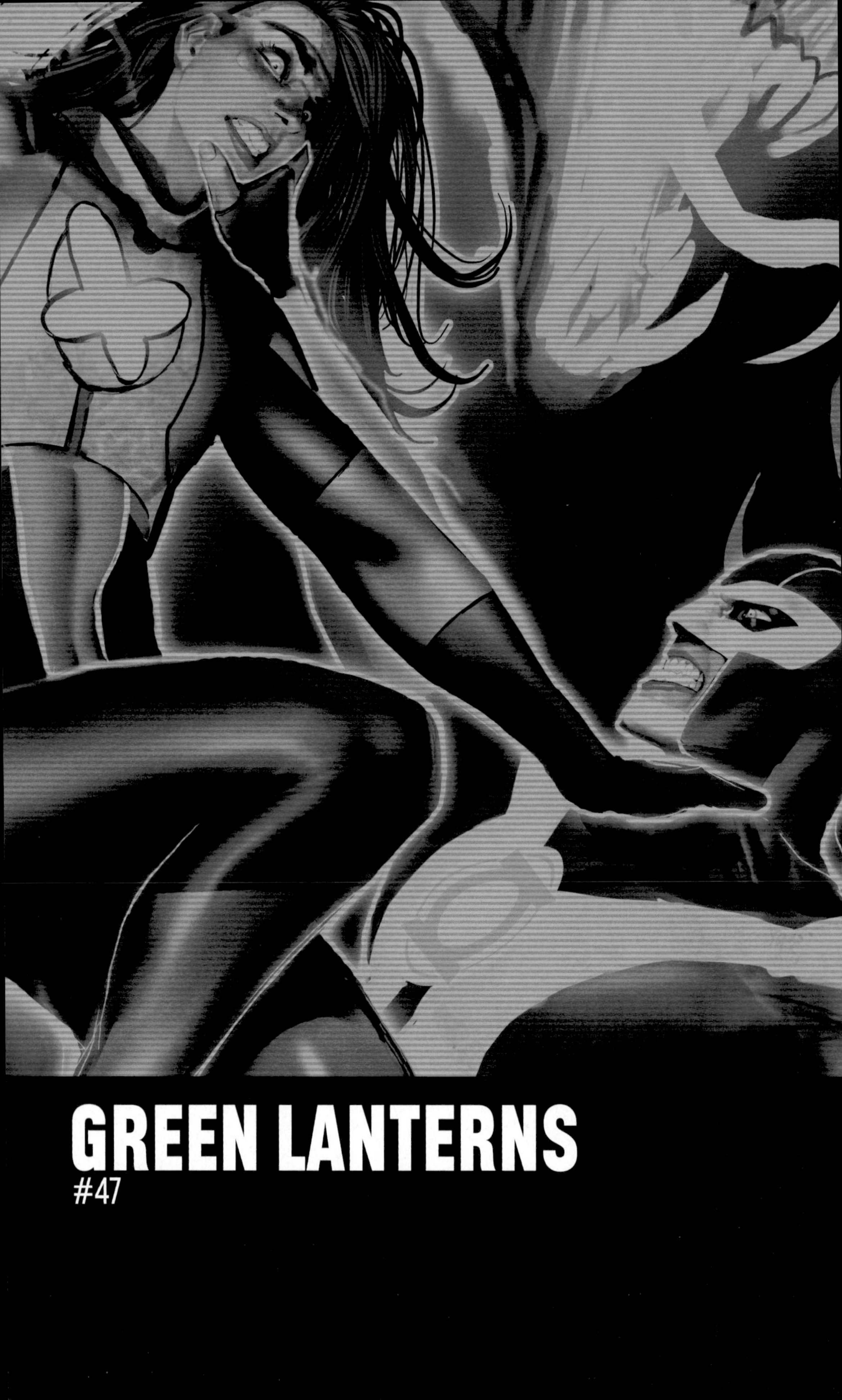

# GREEN LANTERNS
#47

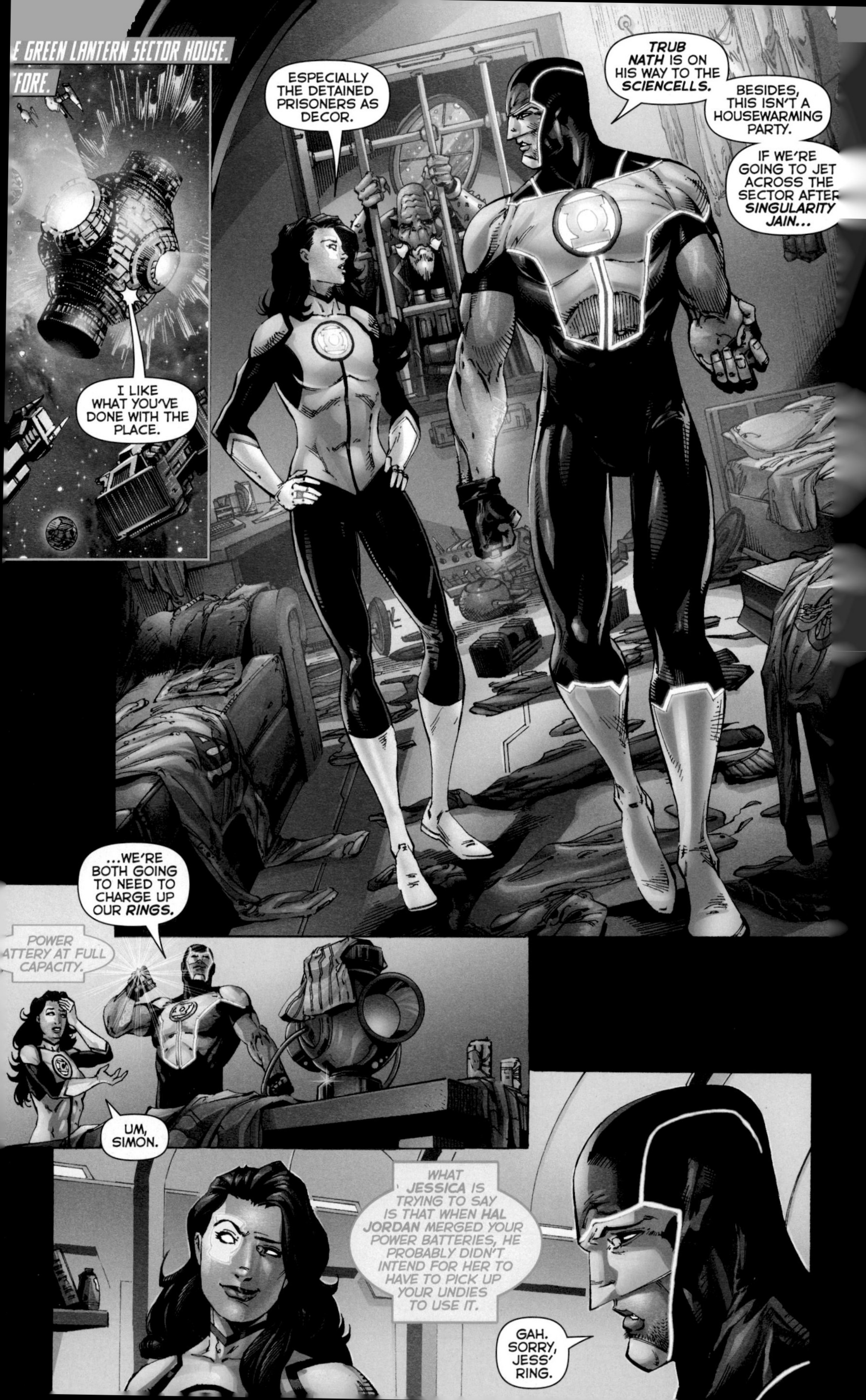
E GREEN LANTERN SECTOR HOUSE.
FORE.
I LIKE WHAT YOU'VE DONE WITH THE PLACE.
ESPECIALLY THE DETAINED PRISONERS AS DECOR.
TRUB NATH IS ON HIS WAY TO THE SCIENCELLS.
BESIDES, THIS ISN'T A HOUSEWARMING PARTY.
IF WE'RE GOING TO JET ACROSS THE SECTOR AFTER SINGULARITY JAIN...
...WE'RE BOTH GOING TO NEED TO CHARGE UP OUR RINGS.
POWER ATTERY AT FULL CAPACITY.
UM, SIMON.
WHAT JESSICA IS TRYING TO SAY IS THAT WHEN HAL JORDAN MERGED YOUR POWER BATTERIES, HE PROBABLY DIDN'T INTEND FOR HER TO HAVE TO PICK UP YOUR UNDIES TO USE IT.
GAH. SORRY, JESS' RING.

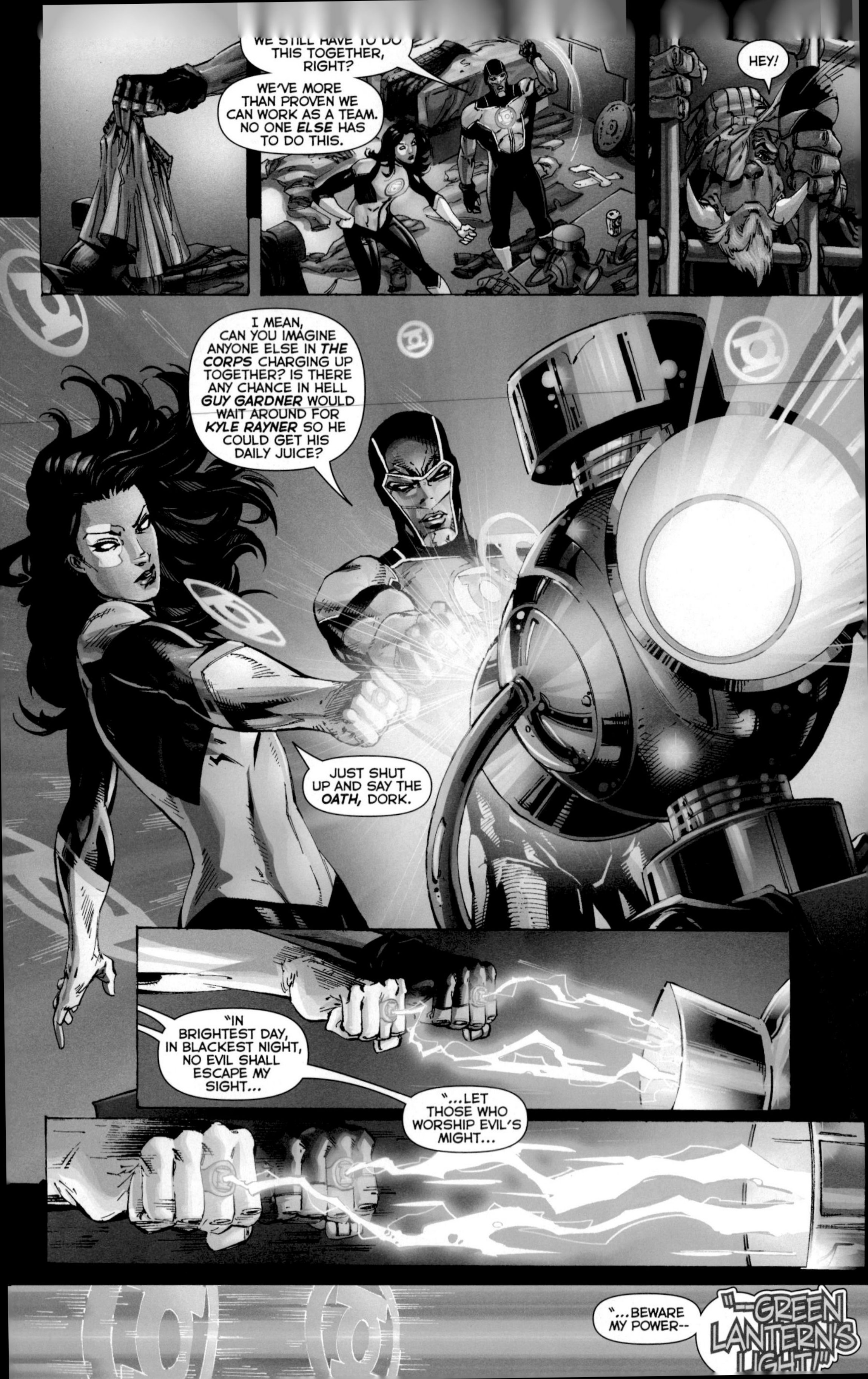
WE STILL HAVE TO DO THIS TOGETHER, RIGHT?
WE'VE MORE THAN PROVEN WE CAN WORK AS A TEAM. NO ONE ELSE HAS TO DO THIS.
HEY!
I MEAN, CAN YOU IMAGINE ANYONE ELSE IN THE CORPS CHARGING UP TOGETHER? IS THERE ANY CHANCE IN HELL GUY GARDNER WOULD WAIT AROUND FOR KYLE RAYNER SO HE COULD GET HIS DAILY JUICE?
JUST SHUT UP AND SAY THE OATH, DORK.
"IN BRIGHTEST DAY, IN BLACKEST NIGHT, NO EVIL SHALL ESCAPE MY SIGHT...
"...LET THOSE WHO WORSHIP EVIL'S MIGHT...
"...BEWARE MY POWER--
"--GREEN LANTERN'S LIGHT!"

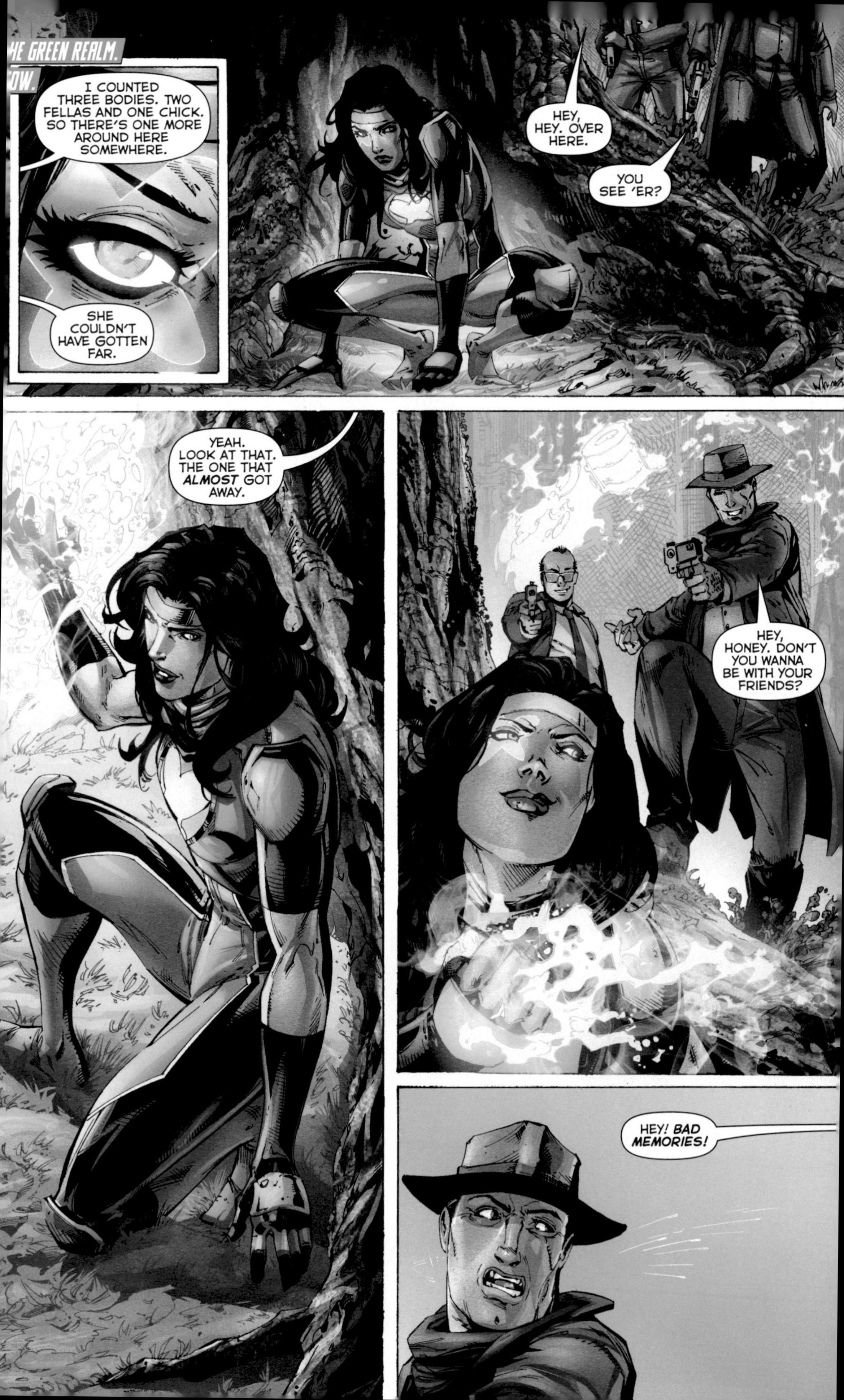

HE GREEN REALM.
OW.
I COUNTED THREE BODIES. TWO FELLAS AND ONE CHICK. SO THERE'S ONE MORE AROUND HERE SOMEWHERE.
SHE COULDN'T HAVE GOTTEN FAR.
HEY, HEY. OVER HERE.
YOU SEE 'ER?
YEAH. LOOK AT THAT. THE ONE THAT *ALMOST* GOT AWAY.
HEY, HONEY. DON'T YOU WANNA BE WITH YOUR FRIENDS?
HEY! *BAD MEMORIES!*

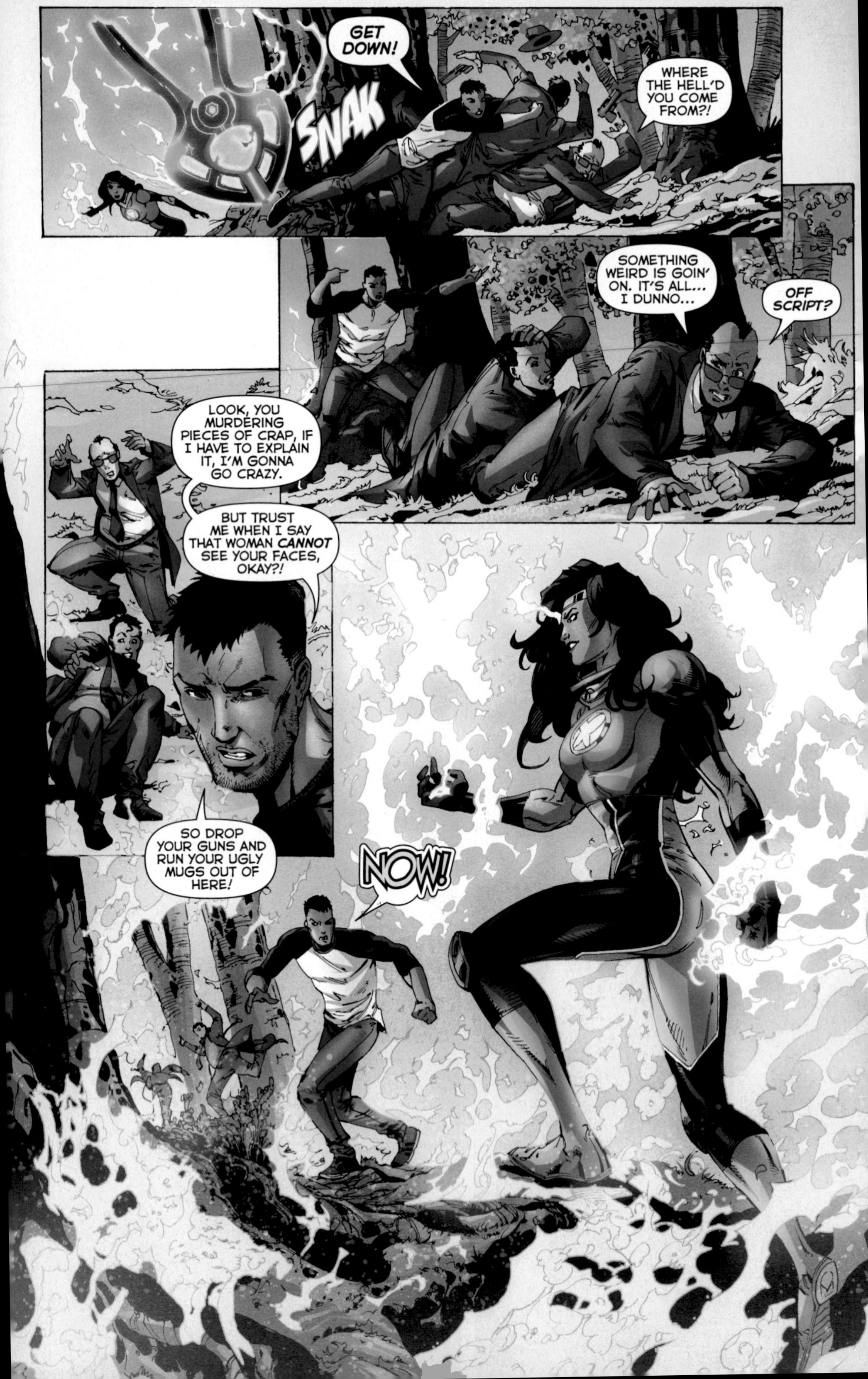
GET DOWN!
SNAK
WHERE THE HELL'D YOU COME FROM?!
SOMETHING WEIRD IS GOIN' ON. IT'S ALL... I DUNNO...
OFF SCRIPT?
LOOK, YOU MURDERING PIECES OF CRAP, IF I HAVE TO EXPLAIN IT, I'M GONNA GO CRAZY.
BUT TRUST ME WHEN I SAY THAT WOMAN *CANNOT* SEE YOUR FACES, OKAY?!
SO DROP YOUR GUNS AND RUN YOUR UGLY MUGS OUT OF HERE!
NOW!

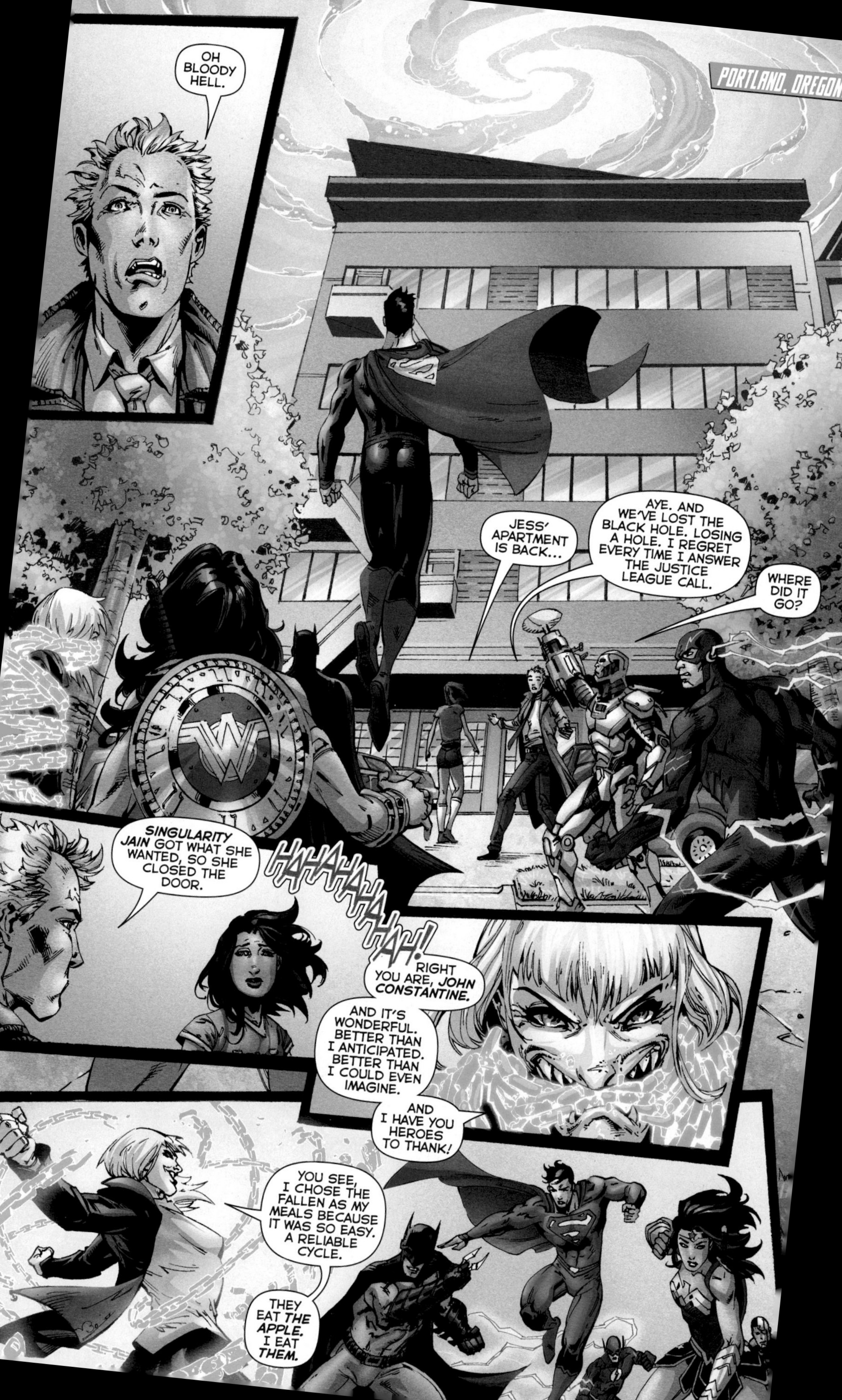

OH BLOODY HELL.
PORTLAND, OREGON
JESS' APARTMENT IS BACK...
AYE. AND WE'VE LOST THE BLACK HOLE. LOSING A HOLE. I REGRET EVERY TIME I ANSWER THE JUSTICE LEAGUE CALL.
WHERE DID IT GO?
SINGULARITY JAIN GOT WHAT SHE WANTED, SO SHE CLOSED THE DOOR.
HAHAHAHAHAHAH!
RIGHT YOU ARE, JOHN CONSTANTINE.
AND IT'S WONDERFUL. BETTER THAN I ANTICIPATED. BETTER THAN I COULD EVEN IMAGINE.
AND I HAVE YOU HEROES TO THANK!
YOU SEE, I CHOSE THE FALLEN AS MY MEALS BECAUSE IT WAS SO EASY. A RELIABLE CYCLE.
THEY EAT THE APPLE. I EAT THEM.

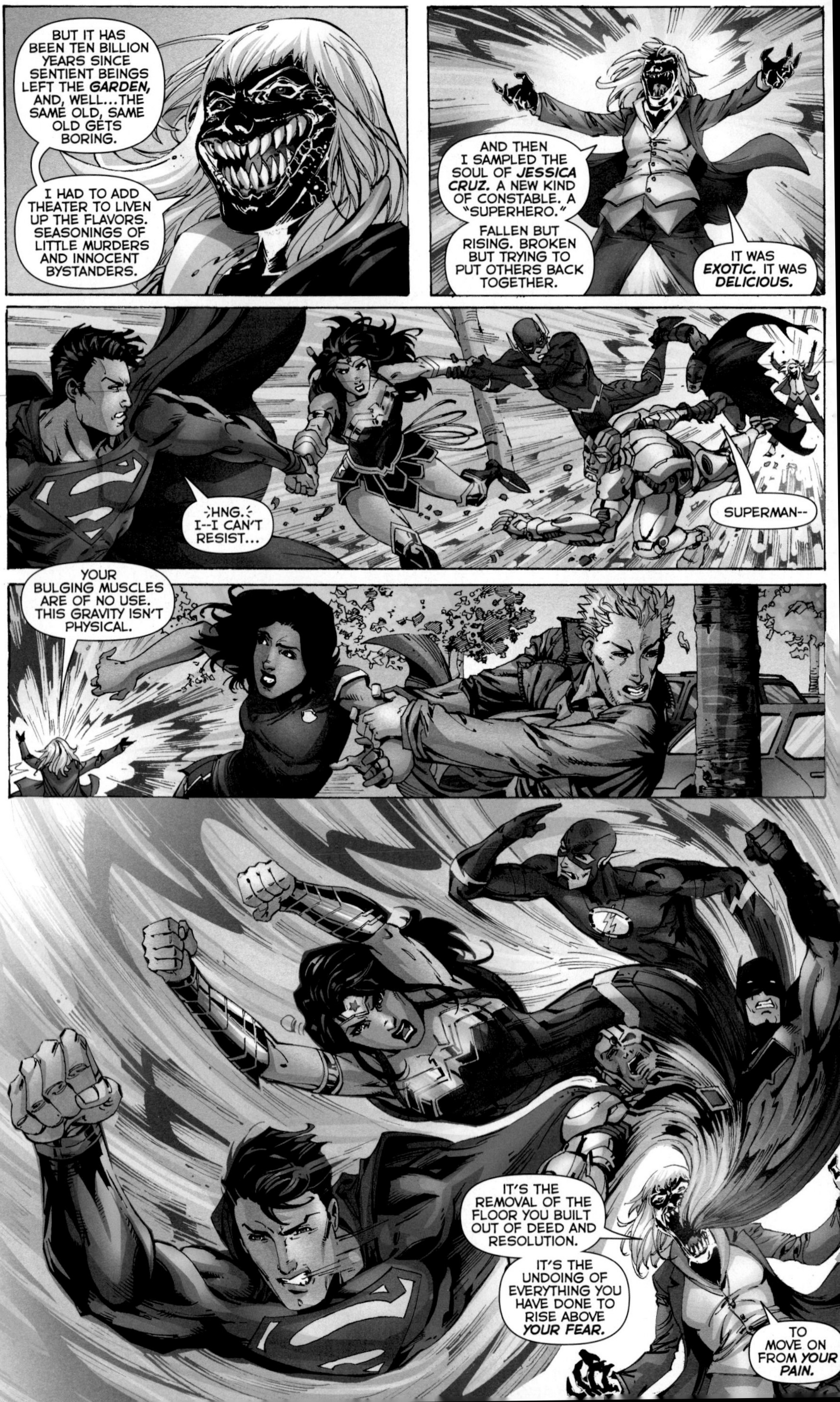

BUT IT HAS BEEN TEN BILLION YEARS SINCE SENTIENT BEINGS LEFT THE GARDEN, AND, WELL...THE SAME OLD, SAME OLD GETS BORING.
I HAD TO ADD THEATER TO LIVEN UP THE FLAVORS. SEASONINGS OF LITTLE MURDERS AND INNOCENT BYSTANDERS.
AND THEN I SAMPLED THE SOUL OF JESSICA CRUZ. A NEW KIND OF CONSTABLE. A "SUPERHERO."
FALLEN BUT RISING. BROKEN BUT TRYING TO PUT OTHERS BACK TOGETHER.
IT WAS EXOTIC. IT WAS DELICIOUS.
HNG. I--I CAN'T RESIST...
SUPERMAN--
YOUR BULGING MUSCLES ARE OF NO USE. THIS GRAVITY ISN'T PHYSICAL.
IT'S THE REMOVAL OF THE FLOOR YOU BUILT OUT OF DEED AND RESOLUTION.
IT'S THE UNDOING OF EVERYTHING YOU HAVE DONE TO RISE ABOVE YOUR FEAR.
TO MOVE ON FROM YOUR PAIN.

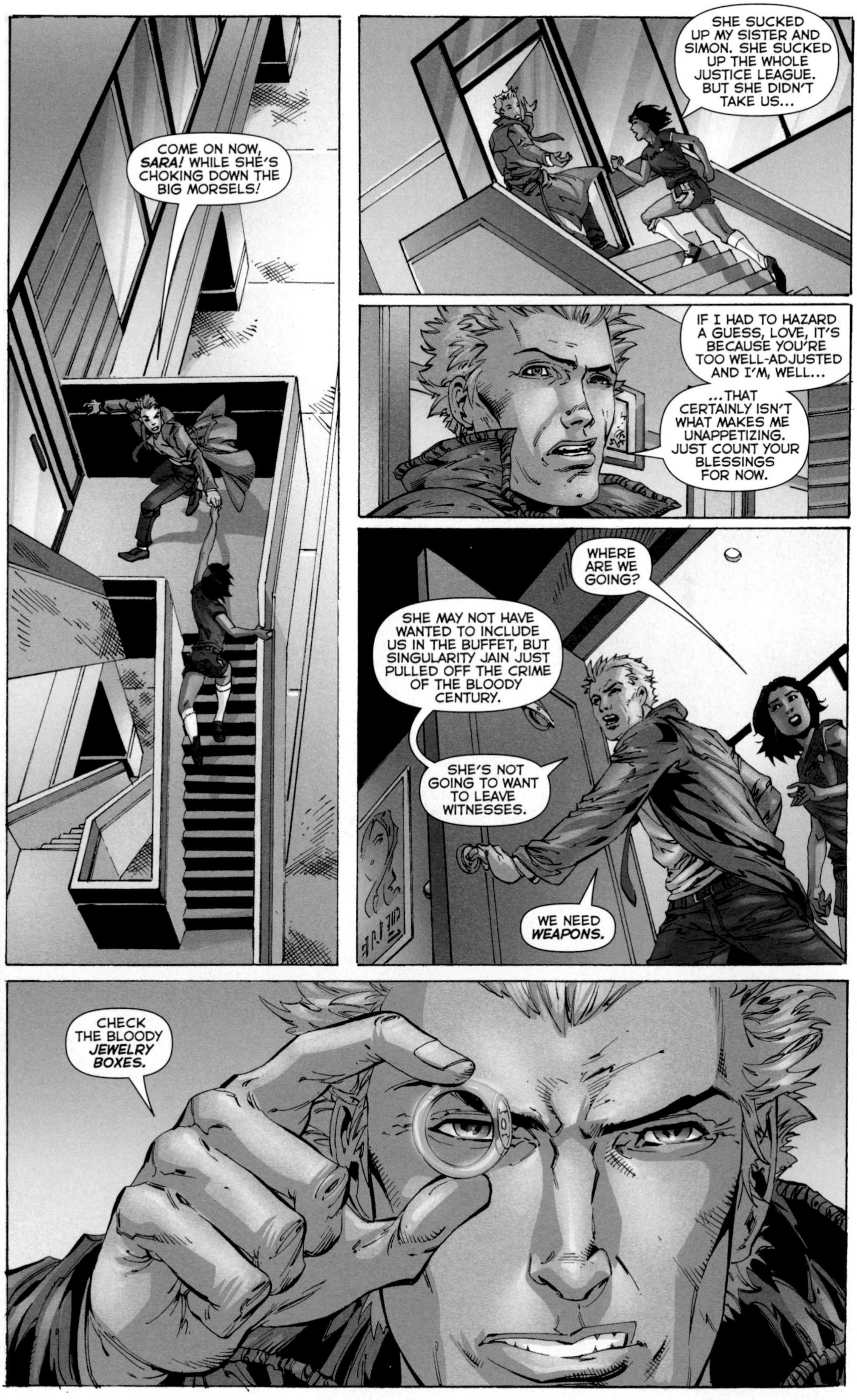
COME ON NOW, SARA! WHILE SHE'S CHOKING DOWN THE BIG MORSELS!
SHE SUCKED UP MY SISTER AND SIMON. SHE SUCKED UP THE WHOLE JUSTICE LEAGUE. BUT SHE DIDN'T TAKE US...
IF I HAD TO HAZARD A GUESS, LOVE, IT'S BECAUSE YOU'RE TOO WELL-ADJUSTED AND I'M, WELL...
...THAT CERTAINLY ISN'T WHAT MAKES ME UNAPPETIZING. JUST COUNT YOUR BLESSINGS FOR NOW.
WHERE ARE WE GOING?
SHE MAY NOT HAVE WANTED TO INCLUDE US IN THE BUFFET, BUT SINGULARITY JAIN JUST PULLED OFF THE CRIME OF THE BLOODY CENTURY.
SHE'S NOT GOING TO WANT TO LEAVE WITNESSES.
WE NEED WEAPONS.
CHECK THE BLOODY JEWELRY BOXES.

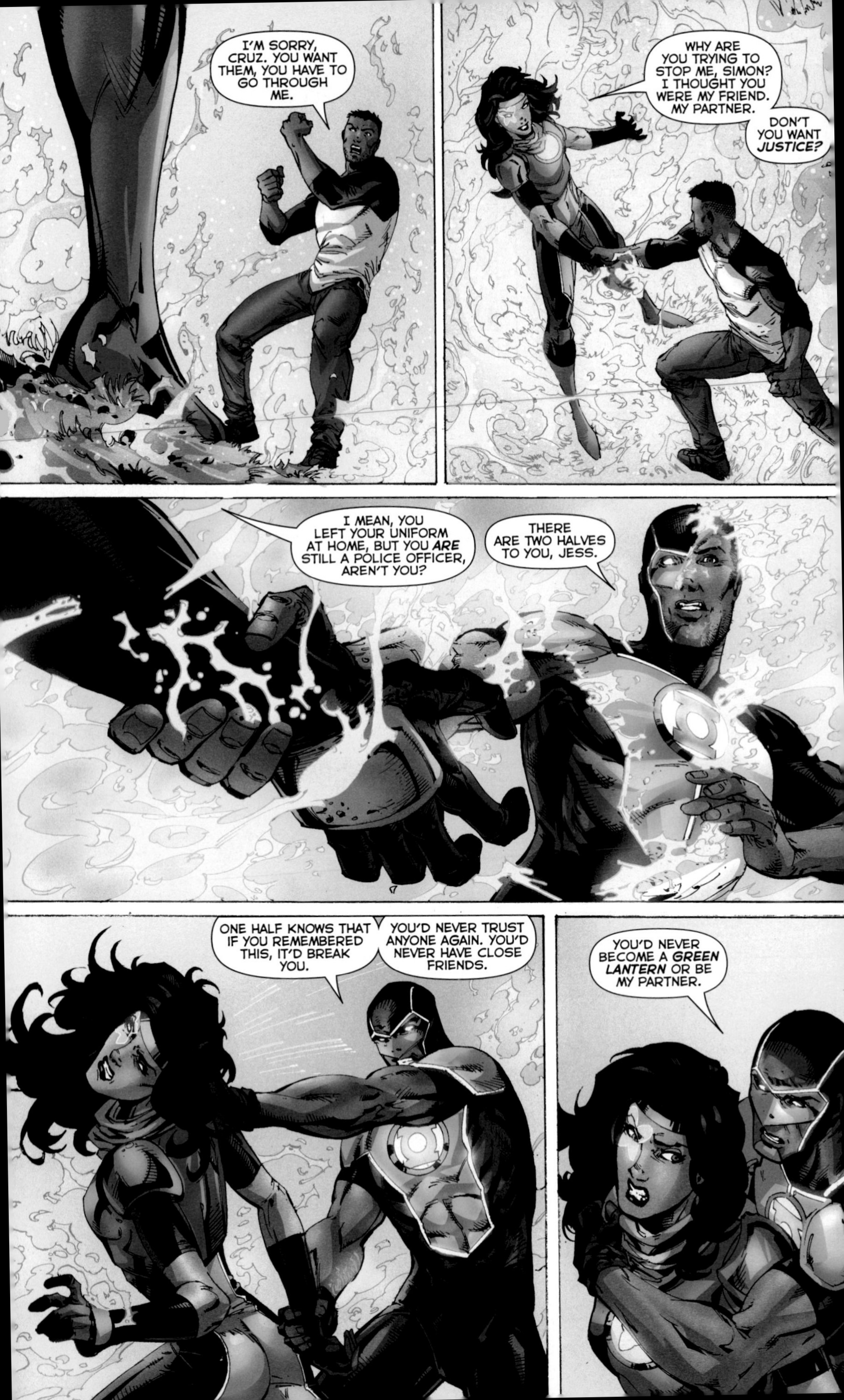
I'M SORRY, CRUZ. YOU WANT THEM, YOU HAVE TO GO THROUGH ME.
WHY ARE YOU TRYING TO STOP ME, SIMON? I THOUGHT YOU WERE MY FRIEND. MY PARTNER.
DON'T YOU WANT JUSTICE?
I MEAN, YOU LEFT YOUR UNIFORM AT HOME, BUT YOU ARE STILL A POLICE OFFICER, AREN'T YOU?
THERE ARE TWO HALVES TO YOU, JESS.
ONE HALF KNOWS THAT IF YOU REMEMBERED THIS, IT'D BREAK YOU.
YOU'D NEVER TRUST ANYONE AGAIN. YOU'D NEVER HAVE CLOSE FRIENDS.
YOU'D NEVER BECOME A GREEN LANTERN OR BE MY PARTNER.

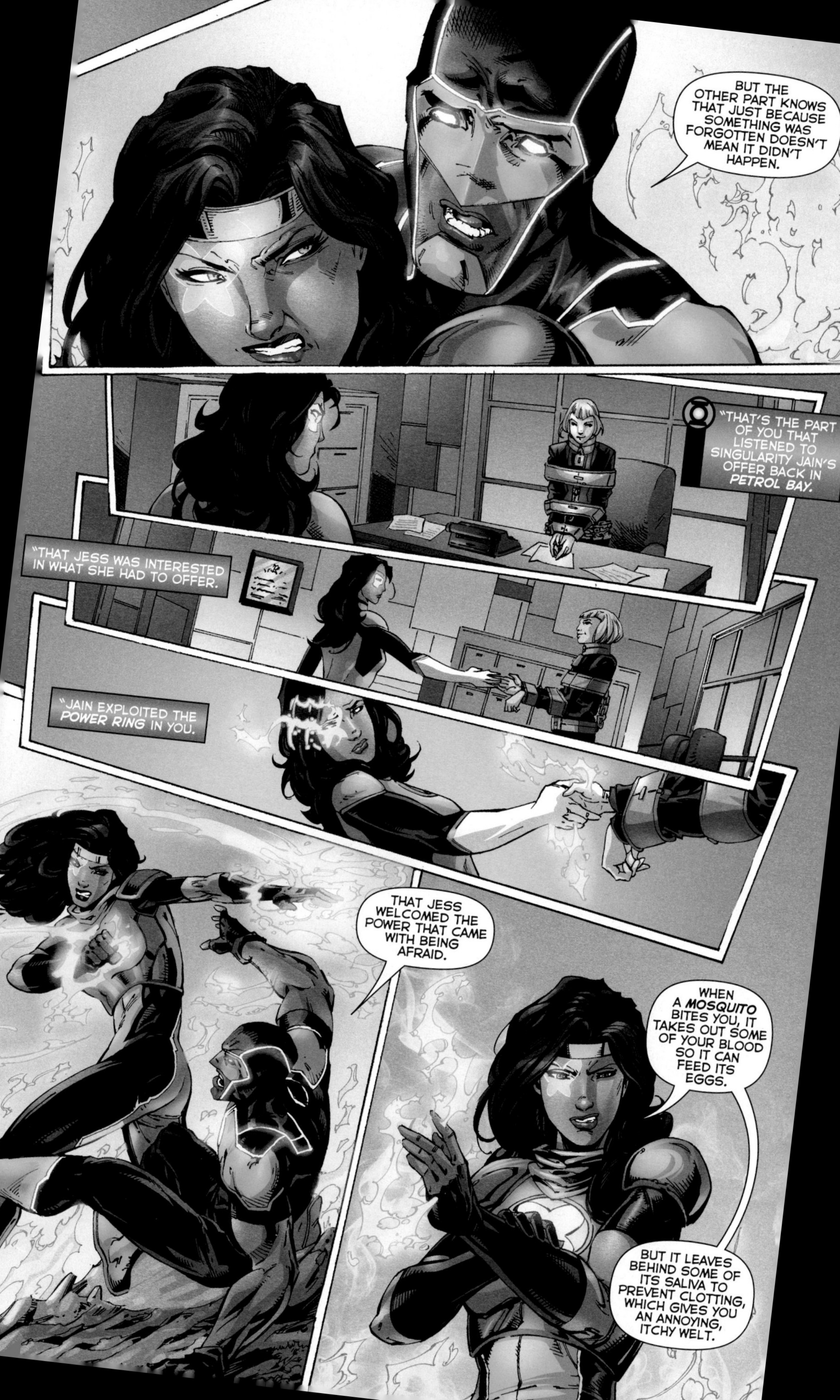
BUT THE OTHER PART KNOWS THAT JUST BECAUSE SOMETHING WAS FORGOTTEN DOESN'T MEAN IT DIDN'T HAPPEN.
"THAT'S THE PART OF YOU THAT LISTENED TO SINGULARITY JAIN'S OFFER BACK IN PETROL BAY.
"THAT JESS WAS INTERESTED IN WHAT SHE HAD TO OFFER.
"JAIN EXPLOITED THE POWER RING IN YOU.
THAT JESS WELCOMED THE POWER THAT CAME WITH BEING AFRAID.
WHEN A MOSQUITO BITES YOU, IT TAKES OUT SOME OF YOUR BLOOD SO IT CAN FEED ITS EGGS.
BUT IT LEAVES BEHIND SOME OF ITS SALIVA TO PREVENT CLOTTING, WHICH GIVES YOU AN ANNOYING, ITCHY WELT.

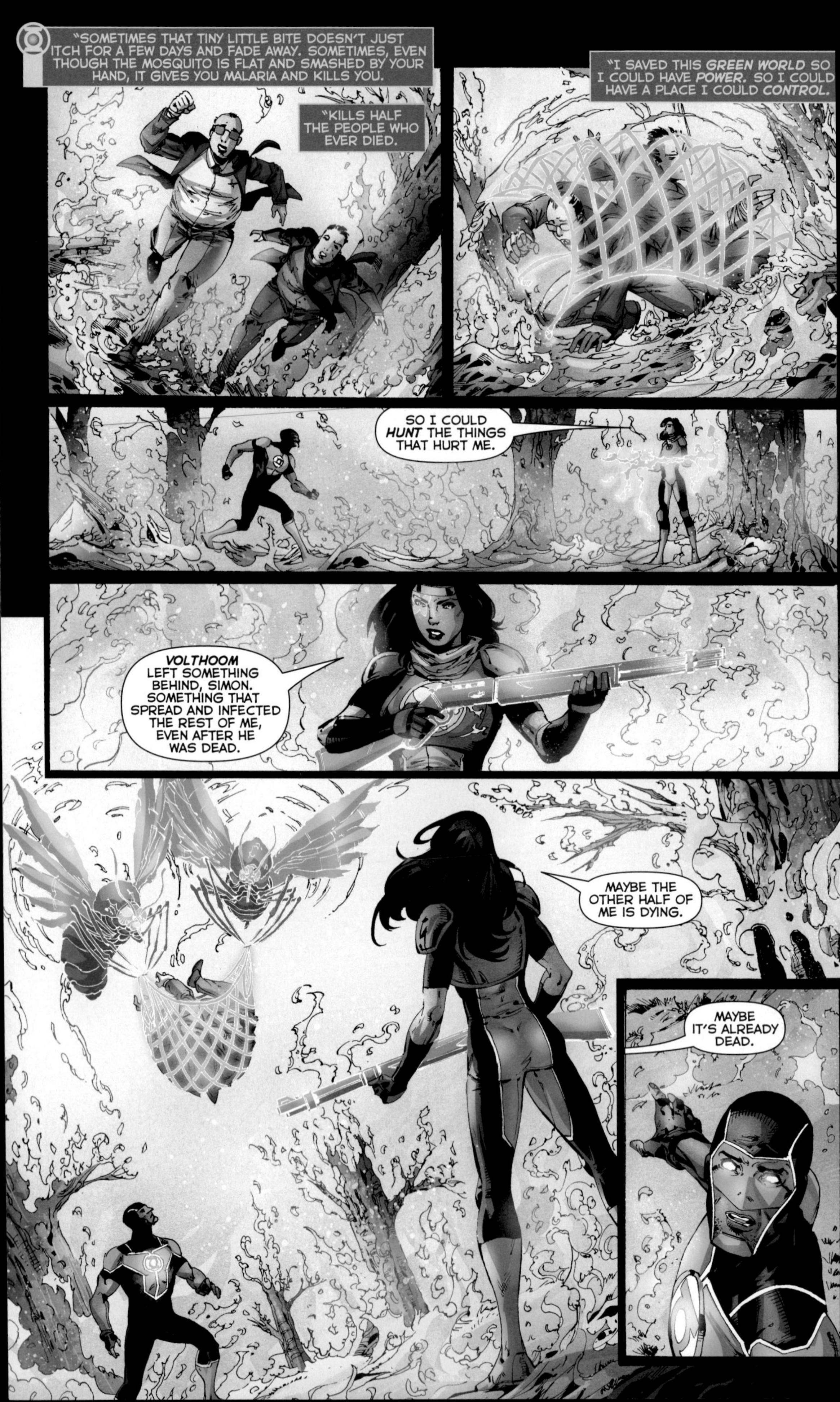
"SOMETIMES THAT TINY LITTLE BITE DOESN'T JUST ITCH FOR A FEW DAYS AND FADE AWAY. SOMETIMES, EVEN THOUGH THE MOSQUITO IS FLAT AND SMASHED BY YOUR HAND, IT GIVES YOU MALARIA AND KILLS YOU.
"KILLS HALF THE PEOPLE WHO EVER DIED.
"I SAVED THIS GREEN WORLD SO I COULD HAVE POWER. SO I COULD HAVE A PLACE I COULD CONTROL.
SO I COULD HUNT THE THINGS THAT HURT ME.
VOLTHOOM LEFT SOMETHING BEHIND, SIMON. SOMETHING THAT SPREAD AND INFECTED THE REST OF ME, EVEN AFTER HE WAS DEAD.
MAYBE THE OTHER HALF OF ME IS DYING.
MAYBE IT'S ALREADY DEAD.

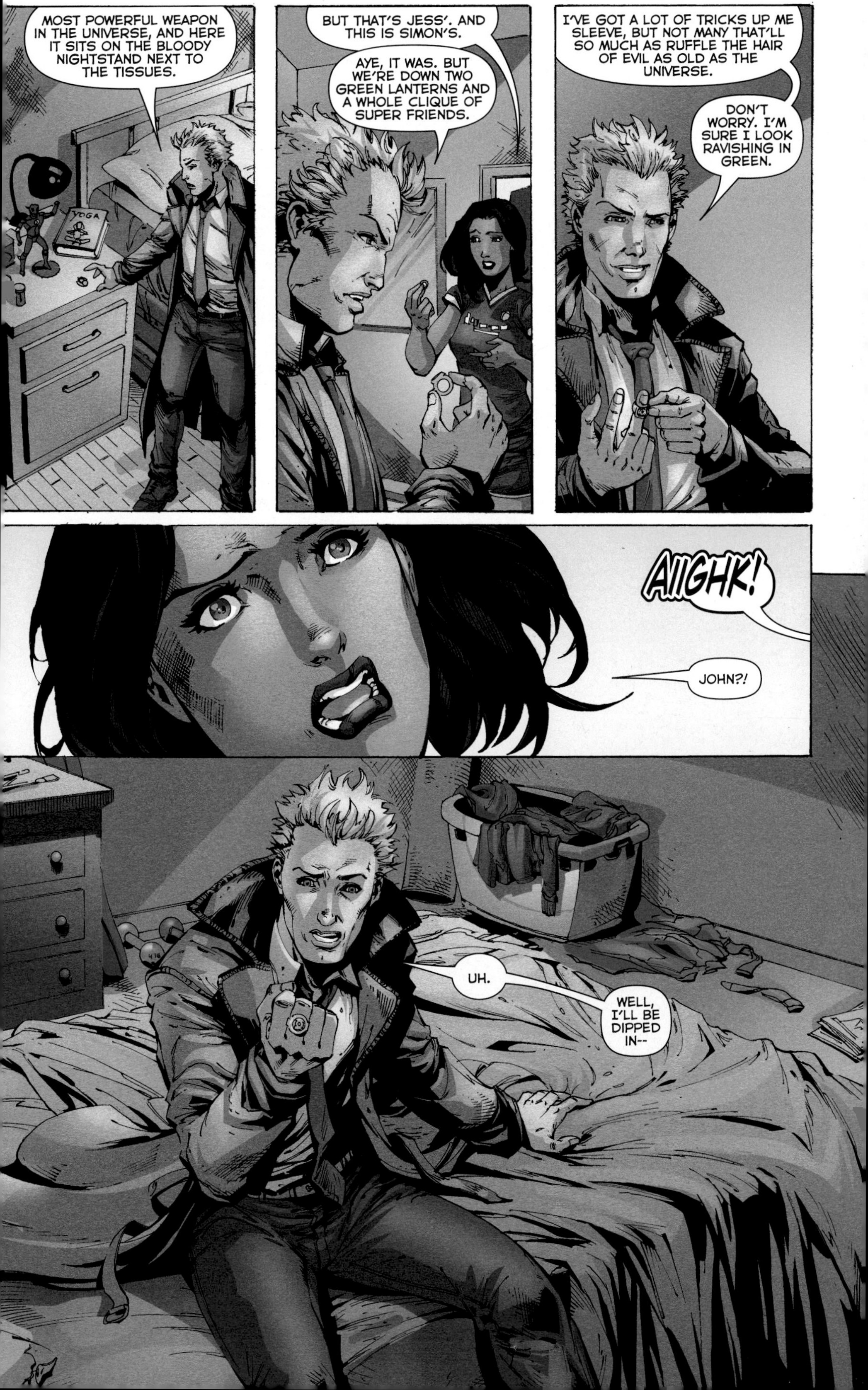
MOST POWERFUL WEAPON IN THE UNIVERSE, AND HERE IT SITS ON THE BLOODY NIGHTSTAND NEXT TO THE TISSUES.
YOGA
BUT THAT'S JESS'. AND THIS IS SIMON'S.
AYE, IT WAS. BUT WE'RE DOWN TWO GREEN LANTERNS AND A WHOLE CLIQUE OF SUPER FRIENDS.
I'VE GOT A LOT OF TRICKS UP ME SLEEVE, BUT NOT MANY THAT'LL SO MUCH AS RUFFLE THE HAIR OF EVIL AS OLD AS THE UNIVERSE.
DON'T WORRY. I'M SURE I LOOK RAVISHING IN GREEN.
AIIGHK!
JOHN?!
UH.
WELL, I'LL BE DIPPED IN--

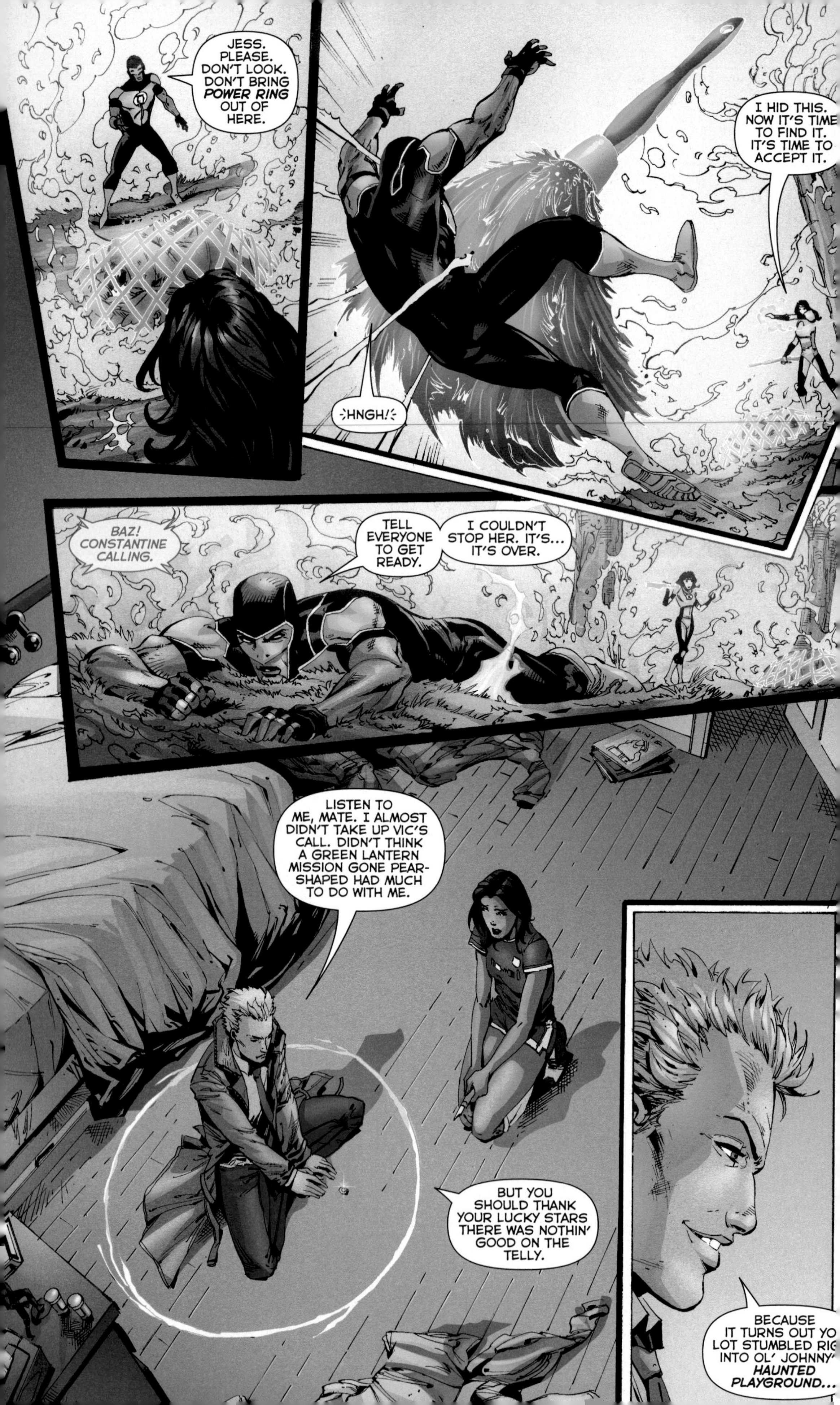
JESS. PLEASE. DON'T LOOK. DON'T BRING POWER RING OUT OF HERE.
I HID THIS. NOW IT'S TIME TO FIND IT. IT'S TIME TO ACCEPT IT.
HNGH!
BAZ! CONSTANTINE CALLING.
TELL EVERYONE TO GET READY.
I COULDN'T STOP HER. IT'S... IT'S OVER.
LISTEN TO ME, MATE. I ALMOST DIDN'T TAKE UP VIC'S CALL. DIDN'T THINK A GREEN LANTERN MISSION GONE PEAR-SHAPED HAD MUCH TO DO WITH ME.
BUT YOU SHOULD THANK YOUR LUCKY STARS THERE WAS NOTHIN' GOOD ON THE TELLY.
BECAUSE IT TURNS OUT YO LOT STUMBLED RIG INTO OL' JOHNNY' HAUNTED PLAYGROUND...

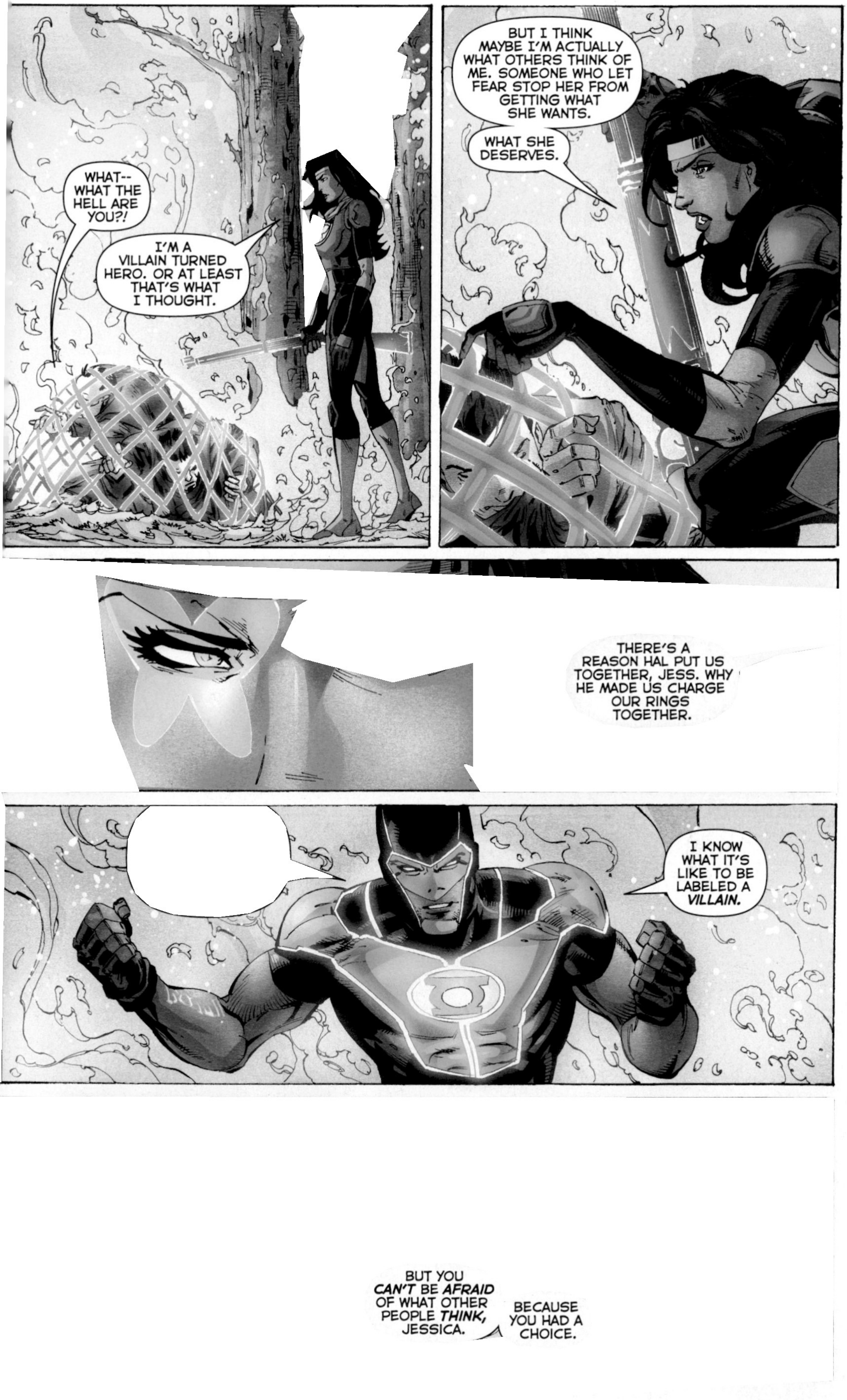
WHAT-- WHAT THE HELL ARE YOU?!
I'M A VILLAIN TURNED HERO. OR AT LEAST THAT'S WHAT I THOUGHT.
BUT I THINK MAYBE I'M ACTUALLY WHAT OTHERS THINK OF ME. SOMEONE WHO LET FEAR STOP HER FROM GETTING WHAT SHE WANTS.
WHAT SHE DESERVES.
THERE'S A REASON HAL PUT US TOGETHER, JESS. WHY HE MADE US CHARGE OUR RINGS TOGETHER.
I KNOW WHAT IT'S LIKE TO BE LABELED A *VILLAIN.*
BUT YOU *CAN'T* BE *AFRAID* OF WHAT OTHER PEOPLE *THINK,* JESSICA.
BECAUSE YOU HAD A CHOICE.

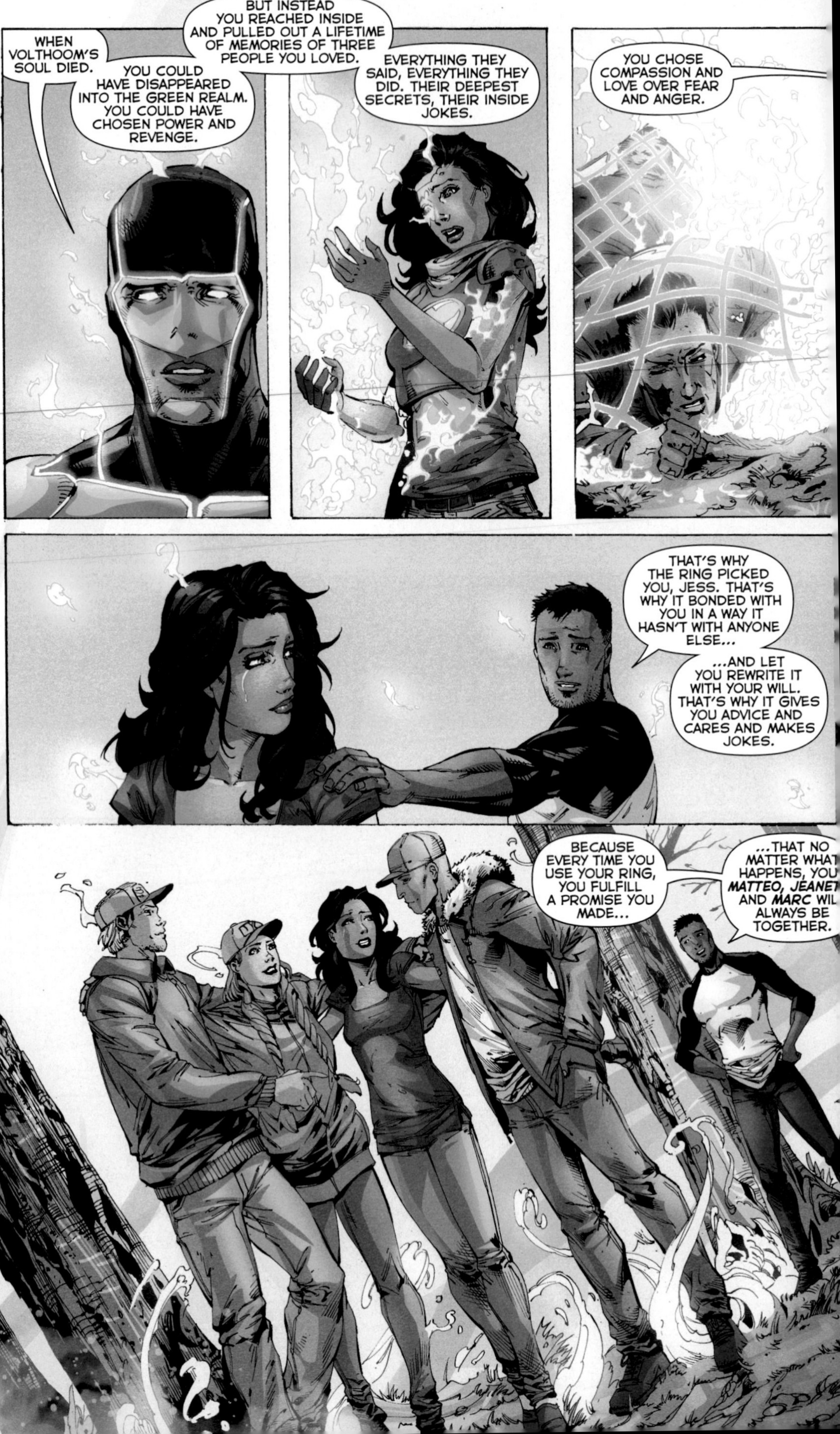

WHEN VOLTHOOM'S SOUL DIED.
YOU COULD HAVE DISAPPEARED INTO THE GREEN REALM. YOU COULD HAVE CHOSEN POWER AND REVENGE.
BUT INSTEAD YOU REACHED INSIDE AND PULLED OUT A LIFETIME OF MEMORIES OF THREE PEOPLE YOU LOVED.
EVERYTHING THEY SAID, EVERYTHING THEY DID. THEIR DEEPEST SECRETS, THEIR INSIDE JOKES.
YOU CHOSE COMPASSION AND LOVE OVER FEAR AND ANGER.
THAT'S WHY THE RING PICKED YOU, JESS. THAT'S WHY IT BONDED WITH YOU IN A WAY IT HASN'T WITH ANYONE ELSE...
...AND LET YOU REWRITE IT WITH YOUR WILL. THAT'S WHY IT GIVES YOU ADVICE AND CARES AND MAKES JOKES.
BECAUSE EVERY TIME YOU USE YOUR RING, YOU FULFILL A PROMISE YOU MADE...
...THAT NO MATTER WHAT HAPPENS, YOU, *MATTEO, JEANET* AND *MARC* WIL ALWAYS BE TOGETHER.

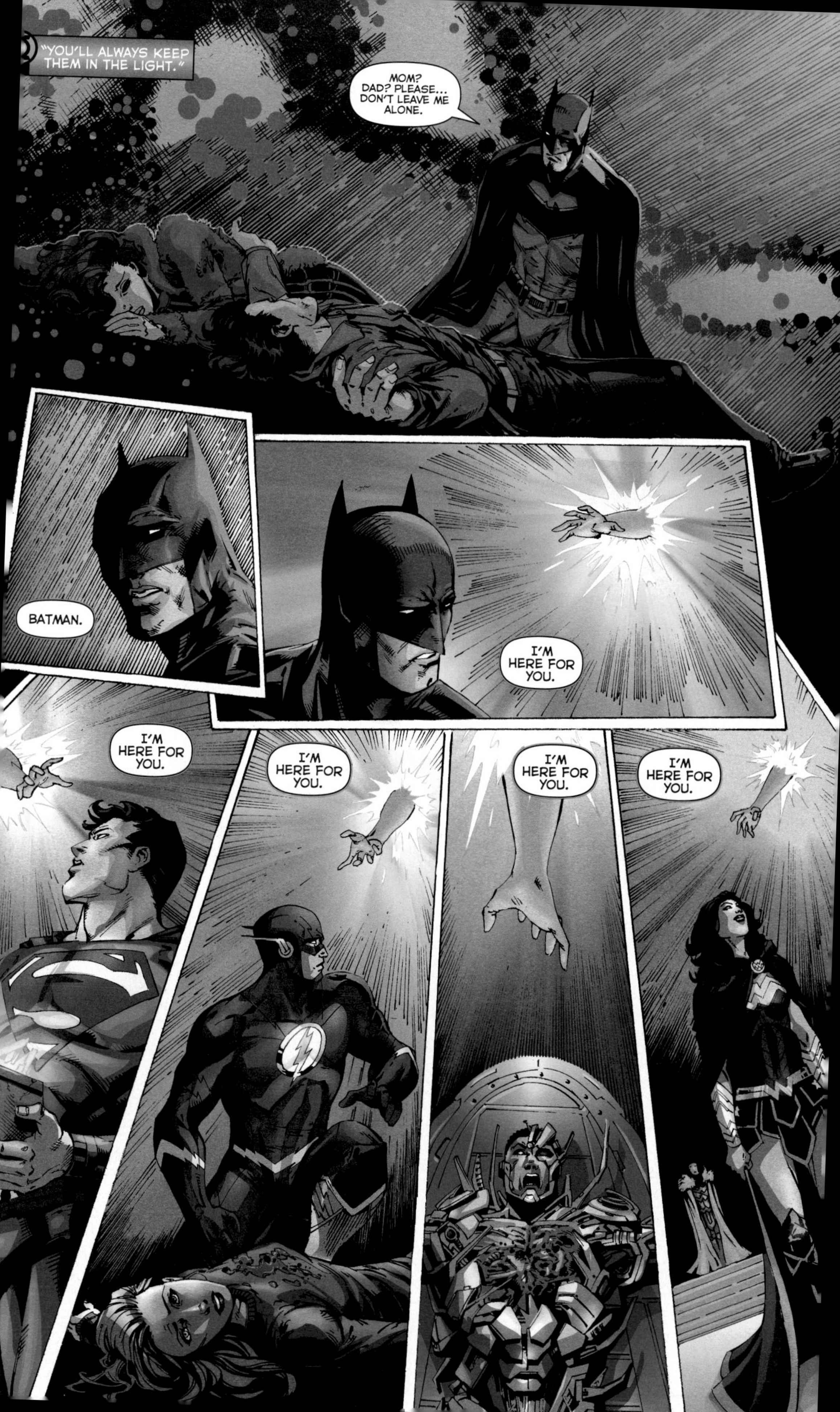
"YOU'LL ALWAYS KEEP THEM IN THE LIGHT."
MOM? DAD? PLEASE... DON'T LEAVE ME ALONE.
BATMAN.
I'M HERE FOR YOU.
I'M HERE FOR YOU.
I'M HERE FOR YOU.
I'M HERE FOR YOU.
I'M HERE FOR YOU.

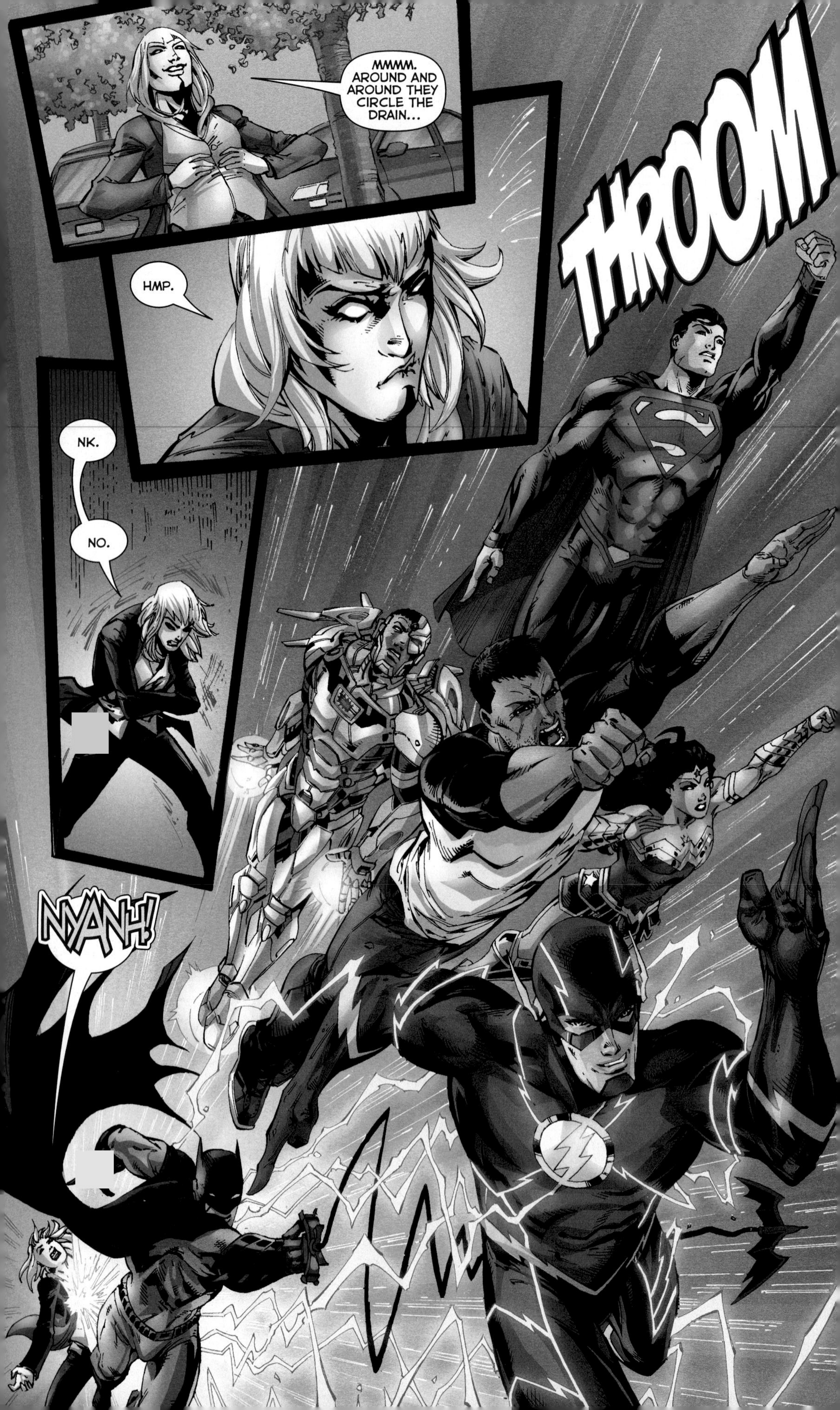
MMMM. AROUND AND AROUND THEY CIRCLE THE DRAIN...
HMP.
NK.
NO.
THROOM
NYANH!

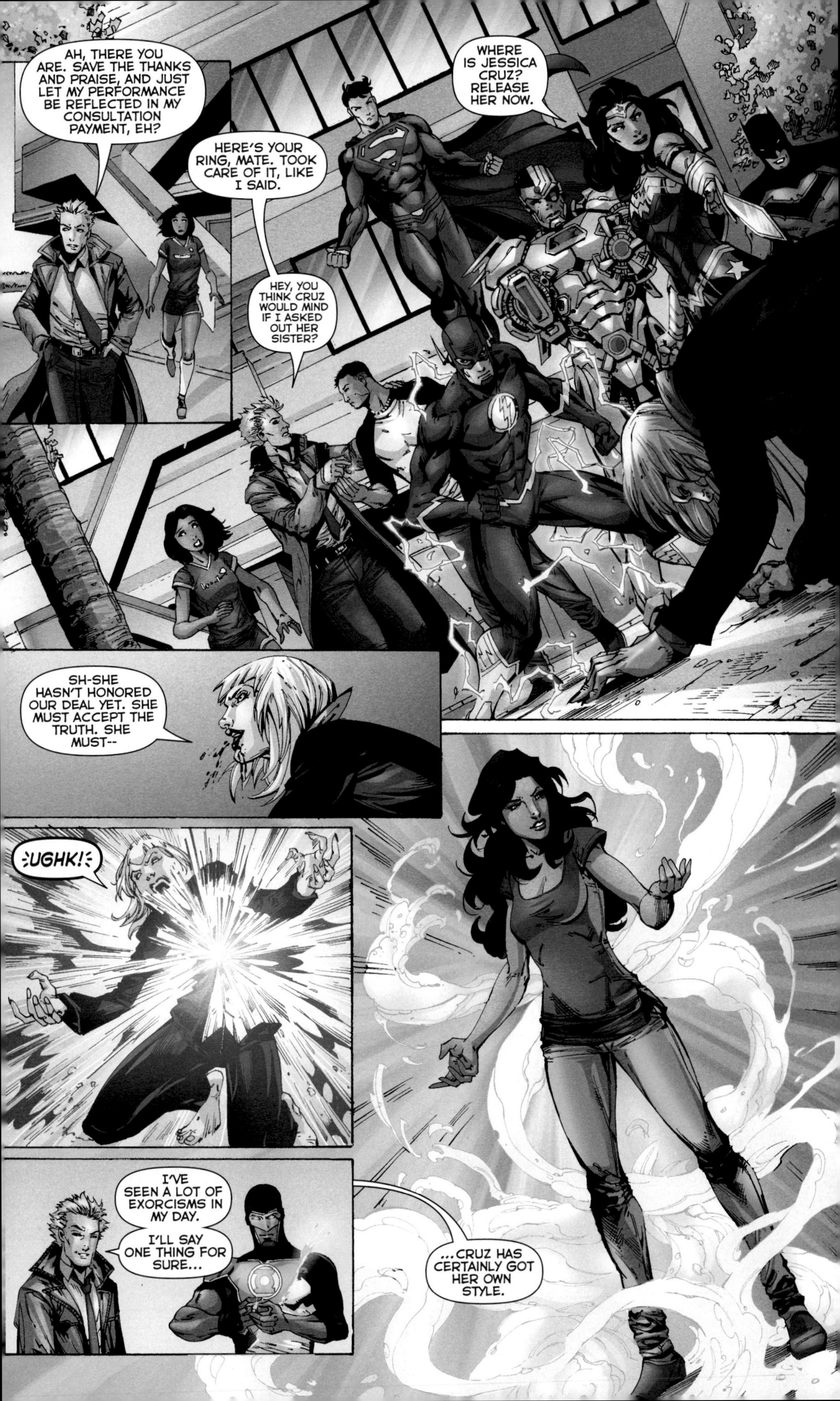

AH, THERE YOU ARE. SAVE THE THANKS AND PRAISE, AND JUST LET MY PERFORMANCE BE REFLECTED IN MY CONSULTATION PAYMENT, EH?
HERE'S YOUR RING, MATE. TOOK CARE OF IT, LIKE I SAID.
WHERE IS JESSICA CRUZ? RELEASE HER NOW.
HEY, YOU THINK CRUZ WOULD MIND IF I ASKED OUT HER SISTER?
SH-SHE HASN'T HONORED OUR DEAL YET. SHE MUST ACCEPT THE TRUTH. SHE MUST--
UGHK!
I'VE SEEN A LOT OF EXORCISMS IN MY DAY.
I'LL SAY ONE THING FOR SURE...
...CRUZ HAS CERTAINLY GOT HER OWN STYLE.

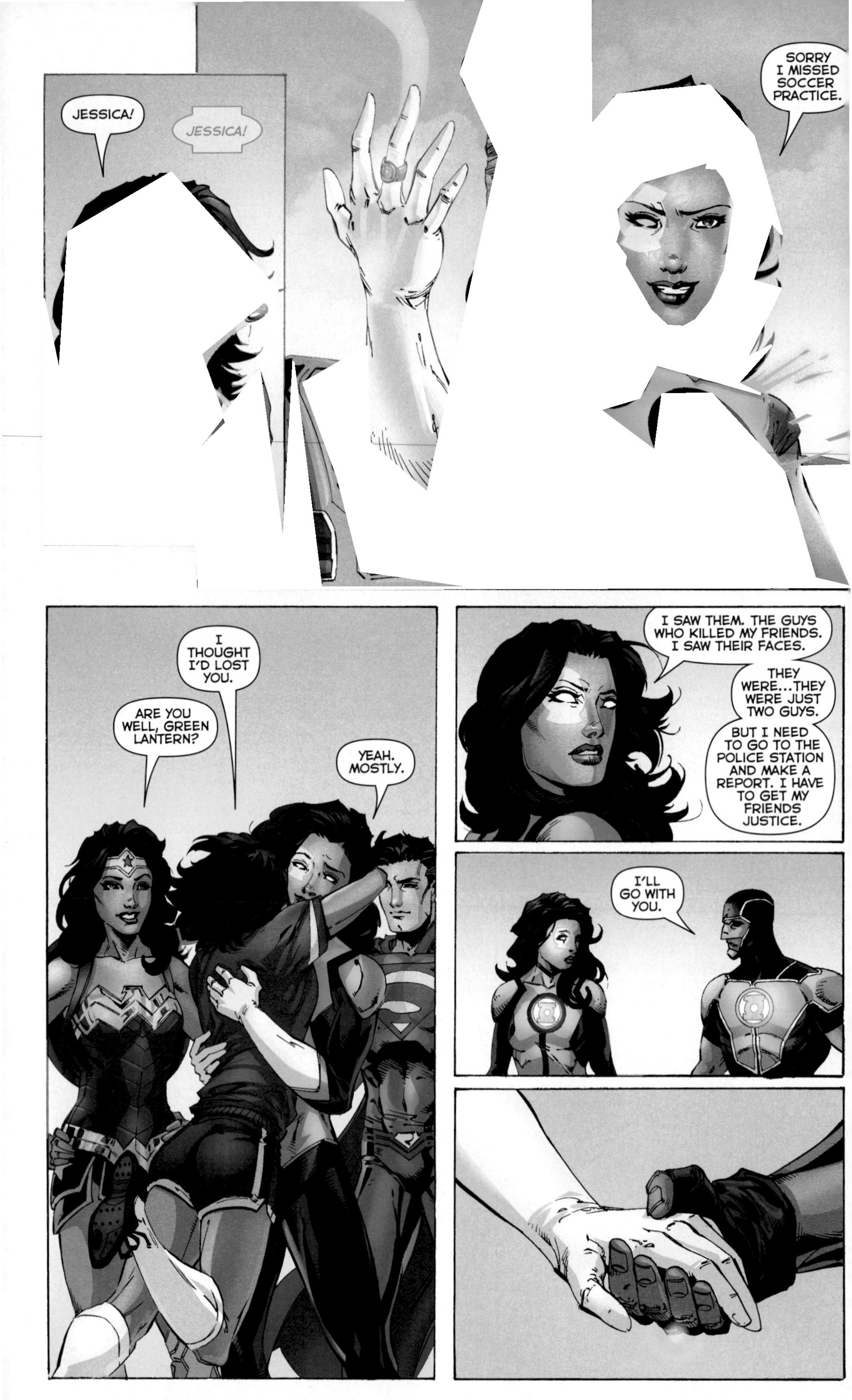
JESSICA!
JESSICA!
SORRY I MISSED SOCCER PRACTICE.
I THOUGHT I'D LOST YOU.
ARE YOU WELL, GREEN LANTERN?
YEAH. MOSTLY.
I SAW THEM. THE GUYS WHO KILLED MY FRIENDS. I SAW THEIR FACES.
THEY WERE...THEY WERE JUST TWO GUYS.
BUT I NEED TO GO TO THE POLICE STATION AND MAKE A REPORT. I HAVE TO GET MY FRIENDS JUSTICE.
I'LL GO WITH YOU.

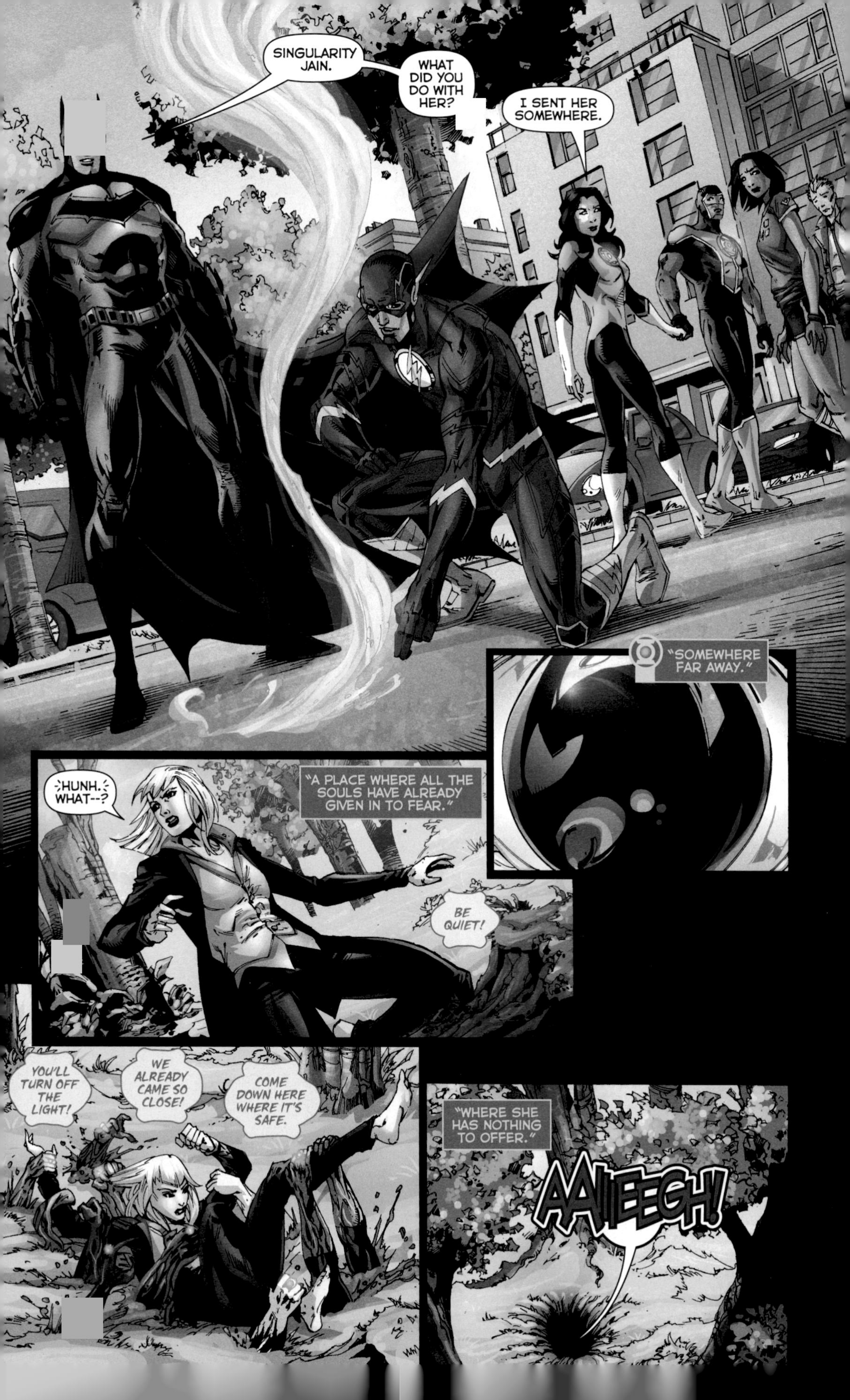
SINGULARITY JAIN.
WHAT DID YOU DO WITH HER?
I SENT HER SOMEWHERE.
"SOMEWHERE FAR AWAY."
HUNH. WHAT--?
"A PLACE WHERE ALL THE SOULS HAVE ALREADY GIVEN IN TO FEAR."
BE QUIET!
YOU'LL TURN OFF THE LIGHT!
WE ALREADY CAME SO CLOSE!
COME DOWN HERE WHERE IT'S SAFE.
"WHERE SHE HAS NOTHING TO OFFER."
AAIIEEGH!

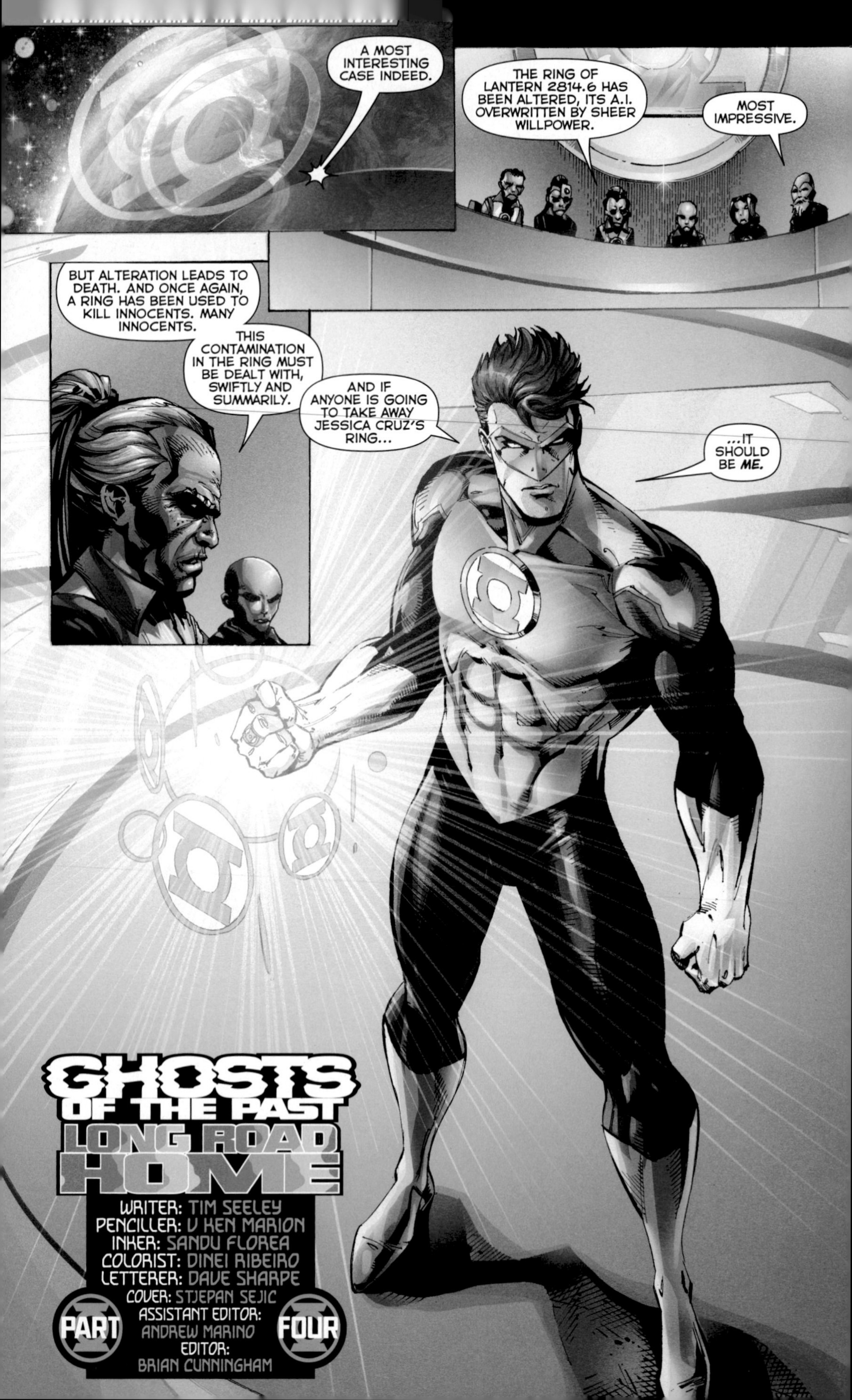
A MOST INTERESTING CASE INDEED.
THE RING OF LANTERN 2814.6 HAS BEEN ALTERED, ITS A.I. OVERWRITTEN BY SHEER WILLPOWER.
MOST IMPRESSIVE.
BUT ALTERATION LEADS TO DEATH. AND ONCE AGAIN, A RING HAS BEEN USED TO KILL INNOCENTS. MANY INNOCENTS.
THIS CONTAMINATION IN THE RING MUST BE DEALT WITH, SWIFTLY AND SUMMARILY.
AND IF ANYONE IS GOING TO TAKE AWAY JESSICA CRUZ'S RING...
...IT SHOULD BE *ME.*
GHOSTS OF THE PAST
LONG ROAD HOME
WRITER: TIM SEELEY
PENCILLER: V KEN MARION
INKER: SANDU FLOREA
COLORIST: DINEI RIBEIRO
LETTERER: DAVE SHARPE
COVER: STJEPAN SEJIC
PART
ASSISTANT EDITOR: ANDREW MARINO
FOUR
EDITOR: BRIAN CUNNINGHAM

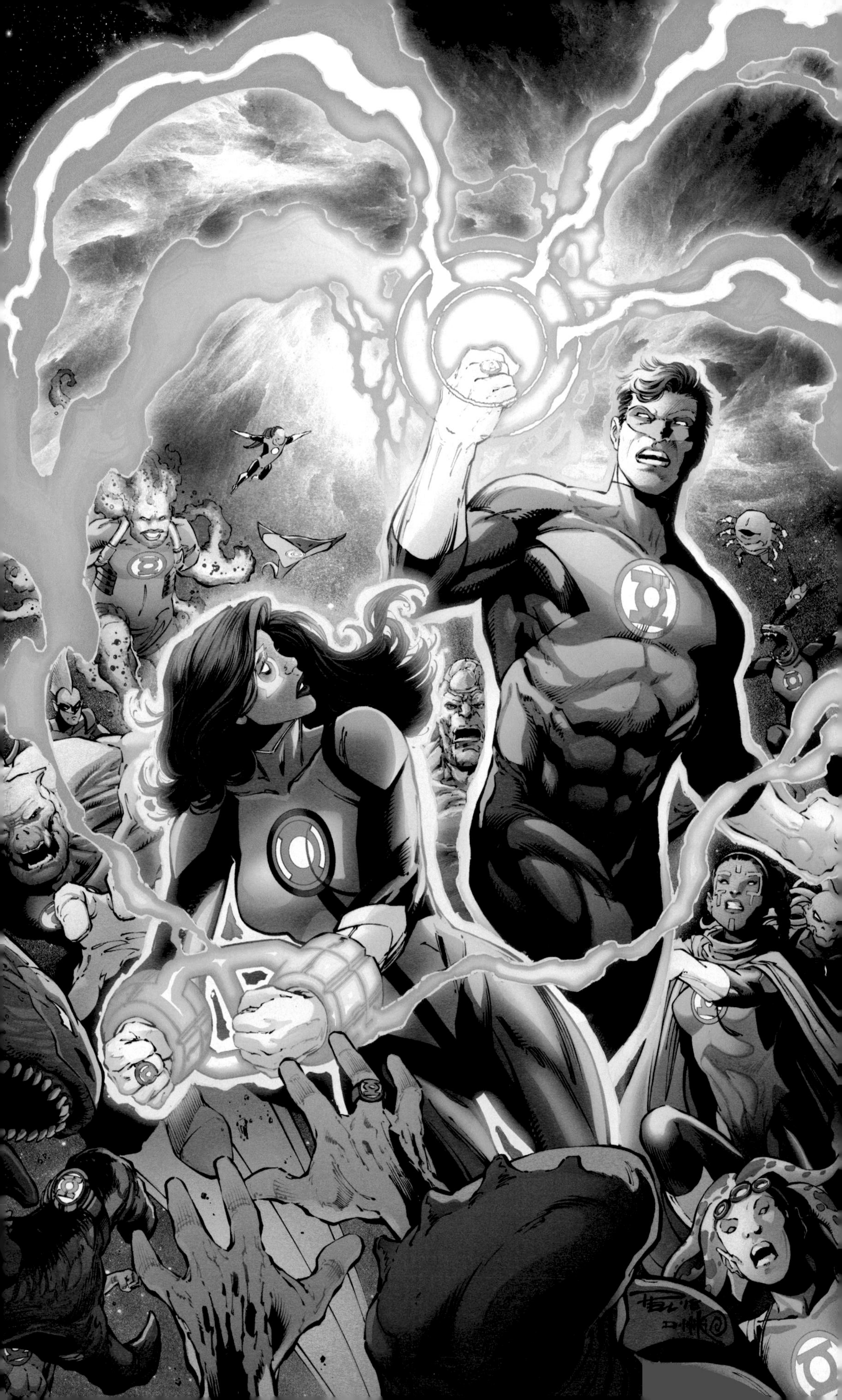

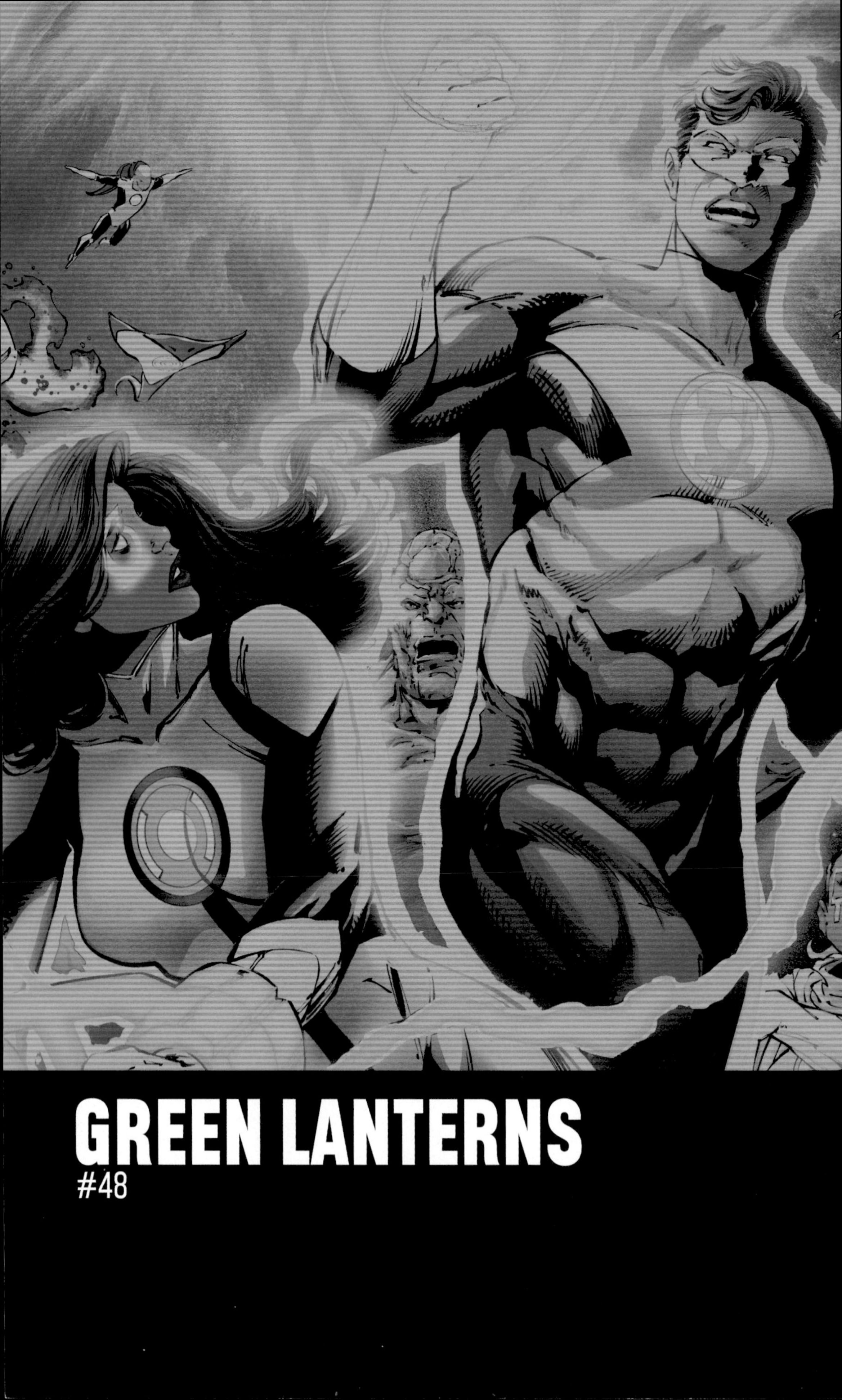

# GREEN LANTERNS
#48

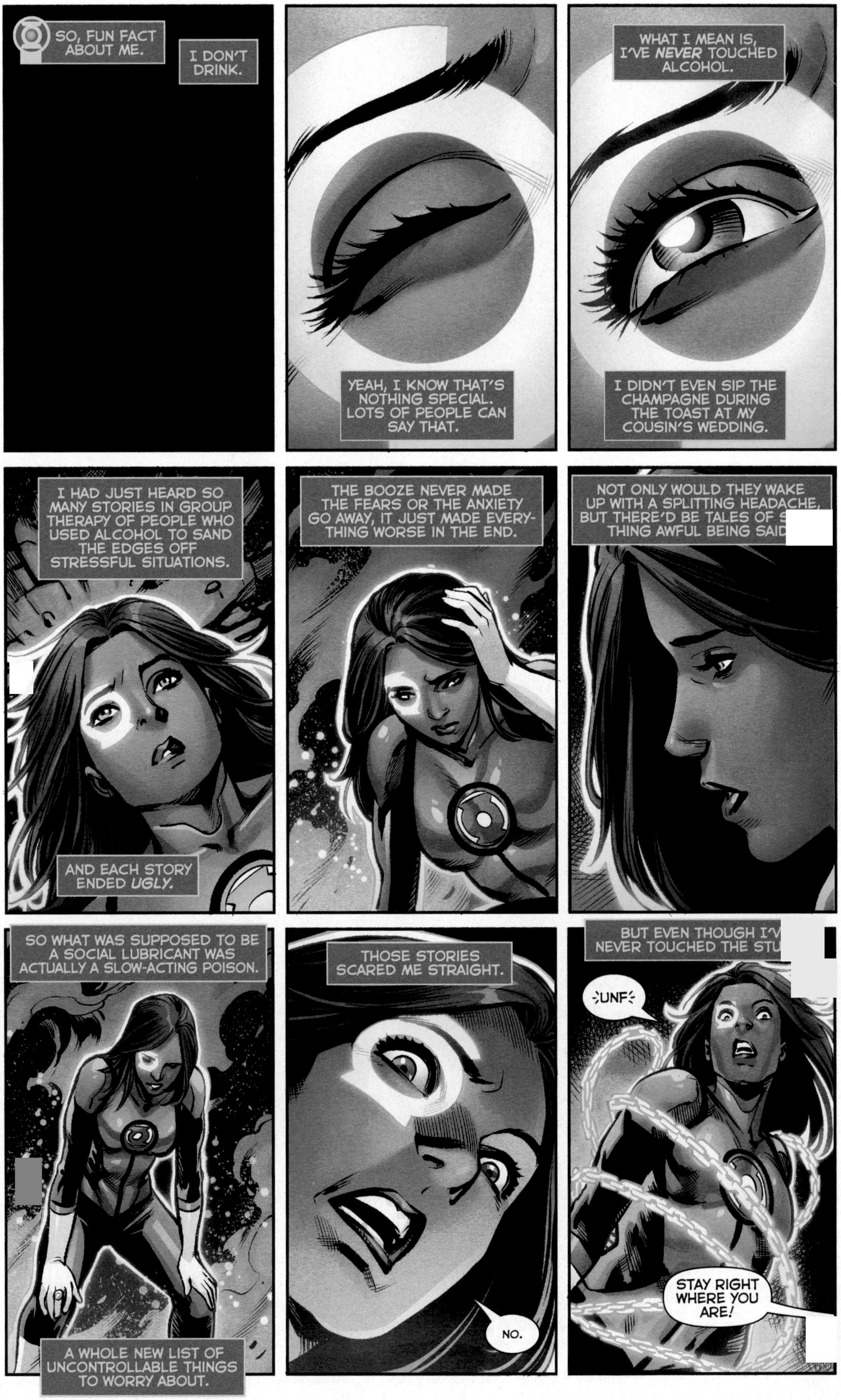
SO, FUN FACT ABOUT ME.
I DON'T DRINK.
YEAH, I KNOW THAT'S NOTHING SPECIAL. LOTS OF PEOPLE CAN SAY THAT.
WHAT I MEAN IS, I'VE *NEVER* TOUCHED ALCOHOL.
I DIDN'T EVEN SIP THE CHAMPAGNE DURING THE TOAST AT MY COUSIN'S WEDDING.
I HAD JUST HEARD SO MANY STORIES IN GROUP THERAPY OF PEOPLE WHO USED ALCOHOL TO SAND THE EDGES OFF STRESSFUL SITUATIONS.
AND EACH STORY ENDED *UGLY.*
THE BOOZE NEVER MADE THE FEARS OR THE ANXIETY GO AWAY, IT JUST MADE EVERY-THING WORSE IN THE END.
NOT ONLY WOULD THEY WAKE UP WITH A SPLITTING HEADACHE, BUT THERE'D BE TALES OF S
THING AWFUL BEING SAID
SO WHAT WAS SUPPOSED TO BE A SOCIAL LUBRICANT WAS ACTUALLY A SLOW-ACTING POISON.
A WHOLE NEW LIST OF UNCONTROLLABLE THINGS TO WORRY ABOUT.
THOSE STORIES SCARED ME STRAIGHT.
NO.
BUT EVEN THOUGH I'V
NEVER TOUCHED THE STU
UNF
STAY RIGHT WHERE YOU ARE!

SPACE SECTOR 2910.
THE PLANET OZRAO.

...I NOW KNOW WHAT THAT NEXT MORNING FEELS LIKE.

# REBEL RUN

## PART ONE

AARON GILLESPIE **WRITER**    RONAN CLIQUET **ARTIST**

HI-FI **COLORIST**    DAVE SHARPE **LETTERER**

PAUL PELLETIER, DANNY MIKI, ADRIANO LUCAS **COVER**

ANDREW MARINO **ASSISTANT EDITOR**    BRIAN CUNNINGHAM **EDITOR**

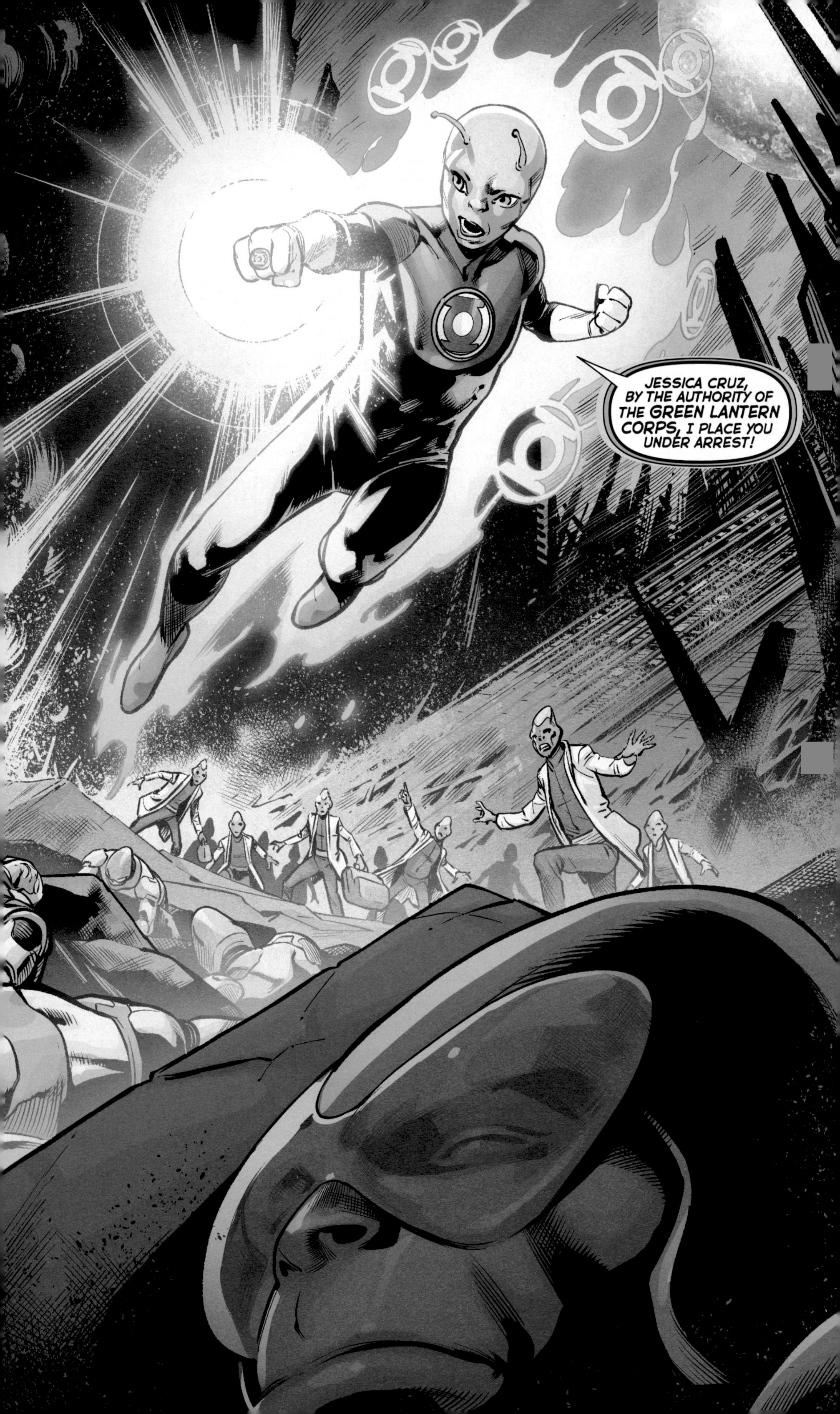
JESSICA CRUZ, BY THE AUTHORITY OF THE GREEN LANTERN CORPS, I PLACE YOU UNDER ARREST!

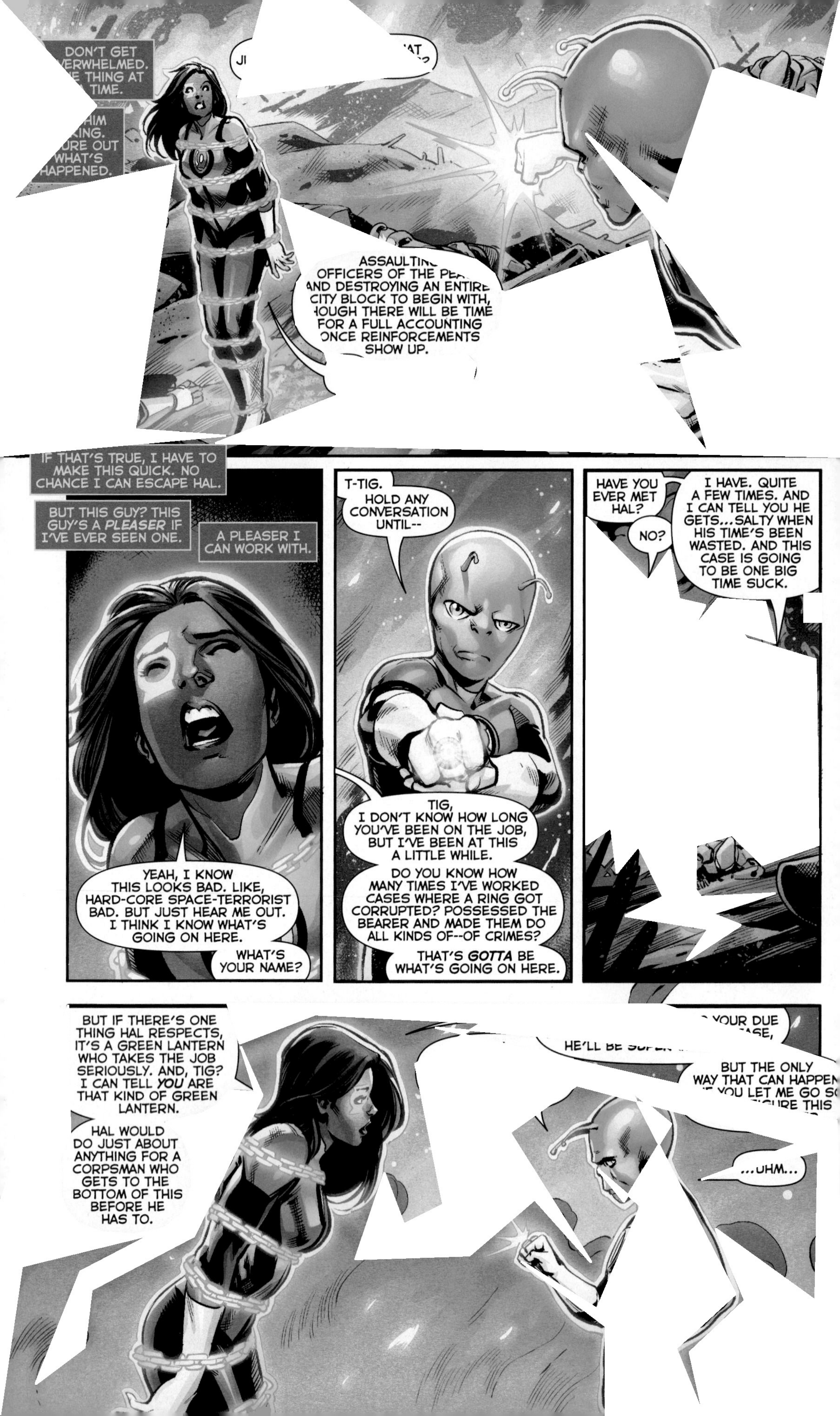

DON'T GET
ERWHELMED.
E THING AT
TIME.
HIM
KING.
URE OUT
WHAT'S
HAPPENED.
ASSAULTIN
OFFICERS OF THE PE
AND DESTROYING AN ENTIRE
CITY BLOCK TO BEGIN WITH,
HOUGH THERE WILL BE TIME
FOR A FULL ACCOUNTING
ONCE REINFORCEMENTS
SHOW UP.
IF THAT'S TRUE, I HAVE TO MAKE THIS QUICK. NO CHANCE I CAN ESCAPE HAL.
BUT THIS GUY? THIS GUY'S A *PLEASER* IF I'VE EVER SEEN ONE.
A PLEASER I CAN WORK WITH.
YEAH, I KNOW THIS LOOKS BAD. LIKE, HARD-CORE SPACE-TERRORIST BAD. BUT JUST HEAR ME OUT. I THINK I KNOW WHAT'S GOING ON HERE.
WHAT'S YOUR NAME?
T-TIG. HOLD ANY CONVERSATION UNTIL--
TIG, I DON'T KNOW HOW LONG YOU'VE BEEN ON THE JOB, BUT I'VE BEEN AT THIS A LITTLE WHILE.
DO YOU KNOW HOW MANY TIMES I'VE WORKED CASES WHERE A RING GOT CORRUPTED? POSSESSED THE BEARER AND MADE THEM DO ALL KINDS OF--OF CRIMES?
THAT'S *GOTTA* BE WHAT'S GOING ON HERE.
HAVE YOU EVER MET HAL?
NO?
I HAVE. QUITE A FEW TIMES. AND I CAN TELL YOU HE GETS...SALTY WHEN HIS TIME'S BEEN WASTED. AND THIS CASE IS GOING TO BE ONE BIG TIME SUCK.
BUT IF THERE'S ONE THING HAL RESPECTS, IT'S A GREEN LANTERN WHO TAKES THE JOB SERIOUSLY. AND, TIG? I CAN TELL *YOU* ARE THAT KIND OF GREEN LANTERN.
HAL WOULD DO JUST ABOUT ANYTHING FOR A CORPSMAN WHO GETS TO THE BOTTOM OF THIS BEFORE HE HAS TO.
YOUR DUE
HE'LL BE
BUT THE ONLY WAY THAT CAN HAPPEN
YOU LET ME GO SO
...UHM...

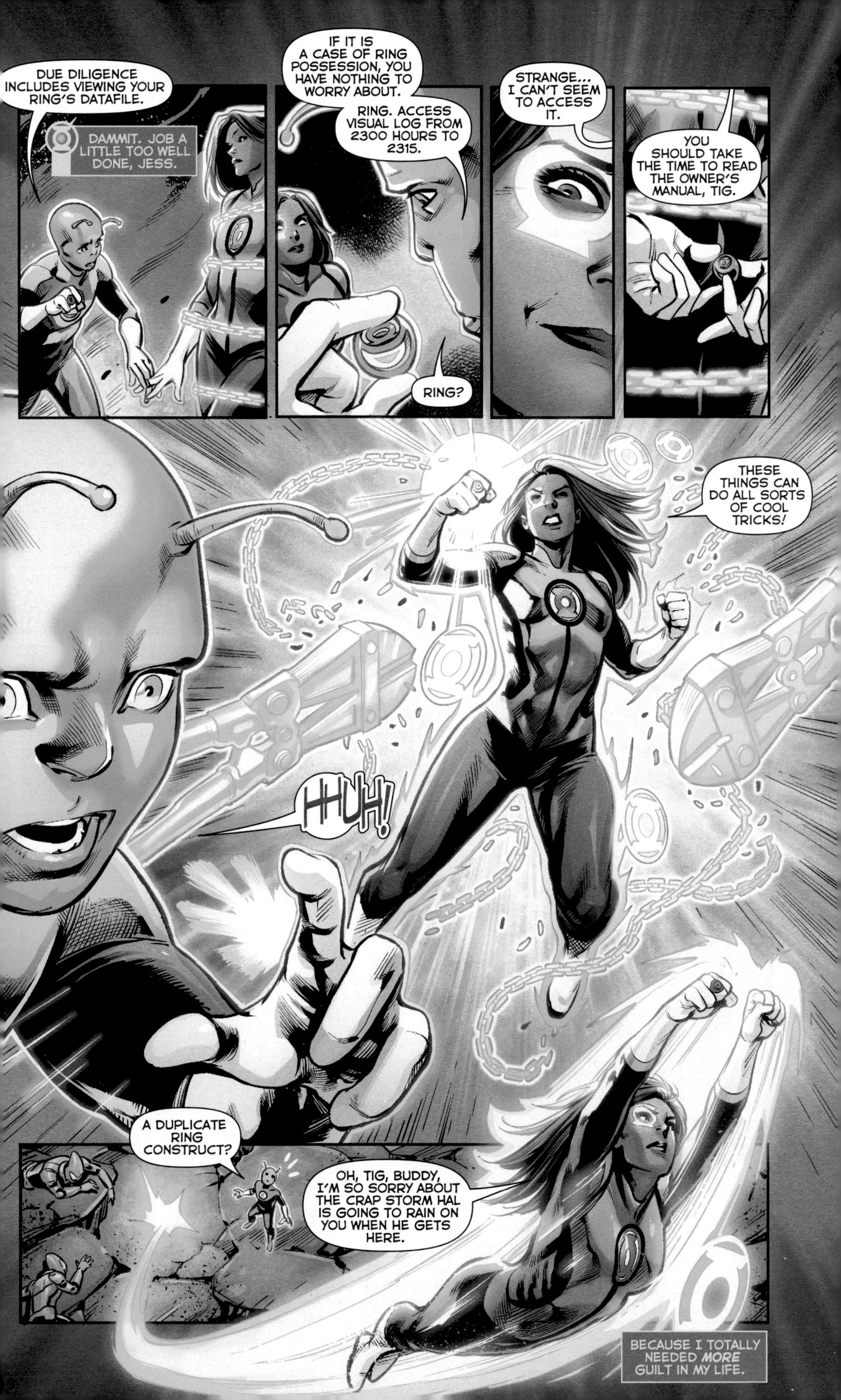
DUE DILIGENCE INCLUDES VIEWING YOUR RING'S DATAFILE.
DAMMIT. JOB A LITTLE TOO WELL DONE, JESS.
IF IT IS A CASE OF RING POSSESSION, YOU HAVE NOTHING TO WORRY ABOUT.
RING. ACCESS VISUAL LOG FROM 2300 HOURS TO 2315.
RING?
STRANGE... I CAN'T SEEM TO ACCESS IT.
YOU SHOULD TAKE THE TIME TO READ THE OWNER'S MANUAL, TIG.
THESE THINGS CAN DO ALL SORTS OF COOL TRICKS!
HHUH!
A DUPLICATE RING CONSTRUCT?
OH, TIG, BUDDY, I'M SO SORRY ABOUT THE CRAP STORM HAL IS GOING TO RAIN ON YOU WHEN HE GETS HERE.
BECAUSE I TOTALLY NEEDED *MORE* GUILT IN MY LIFE.

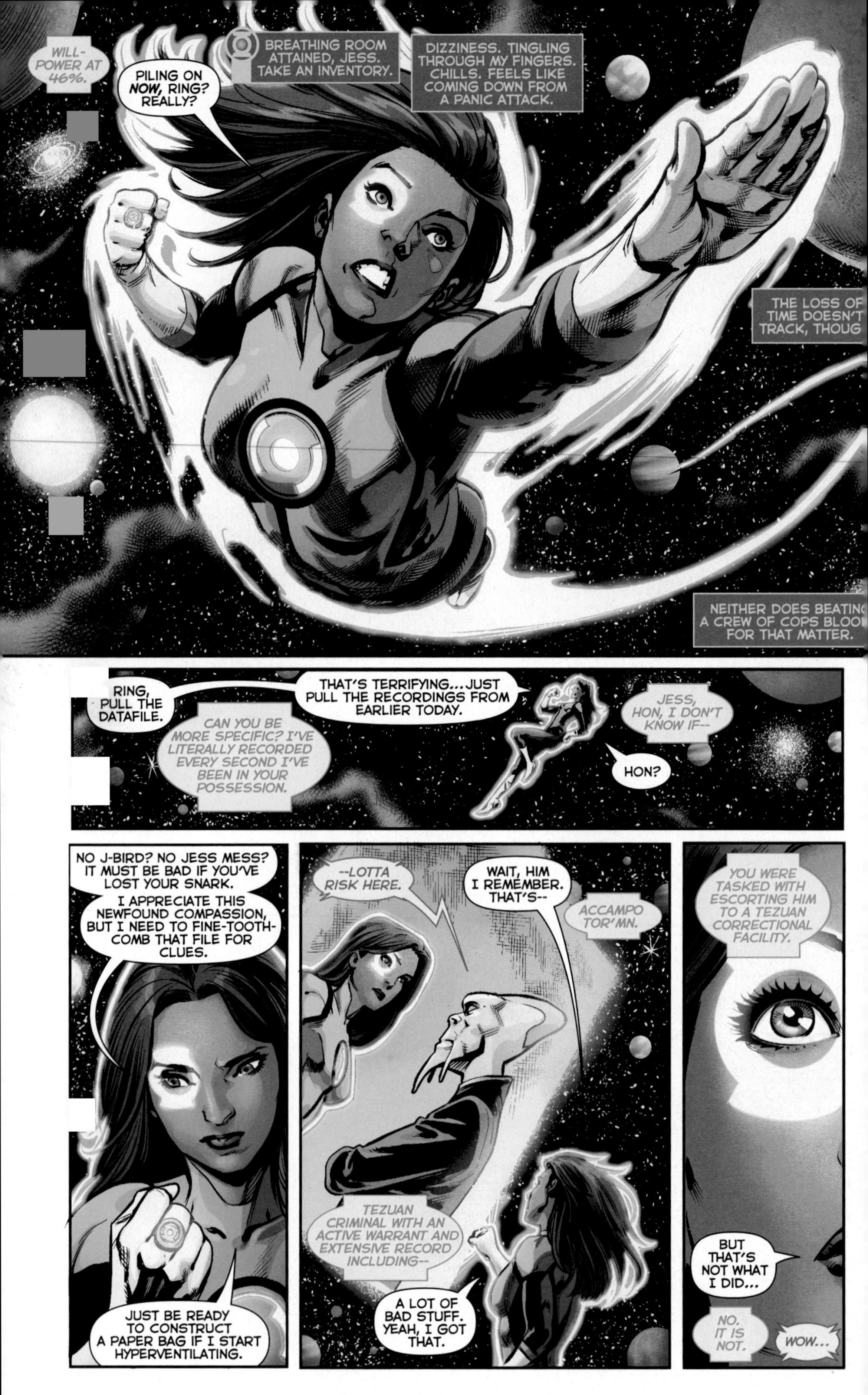
WILL-POWER AT 46%.
PILING ON NOW, RING? REALLY?
BREATHING ROOM ATTAINED, JESS. TAKE AN INVENTORY.
DIZZINESS. TINGLING THROUGH MY FINGERS. CHILLS. FEELS LIKE COMING DOWN FROM A PANIC ATTACK.
THE LOSS OF TIME DOESN'T TRACK, THOUG
NEITHER DOES BEATIN A CREW OF COPS BLOO FOR THAT MATTER.
RING, PULL THE DATAFILE.
CAN YOU BE MORE SPECIFIC? I'VE LITERALLY RECORDED EVERY SECOND I'VE BEEN IN YOUR POSSESSION.
THAT'S TERRIFYING... JUST PULL THE RECORDINGS FROM EARLIER TODAY.
JESS, HON, I DON'T KNOW IF--
HON?
NO J-BIRD? NO JESS MESS? IT MUST BE BAD IF YOU'VE LOST YOUR SNARK.
I APPRECIATE THIS NEWFOUND COMPASSION, BUT I NEED TO FINE-TOOTH-COMB THAT FILE FOR CLUES.
JUST BE READY TO CONSTRUCT A PAPER BAG IF I START HYPERVENTILATING.
--LOTTA RISK HERE.
WAIT, HIM I REMEMBER. THAT'S--
ACCAMPO TOR'MN.
TEZUAN CRIMINAL WITH AN ACTIVE WARRANT AND EXTENSIVE RECORD INCLUDING--
A LOT OF BAD STUFF. YEAH, I GOT THAT.
YOU WERE TASKED WITH ESCORTING HIM TO A TEZUAN CORRECTIONAL FACILITY.
BUT THAT'S NOT WHAT I DID...
NO. IT IS NOT.
WOW...

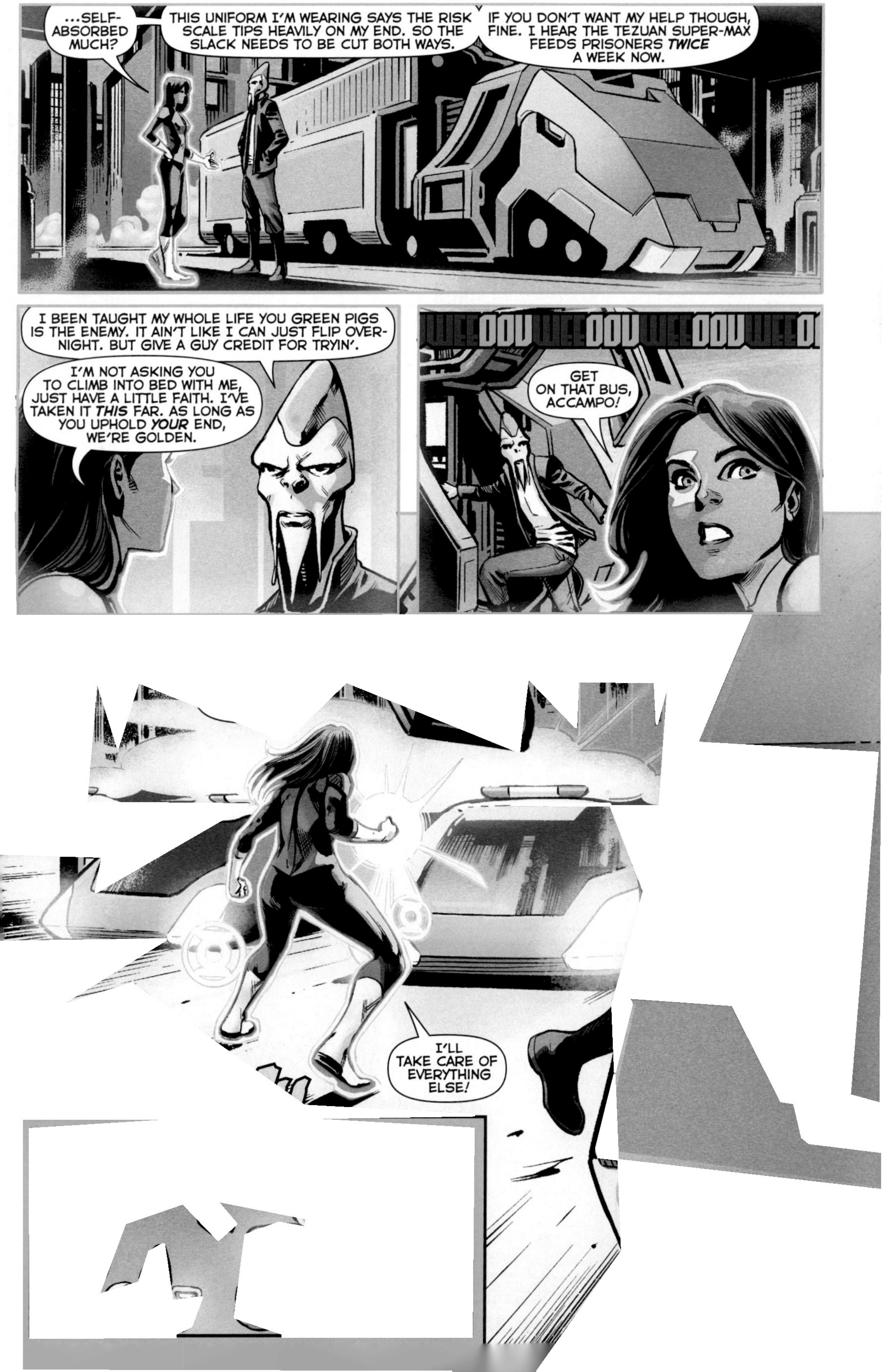
...SELF-ABSORBED MUCH?
THIS UNIFORM I'M WEARING SAYS THE RISK SCALE TIPS HEAVILY ON MY END. SO THE SLACK NEEDS TO BE CUT BOTH WAYS.
IF YOU DON'T WANT MY HELP THOUGH, FINE. I HEAR THE TEZUAN SUPER-MAX FEEDS PRISONERS *TWICE* A WEEK NOW.
I BEEN TAUGHT MY WHOLE LIFE YOU GREEN PIGS IS THE ENEMY. IT AIN'T LIKE I CAN JUST FLIP OVER-NIGHT. BUT GIVE A GUY CREDIT FOR TRYIN'.
I'M NOT ASKING YOU TO CLIMB INTO BED WITH ME, JUST HAVE A LITTLE FAITH. I'VE TAKEN IT *THIS* FAR. AS LONG AS YOU UPHOLD *YOUR* END, WE'RE GOLDEN.
WEEOOV WEEOOV WEEOOV WEEO
GET ON THAT BUS, ACCAMPO!
I'LL TAKE CARE OF EVERYTHING ELSE!

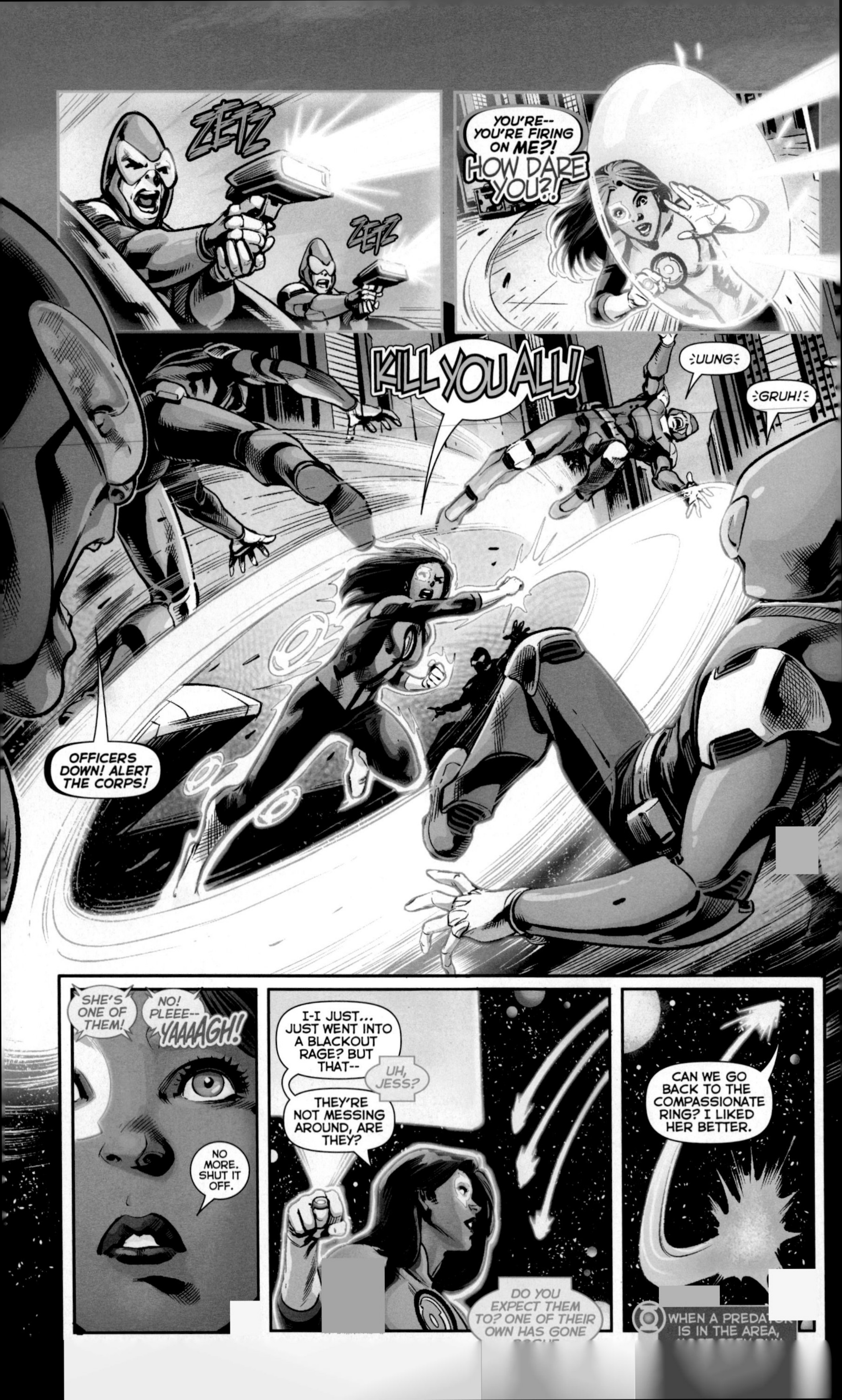
ZETZ
ZETZ
YOU'RE-- YOU'RE FIRING ON ME?! HOW DARE YOU?!
KILL YOU ALL!
UUNG
GRUH!
OFFICERS DOWN! ALERT THE CORPS!
SHE'S ONE OF THEM!
NO! PLEEE-- YAAAAGH!
NO MORE. SHUT IT OFF.
I-I JUST... JUST WENT INTO A BLACKOUT RAGE? BUT THAT--
UH, JESS?
THEY'RE NOT MESSING AROUND, ARE THEY?
DO YOU EXPECT THEM TO? ONE OF THEIR OWN HAS GONE
CAN WE GO BACK TO THE COMPASSIONATE RING? I LIKED HER BETTER.
WHEN A PREDA
IS IN THE AREA,

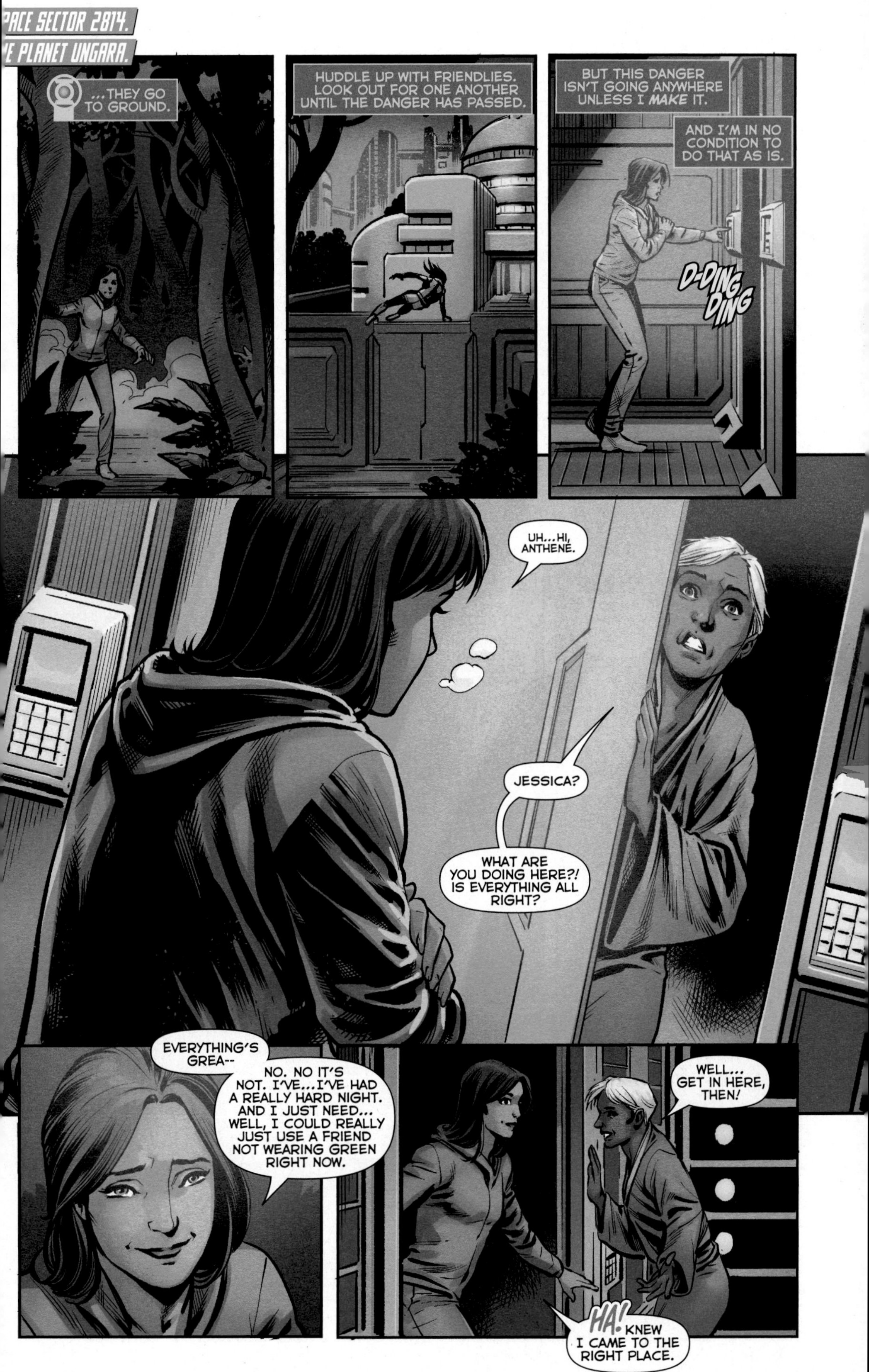

PACE SECTOR 2814.
E PLANET UNGARA.
...THEY GO TO GROUND.
HUDDLE UP WITH FRIENDLIES. LOOK OUT FOR ONE ANOTHER UNTIL THE DANGER HAS PASSED.
BUT THIS DANGER ISN'T GOING ANYWHERE UNLESS I *MAKE* IT.
AND I'M IN NO CONDITION TO DO THAT AS IS.
D-DING DING
UH...HI, ANTHENE.
JESSICA?
WHAT ARE YOU DOING HERE?! IS EVERYTHING ALL RIGHT?
EVERYTHING'S GREA--
NO. NO IT'S NOT. I'VE...I'VE HAD A REALLY HARD NIGHT. AND I JUST NEED... WELL, I COULD REALLY JUST USE A FRIEND NOT WEARING GREEN RIGHT NOW.
WELL... GET IN HERE, THEN!
HA! KNEW I CAME TO THE RIGHT PLACE.

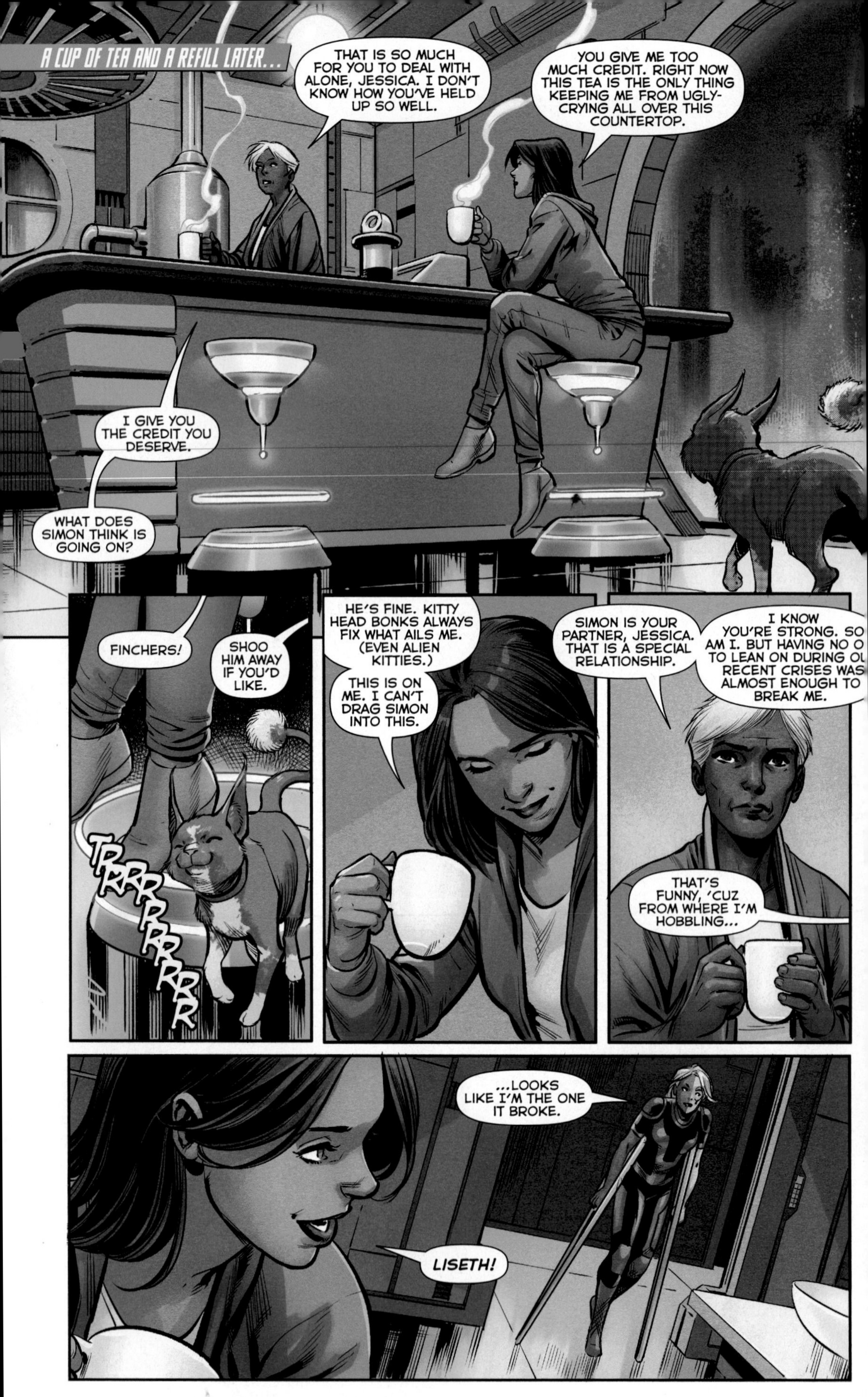

A CUP OF TEA AND A REFILL LATER...
THAT IS SO MUCH FOR YOU TO DEAL WITH ALONE, JESSICA. I DON'T KNOW HOW YOU'VE HELD UP SO WELL.
YOU GIVE ME TOO MUCH CREDIT. RIGHT NOW THIS TEA IS THE ONLY THING KEEPING ME FROM UGLY-CRYING ALL OVER THIS COUNTERTOP.
I GIVE YOU THE CREDIT YOU DESERVE.
WHAT DOES SIMON THINK IS GOING ON?
FINCHERS!
SHOO HIM AWAY IF YOU'D LIKE.
TRRRRRRRRR
HE'S FINE. KITTY HEAD BONKS ALWAYS FIX WHAT AILS ME. (EVEN ALIEN KITTIES.)
THIS IS ON ME. I CAN'T DRAG SIMON INTO THIS.
SIMON IS YOUR PARTNER, JESSICA. THAT IS A SPECIAL RELATIONSHIP.
I KNOW YOU'RE STRONG. SO AM I. BUT HAVING NO O TO LEAN ON DURING OU RECENT CRISES WAS ALMOST ENOUGH TO BREAK ME.
THAT'S FUNNY, 'CUZ FROM WHERE I'M HOBBLING...
...LOOKS LIKE I'M THE ONE IT BROKE.
LISETH!

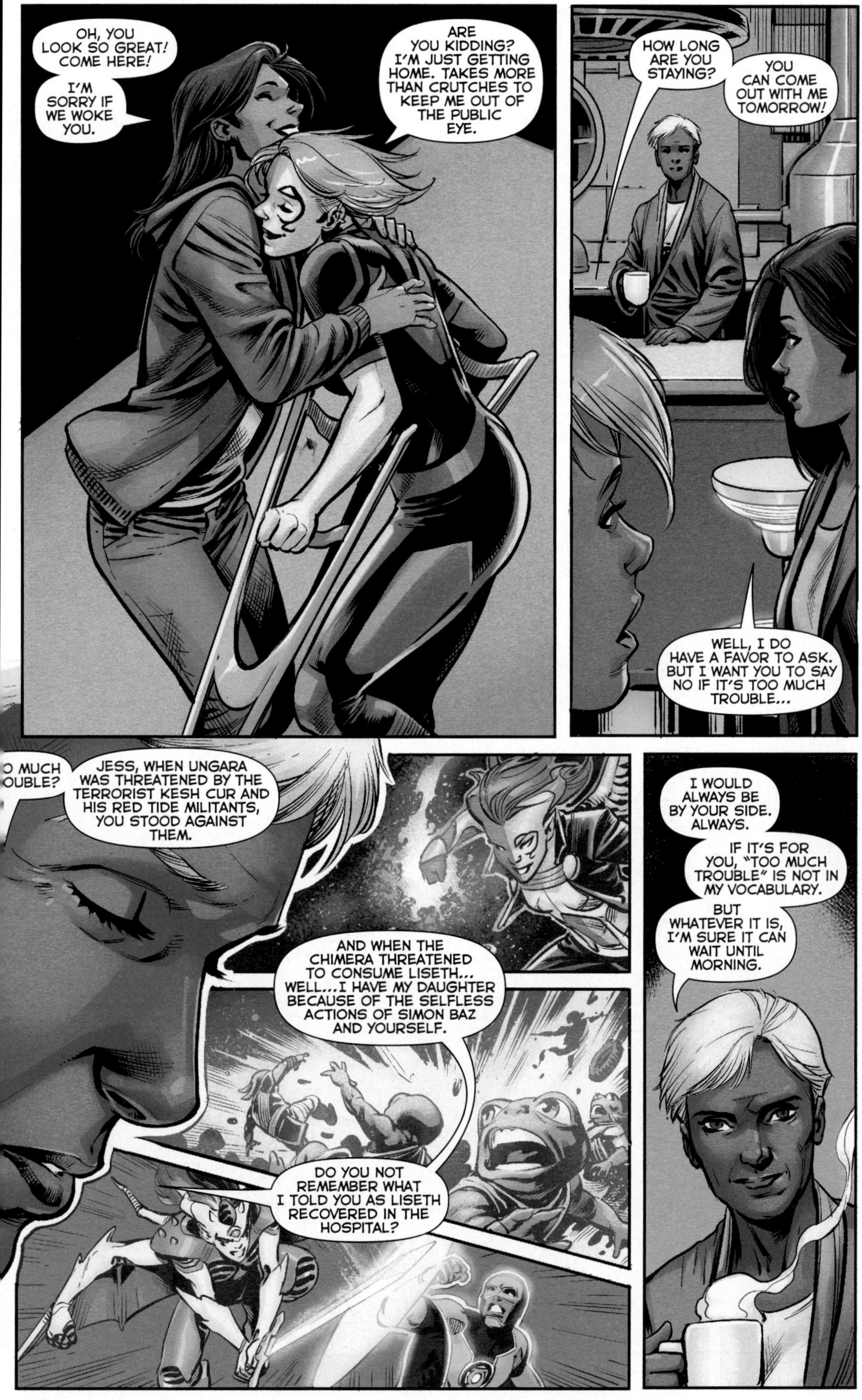

OH, YOU LOOK SO GREAT! COME HERE!
I'M SORRY IF WE WOKE YOU.
ARE YOU KIDDING? I'M JUST GETTING HOME. TAKES MORE THAN CRUTCHES TO KEEP ME OUT OF THE PUBLIC EYE.
HOW LONG ARE YOU STAYING?
YOU CAN COME OUT WITH ME TOMORROW!
WELL, I DO HAVE A FAVOR TO ASK. BUT I WANT YOU TO SAY NO IF IT'S TOO MUCH TROUBLE...
O MUCH OUBLE?
JESS, WHEN UNGARA WAS THREATENED BY THE TERRORIST KESH CUR AND HIS RED TIDE MILITANTS, YOU STOOD AGAINST THEM.
AND WHEN THE CHIMERA THREATENED TO CONSUME LISETH... WELL...I HAVE MY DAUGHTER BECAUSE OF THE SELFLESS ACTIONS OF SIMON BAZ AND YOURSELF.
DO YOU NOT REMEMBER WHAT I TOLD YOU AS LISETH RECOVERED IN THE HOSPITAL?
I WOULD ALWAYS BE BY YOUR SIDE. ALWAYS.
IF IT'S FOR YOU, "TOO MUCH TROUBLE" IS NOT IN MY VOCABULARY.
BUT WHATEVER IT IS, I'M SURE IT CAN WAIT UNTIL MORNING.

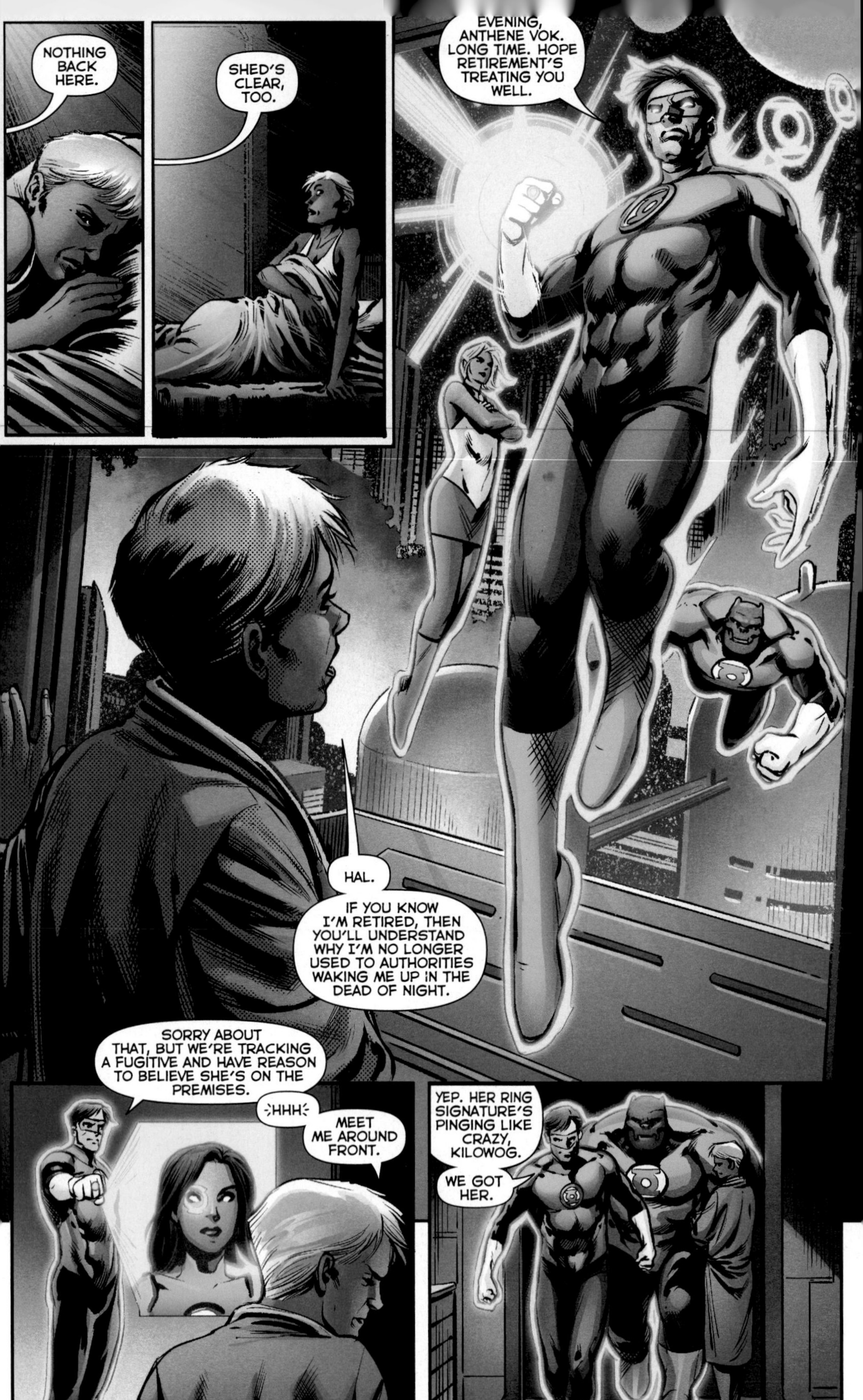
NOTHING BACK HERE.
SHED'S CLEAR, TOO.
EVENING, ANTHENE VOK. LONG TIME. HOPE RETIREMENT'S TREATING YOU WELL.
HAL.
IF YOU KNOW I'M RETIRED, THEN YOU'LL UNDERSTAND WHY I'M NO LONGER USED TO AUTHORITIES WAKING ME UP IN THE DEAD OF NIGHT.
SORRY ABOUT THAT, BUT WE'RE TRACKING A FUGITIVE AND HAVE REASON TO BELIEVE SHE'S ON THE PREMISES.
HHH
MEET ME AROUND FRONT.
YEP. HER RING SIGNATURE'S PINGING LIKE CRAZY, KILOWOG.
WE GOT HER.

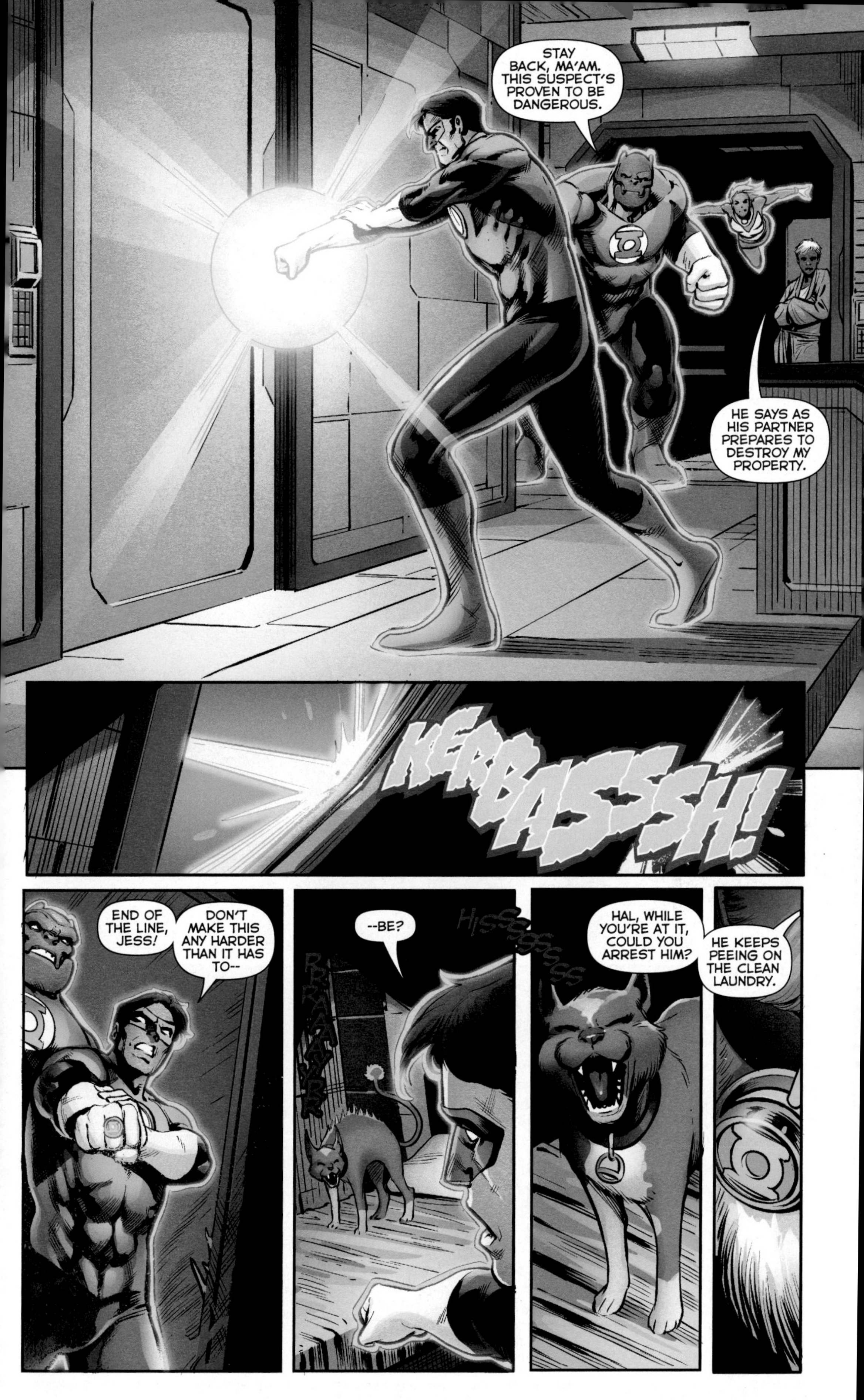
STAY BACK, MA'AM. THIS SUSPECT'S PROVEN TO BE DANGEROUS.
HE SAYS AS HIS PARTNER PREPARES TO DESTROY MY PROPERTY.
KERBASSSH!
END OF THE LINE, JESS!
DON'T MAKE THIS ANY HARDER THAN IT HAS TO--
--BE?
HISSSSSSSS
HAL, WHILE YOU'RE AT IT, COULD YOU ARREST HIM?
HE KEEPS PEEING ON THE CLEAN LAUNDRY.

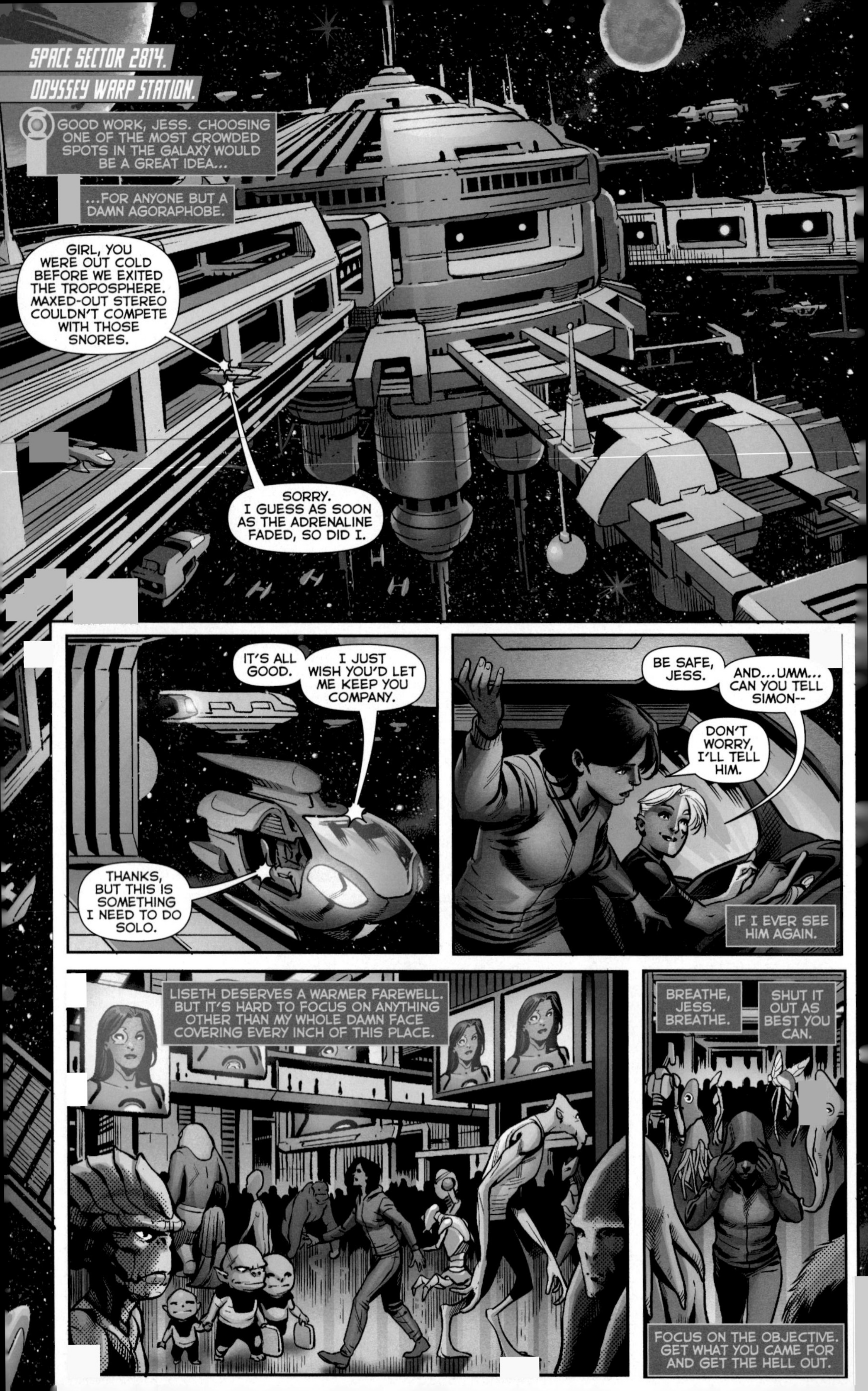
SPACE SECTOR 2814.
ODYSSEY WARP STATION.
GOOD WORK, JESS. CHOOSING ONE OF THE MOST CROWDED SPOTS IN THE GALAXY WOULD BE A GREAT IDEA...
...FOR ANYONE BUT A DAMN AGORAPHOBE.
GIRL, YOU WERE OUT COLD BEFORE WE EXITED THE TROPOSPHERE. MAXED-OUT STEREO COULDN'T COMPETE WITH THOSE SNORES.
SORRY. I GUESS AS SOON AS THE ADRENALINE FADED, SO DID I.
IT'S ALL GOOD.
I JUST WISH YOU'D LET ME KEEP YOU COMPANY.
THANKS, BUT THIS IS SOMETHING I NEED TO DO SOLO.
BE SAFE, JESS.
AND...UMM... CAN YOU TELL SIMON--
DON'T WORRY, I'LL TELL HIM.
IF I EVER SEE HIM AGAIN.
LISETH DESERVES A WARMER FAREWELL. BUT IT'S HARD TO FOCUS ON ANYTHING OTHER THAN MY WHOLE DAMN FACE COVERING EVERY INCH OF THIS PLACE.
BREATHE, JESS. BREATHE.
SHUT IT OUT AS BEST YOU CAN.
FOCUS ON THE OBJECTIVE. GET WHAT YOU CAME FOR AND GET THE HELL OUT.

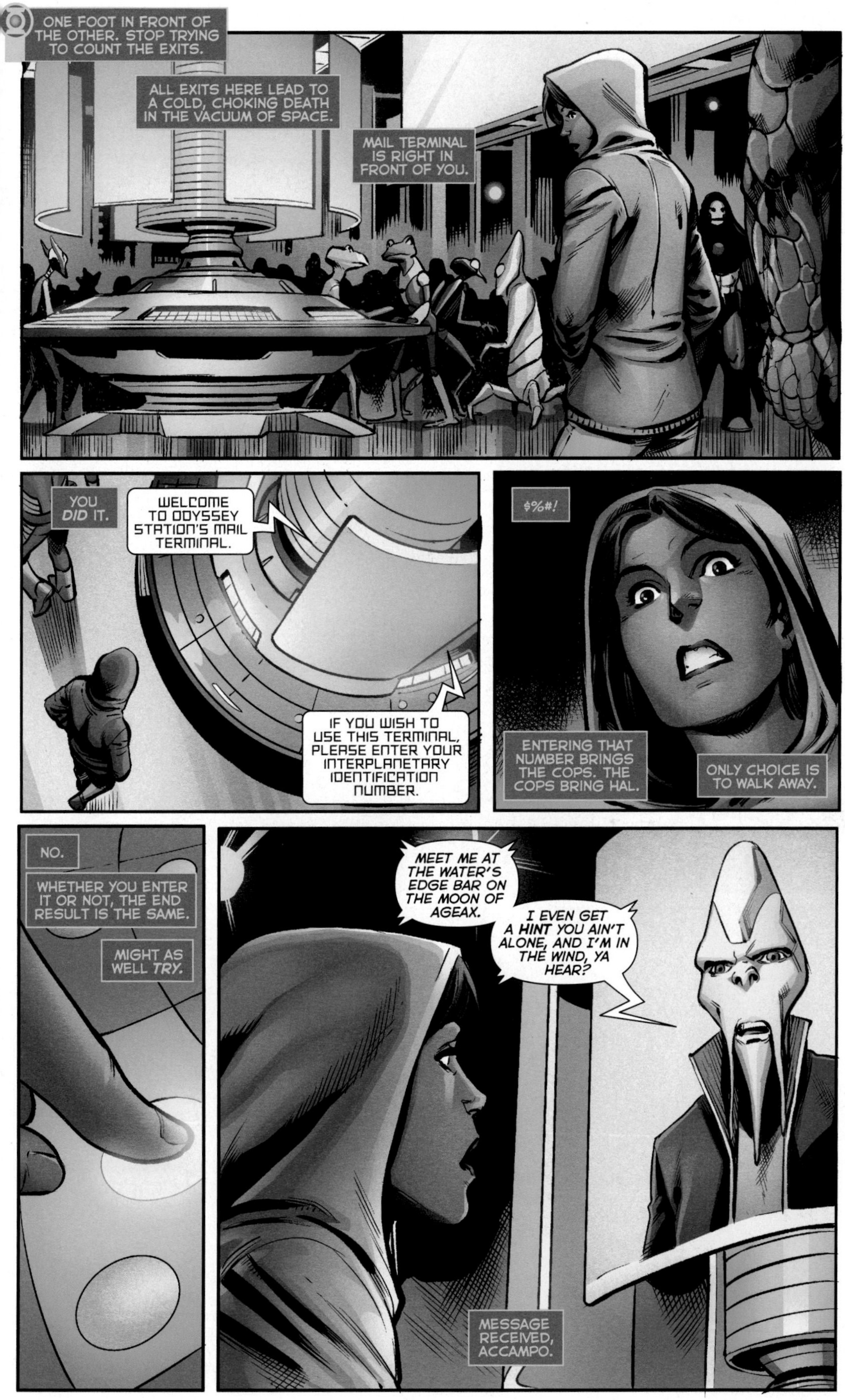
ONE FOOT IN FRONT OF THE OTHER. STOP TRYING TO COUNT THE EXITS.
ALL EXITS HERE LEAD TO A COLD, CHOKING DEATH IN THE VACUUM OF SPACE.
MAIL TERMINAL IS RIGHT IN FRONT OF YOU.
YOU *DID* IT.
WELCOME TO ODYSSEY STATION'S MAIL TERMINAL.
IF YOU WISH TO USE THIS TERMINAL, PLEASE ENTER YOUR INTERPLANETARY IDENTIFICATION NUMBER.
$%#!
ENTERING THAT NUMBER BRINGS THE COPS. THE COPS BRING HAL.
ONLY CHOICE IS TO WALK AWAY.
NO.
WHETHER YOU ENTER IT OR NOT, THE END RESULT IS THE SAME.
MIGHT AS WELL *TRY*.
*MEET ME AT THE WATER'S EDGE BAR ON THE MOON OF AGEAX.*
*I EVEN GET A **HINT** YOU AIN'T ALONE, AND I'M IN THE WIND, YA HEAR?*
MESSAGE RECEIVED, ACCAMPO.

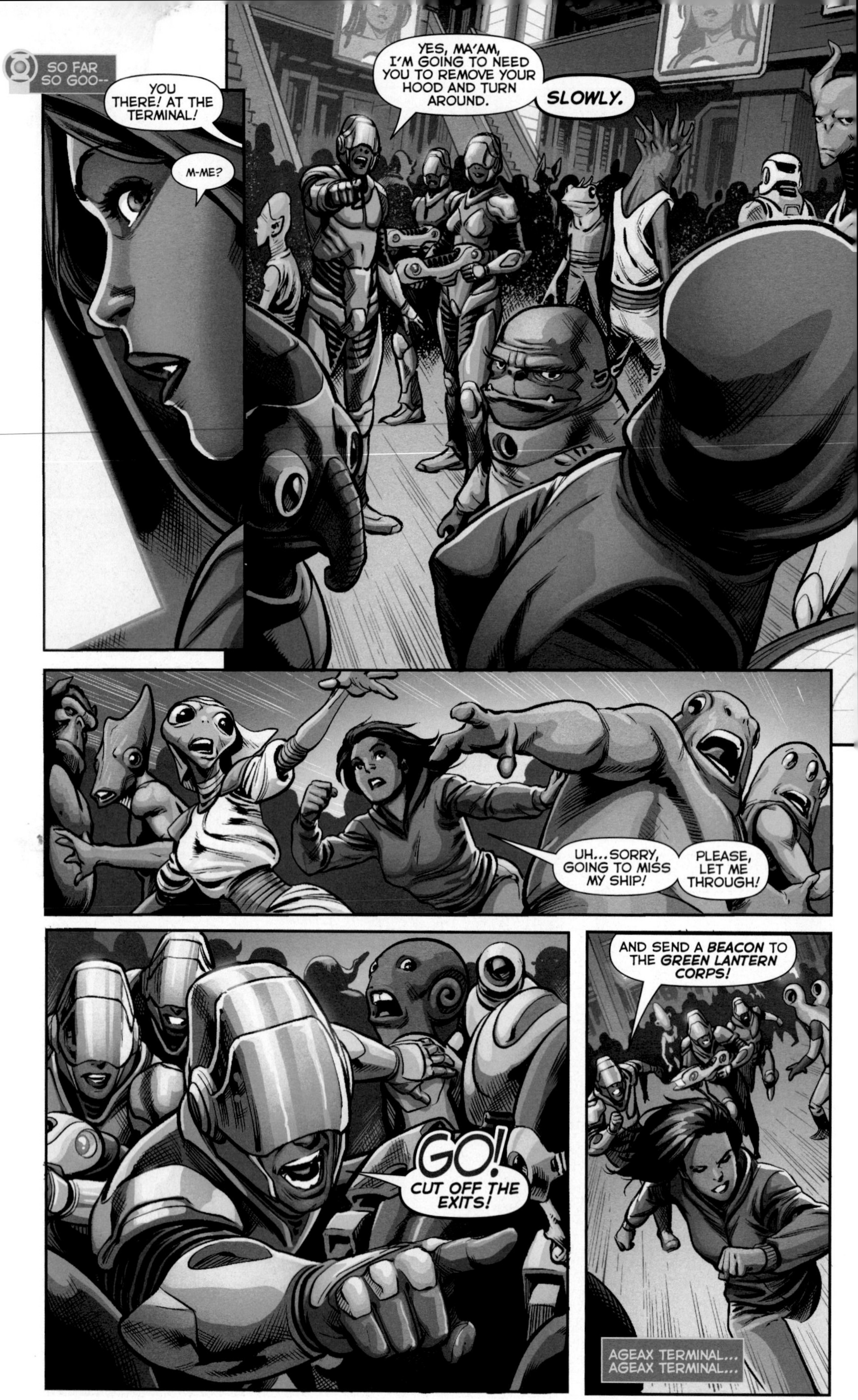
SO FAR SO GOO--
YOU THERE! AT THE TERMINAL!
M-ME?
YES, MA'AM, I'M GOING TO NEED YOU TO REMOVE YOUR HOOD AND TURN AROUND.
SLOWLY.
UH...SORRY, GOING TO MISS MY SHIP!
PLEASE, LET ME THROUGH!
GO! CUT OFF THE EXITS!
AND SEND A BEACON TO THE GREEN LANTERN CORPS!
AGEAX TERMINAL...
AGEAX TERMINAL...

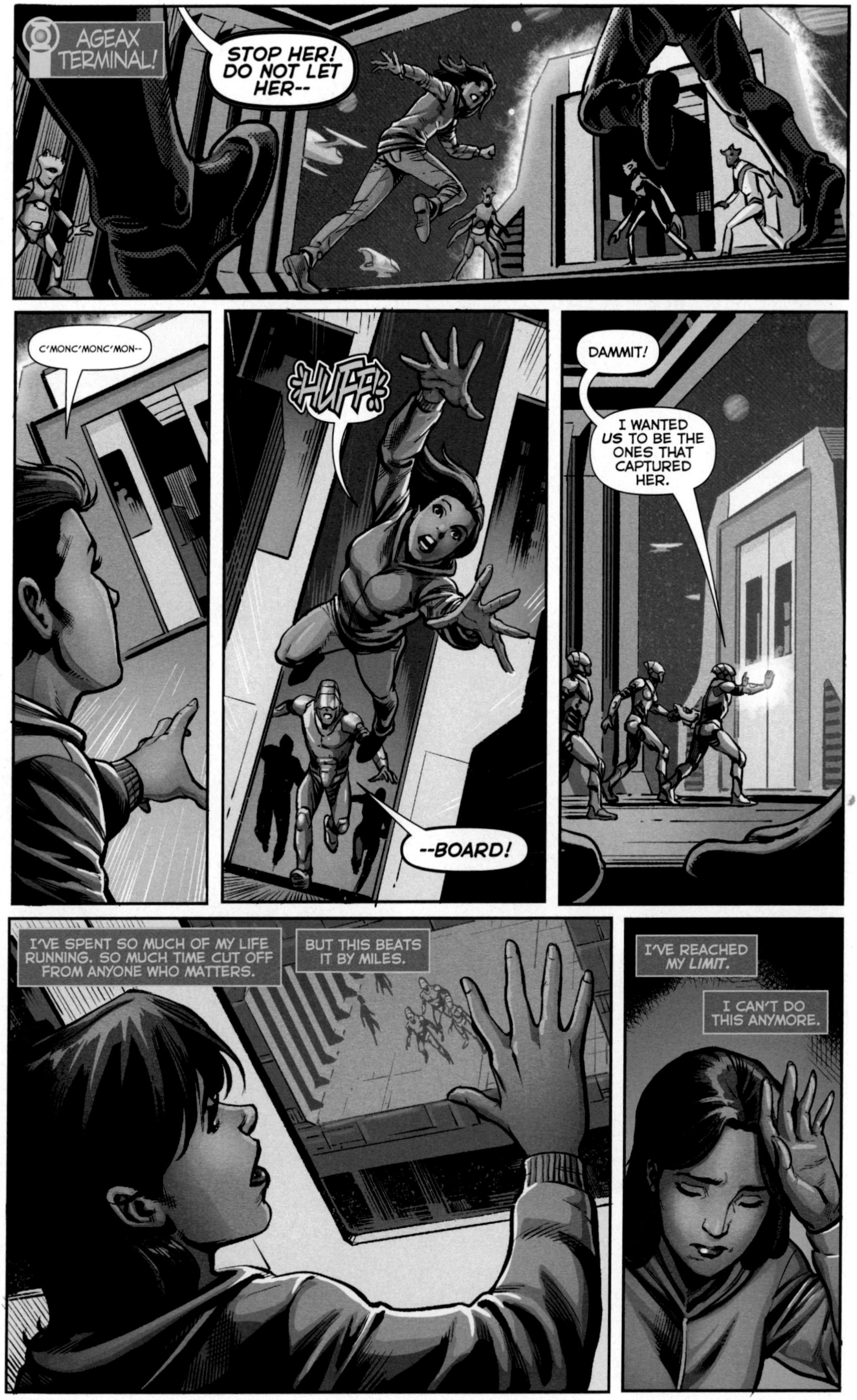
AGEAX TERMINAL!
STOP HER! DO NOT LET HER--
C'MONC'MONC'MON--
HUFF!
--BOARD!
DAMMIT!
I WANTED US TO BE THE ONES THAT CAPTURED HER.
I'VE SPENT SO MUCH OF MY LIFE RUNNING. SO MUCH TIME CUT OFF FROM ANYONE WHO MATTERS.
BUT THIS BEATS IT BY MILES.
I'VE REACHED MY LIMIT.
I CAN'T DO THIS ANYMORE.

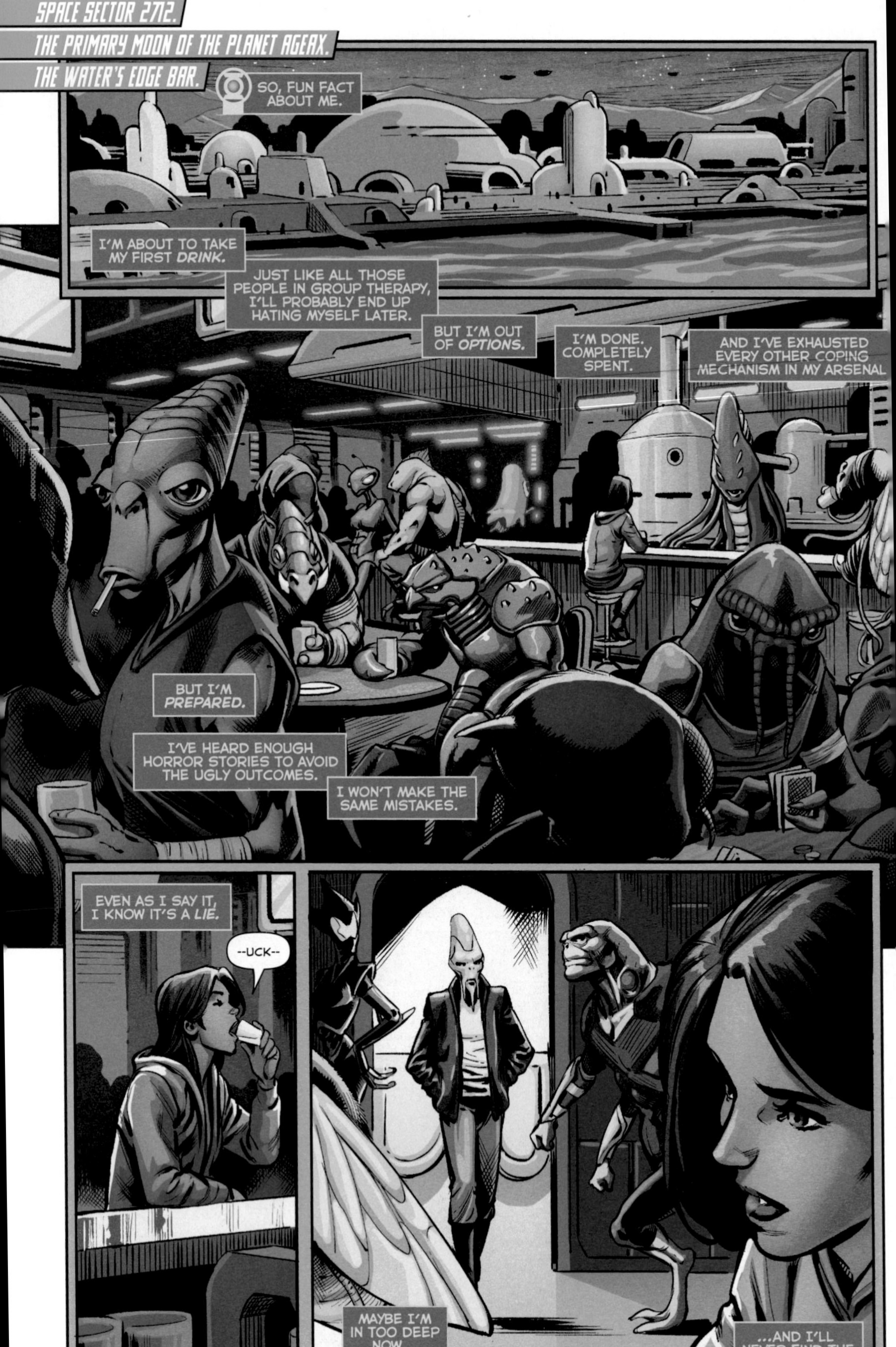

SPACE SECTOR 2712.
THE PRIMARY MOON OF THE PLANET AGEAX.
THE WATER'S EDGE BAR.
SO, FUN FACT ABOUT ME.
I'M ABOUT TO TAKE MY FIRST DRINK.
JUST LIKE ALL THOSE PEOPLE IN GROUP THERAPY, I'LL PROBABLY END UP HATING MYSELF LATER.
BUT I'M OUT OF OPTIONS.
I'M DONE. COMPLETELY SPENT.
AND I'VE EXHAUSTED EVERY OTHER COPING MECHANISM IN MY ARSENAL.
BUT I'M PREPARED.
I'VE HEARD ENOUGH HORROR STORIES TO AVOID THE UGLY OUTCOMES.
I WON'T MAKE THE SAME MISTAKES.
EVEN AS I SAY IT, I KNOW IT'S A LIE.
--UCK--
MAYBE I'M IN TOO DEEP NOW...
...AND I'LL NEVER FIND THE LIGHT AGAIN.

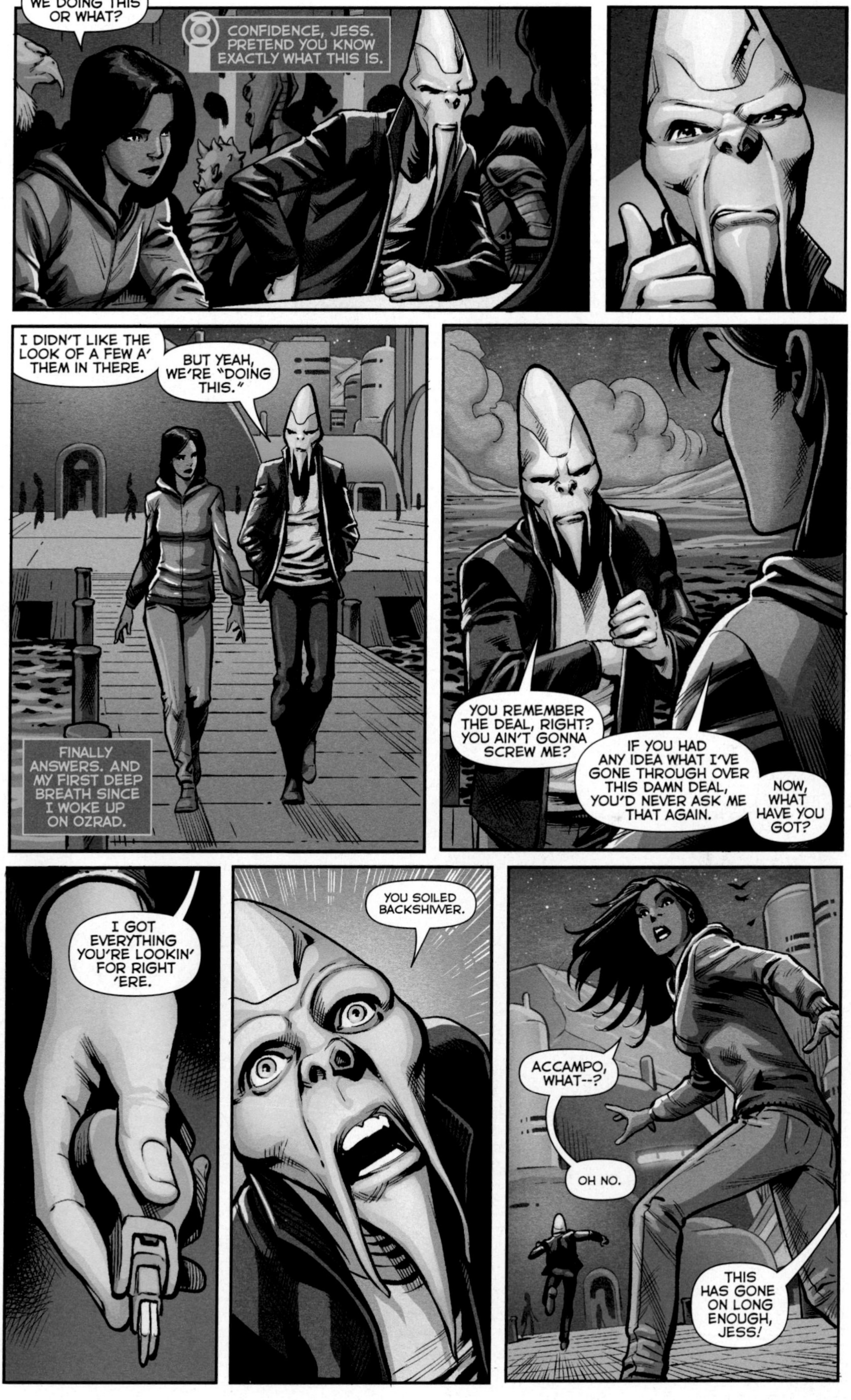
ACCAMPO. WE DOING THIS OR WHAT?
CONFIDENCE, JESS. PRETEND YOU KNOW EXACTLY WHAT THIS IS.
I DIDN'T LIKE THE LOOK OF A FEW A' THEM IN THERE.
BUT YEAH, WE'RE "DOING THIS."
FINALLY ANSWERS. AND MY FIRST DEEP BREATH SINCE I WOKE UP ON OZRAD.
YOU REMEMBER THE DEAL, RIGHT? YOU AIN'T GONNA SCREW ME?
IF YOU HAD ANY IDEA WHAT I'VE GONE THROUGH OVER THIS DAMN DEAL, YOU'D NEVER ASK ME THAT AGAIN.
NOW, WHAT HAVE YOU GOT?
I GOT EVERYTHING YOU'RE LOOKIN' FOR RIGHT 'ERE.
YOU SOILED BACKSHIVVER.
ACCAMPO, WHAT--?
OH NO.
THIS HAS GONE ON LONG ENOUGH, JESS!

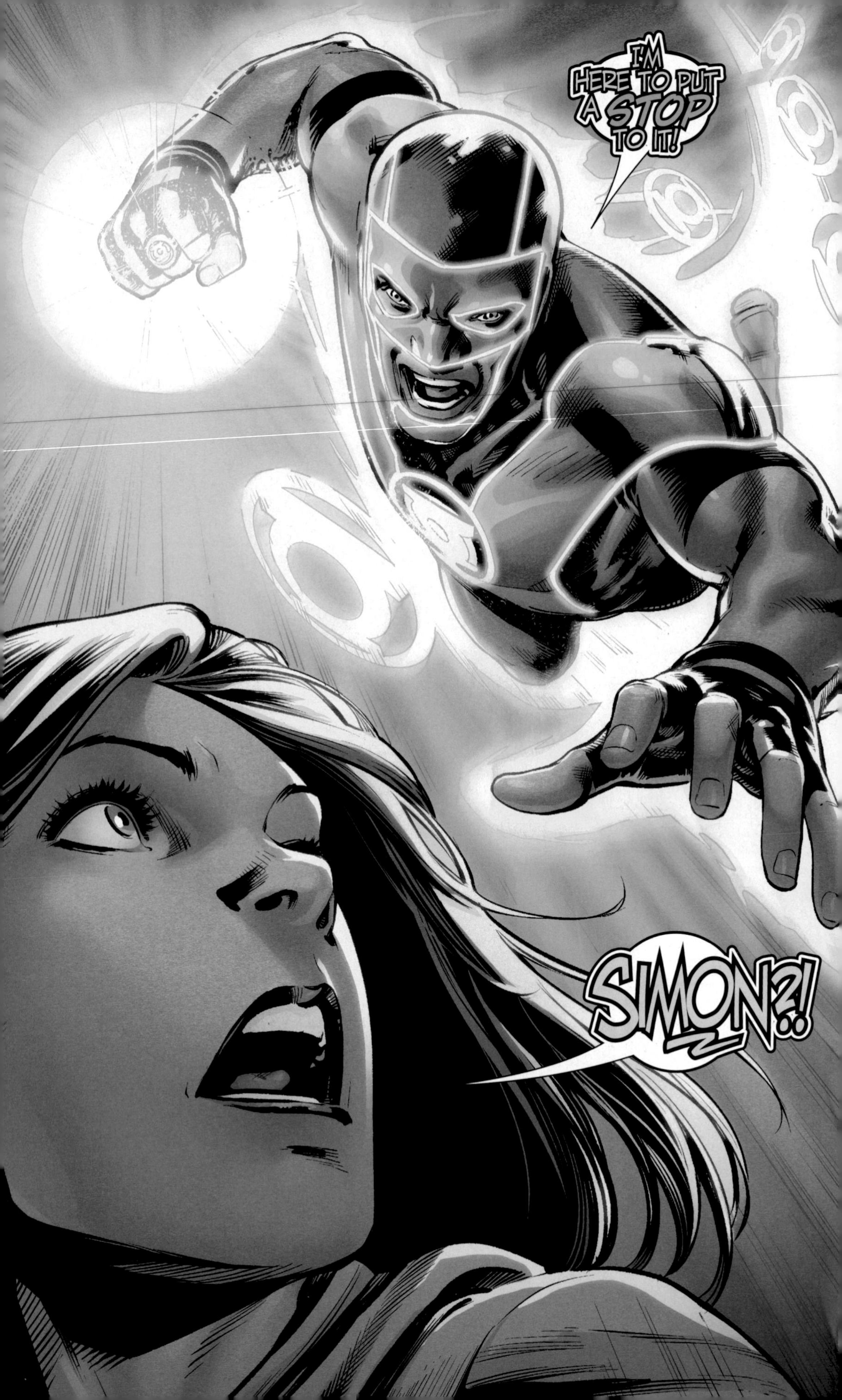
I'M HERE TO PUT A STOP TO IT!
SIMON?!

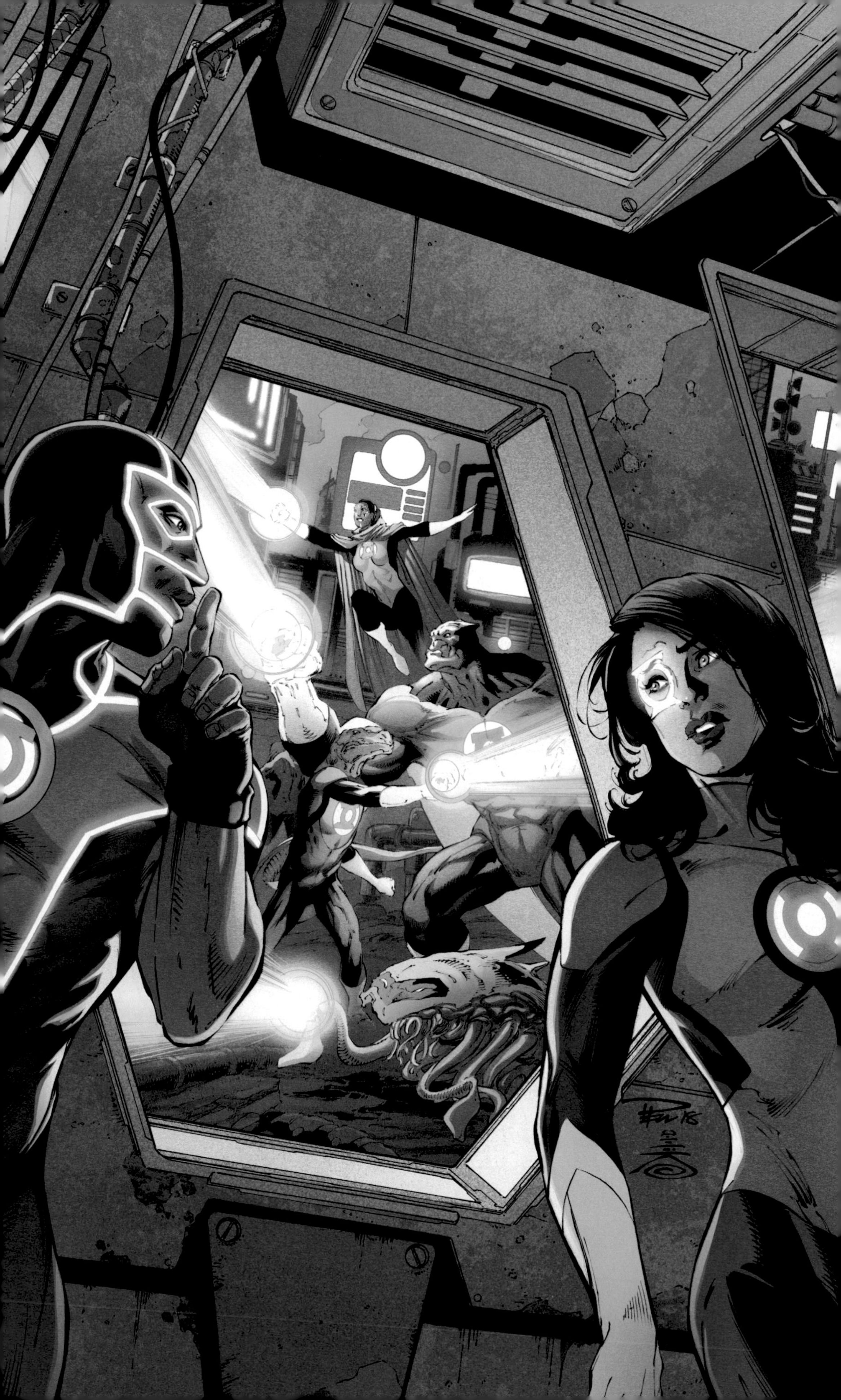

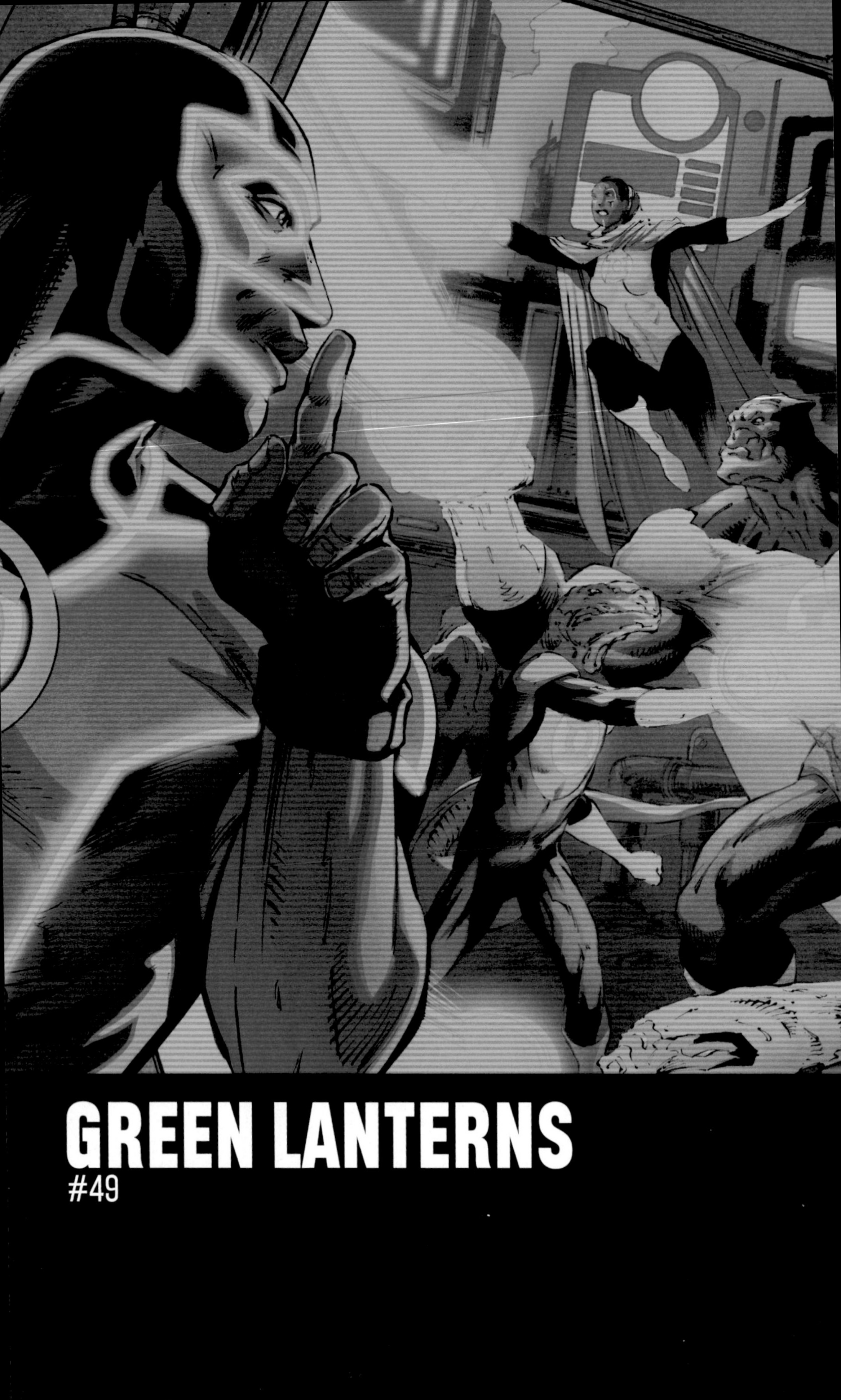

# GREEN LANTERNS
#49

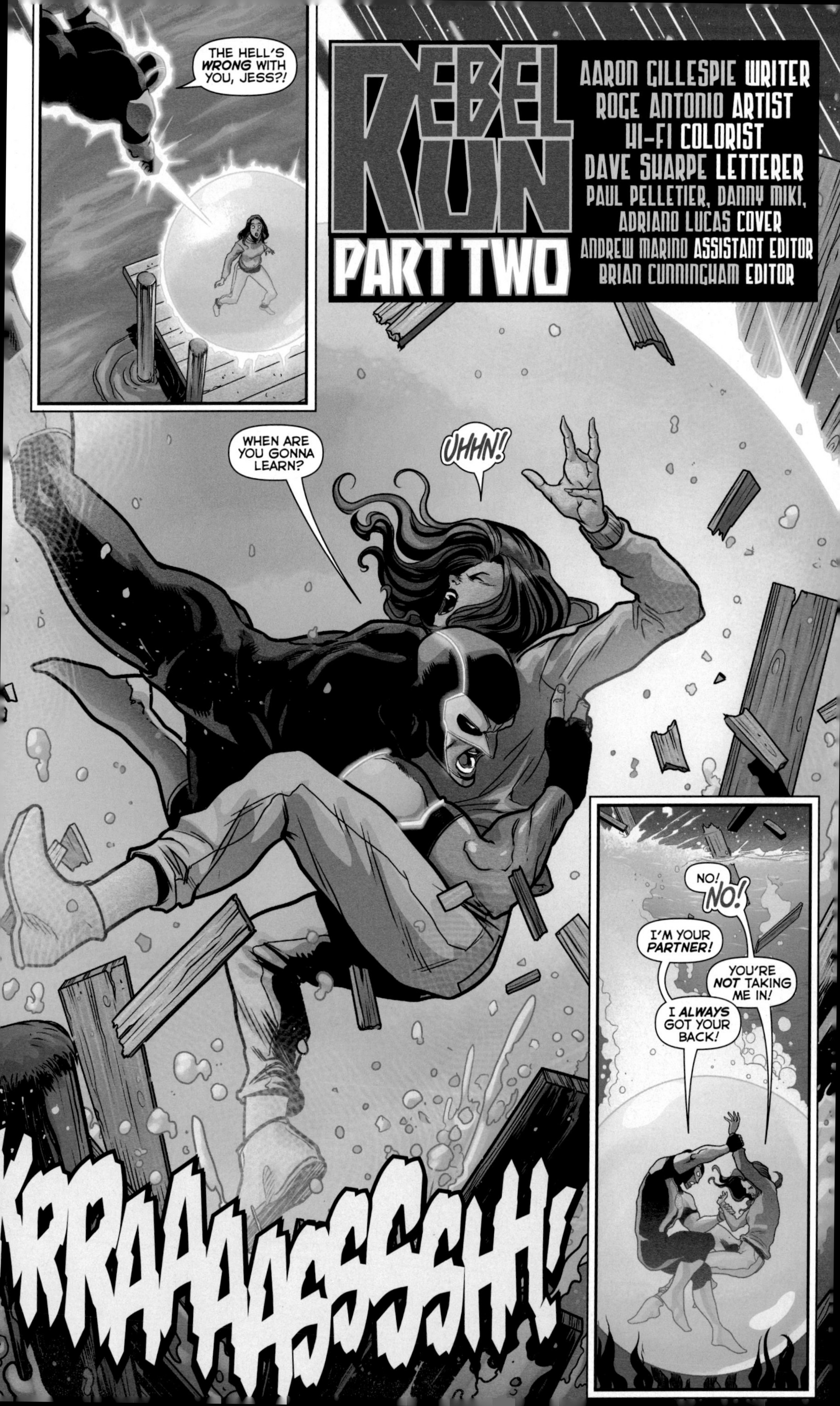
THE HELL'S WRONG WITH YOU, JESS?!
REBEL RUN
PART TWO
AARON GILLESPIE WRITER
ROGE ANTONIO ARTIST
HI-FI COLORIST
DAVE SHARPE LETTERER
PAUL PELLETIER, DANNY MIKI, ADRIANO LUCAS COVER
ANDREW MARINO ASSISTANT EDITOR
BRIAN CUNNINGHAM EDITOR
WHEN ARE YOU GONNA LEARN?
UHHN!
KRAAASSSH!
NO! NO!
I'M YOUR PARTNER!
YOU'RE NOT TAKING ME IN!
I ALWAYS GOT YOUR BACK!

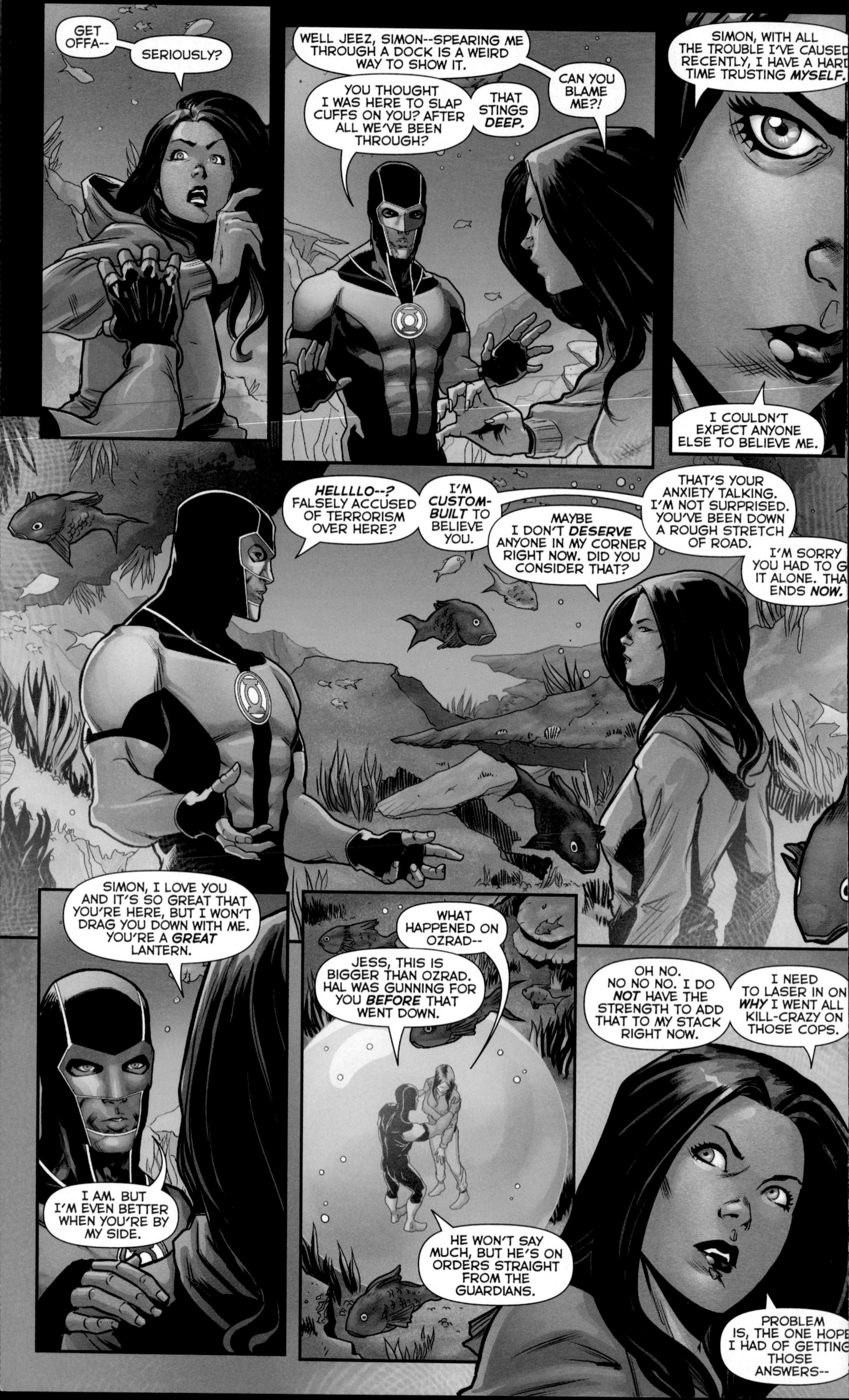
GET OFFA--
SERIOUSLY?
WELL JEEZ, SIMON--SPEARING ME THROUGH A DOCK IS A WEIRD WAY TO SHOW IT.
CAN YOU BLAME ME?!
YOU THOUGHT I WAS HERE TO SLAP CUFFS ON YOU? AFTER ALL WE'VE BEEN THROUGH?
THAT STINGS DEEP.
SIMON, WITH ALL THE TROUBLE I'VE CAUSED RECENTLY, I HAVE A HARD TIME TRUSTING MYSELF.
I COULDN'T EXPECT ANYONE ELSE TO BELIEVE ME.
HELLLLO--? FALSELY ACCUSED OF TERRORISM OVER HERE?
I'M CUSTOM-BUILT TO BELIEVE YOU.
MAYBE I DON'T DESERVE ANYONE IN MY CORNER RIGHT NOW. DID YOU CONSIDER THAT?
THAT'S YOUR ANXIETY TALKING. I'M NOT SURPRISED. YOU'VE BEEN DOWN A ROUGH STRETCH OF ROAD.
I'M SORRY YOU HAD TO G IT ALONE. THA ENDS NOW.
SIMON, I LOVE YOU AND IT'S SO GREAT THAT YOU'RE HERE, BUT I WON'T DRAG YOU DOWN WITH ME. YOU'RE A GREAT LANTERN.
I AM. BUT I'M EVEN BETTER WHEN YOU'RE BY MY SIDE.
WHAT HAPPENED ON OZRAD--
JESS, THIS IS BIGGER THAN OZRAD. HAL WAS GUNNING FOR YOU BEFORE THAT WENT DOWN.
HE WON'T SAY MUCH, BUT HE'S ON ORDERS STRAIGHT FROM THE GUARDIANS.
OH NO. NO NO NO. I DO NOT HAVE THE STRENGTH TO ADD THAT TO MY STACK RIGHT NOW.
I NEED TO LASER IN ON WHY I WENT ALL KILL-CRAZY ON THOSE COPS.
PROBLEM IS, THE ONE HOPE I HAD OF GETTING THOSE ANSWERS--

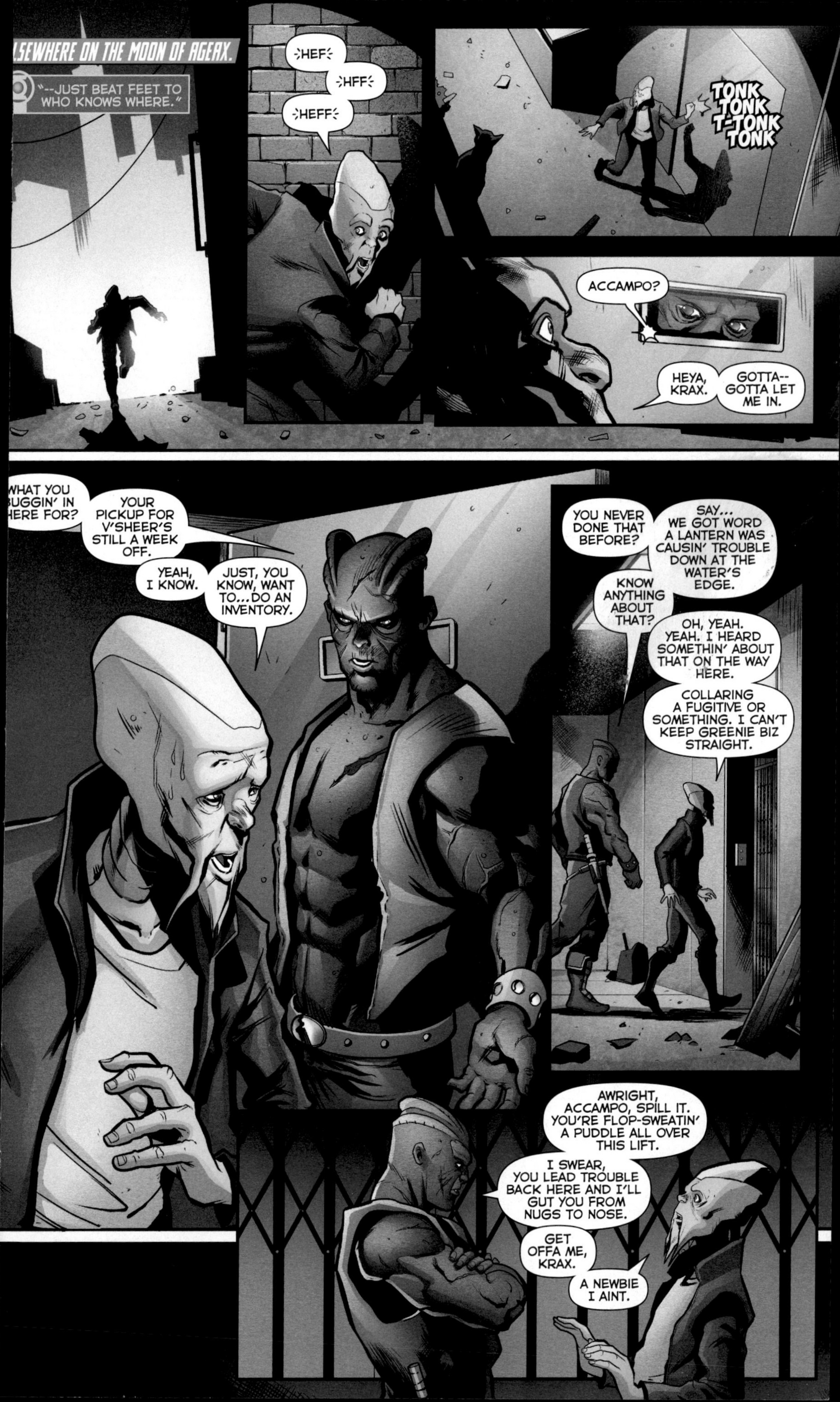
ELSEWHERE ON THE MOON OF AGEAX.
"--JUST BEAT FEET TO WHO KNOWS WHERE."
HEF
HFF
HEFF
TONK TONK T-TONK TONK
ACCAMPO?
HEYA, KRAX.
GOTTA-- GOTTA LET ME IN.
WHAT YOU BUGGIN' IN HERE FOR?
YOUR PICKUP FOR V'SHEER'S STILL A WEEK OFF.
YEAH, I KNOW.
JUST, YOU KNOW, WANT TO...DO AN INVENTORY.
YOU NEVER DONE THAT BEFORE?
SAY... WE GOT WORD A LANTERN WAS CAUSIN' TROUBLE DOWN AT THE WATER'S EDGE.
KNOW ANYTHING ABOUT THAT?
OH, YEAH. YEAH. I HEARD SOMETHIN' ABOUT THAT ON THE WAY HERE.
COLLARING A FUGITIVE OR SOMETHING. I CAN'T KEEP GREENIE BIZ STRAIGHT.
AWRIGHT, ACCAMPO, SPILL IT. YOU'RE FLOP-SWEATIN' A PUDDLE ALL OVER THIS LIFT.
I SWEAR, YOU LEAD TROUBLE BACK HERE AND I'LL GUT YOU FROM NUGS TO NOSE.
GET OFFA ME, KRAX.
A NEWBIE I AINT.

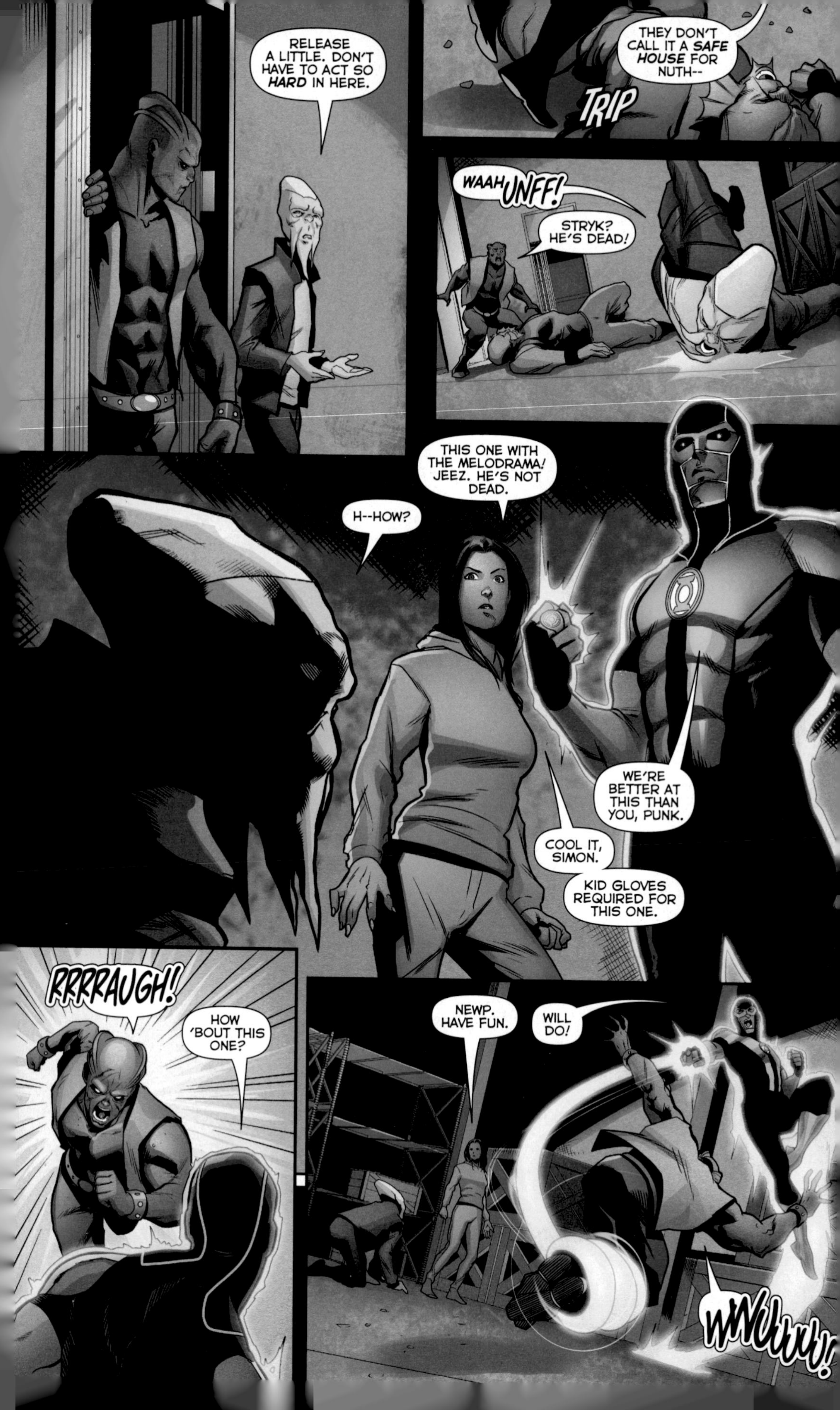

RELEASE A LITTLE. DON'T HAVE TO ACT SO HARD IN HERE.
THEY DON'T CALL IT A SAFE HOUSE FOR NUTH--
TRIP
WAAH UNFF!
STRYK? HE'S DEAD!
THIS ONE WITH THE MELODRAMA! JEEZ. HE'S NOT DEAD.
H--HOW?
WE'RE BETTER AT THIS THAN YOU, PUNK.
COOL IT, SIMON.
KID GLOVES REQUIRED FOR THIS ONE.
RRRRAUGH!
HOW 'BOUT THIS ONE?
NEWP. HAVE FUN.
WILL DO!
WNNUUU!

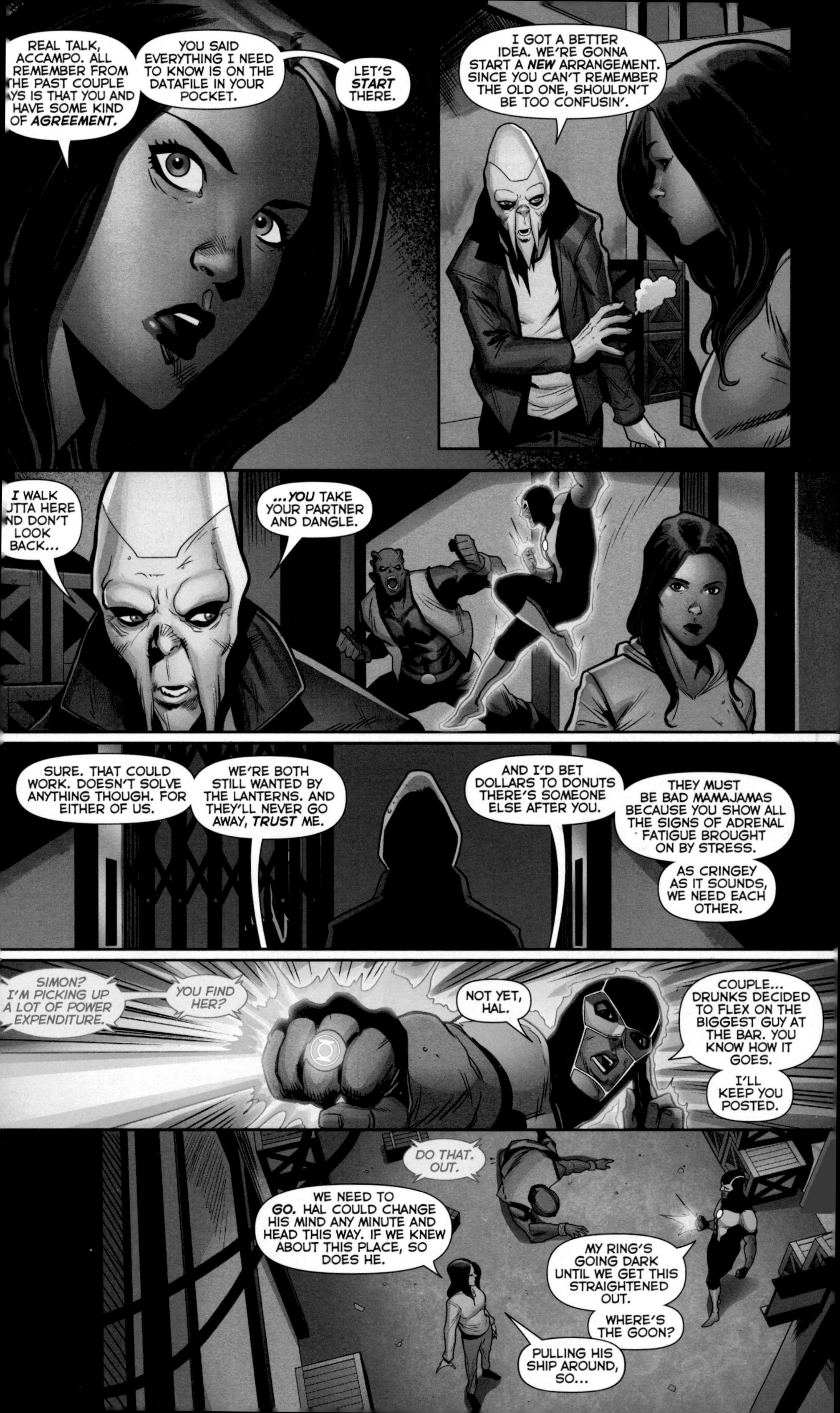
REAL TALK, ACCAMPO. ALL I REMEMBER FROM THE PAST COUPLE DAYS IS THAT YOU AND I HAVE SOME KIND OF AGREEMENT.
YOU SAID EVERYTHING I NEED TO KNOW IS ON THE DATAFILE IN YOUR POCKET.
LET'S START THERE.
I GOT A BETTER IDEA. WE'RE GONNA START A NEW ARRANGEMENT. SINCE YOU CAN'T REMEMBER THE OLD ONE, SHOULDN'T BE TOO CONFUSIN'.
I WALK OUTTA HERE AND DON'T LOOK BACK...
...YOU TAKE YOUR PARTNER AND DANGLE.
SURE. THAT COULD WORK. DOESN'T SOLVE ANYTHING THOUGH. FOR EITHER OF US.
WE'RE BOTH STILL WANTED BY THE LANTERNS. AND THEY'LL NEVER GO AWAY, TRUST ME.
AND I'D BET DOLLARS TO DONUTS THERE'S SOMEONE ELSE AFTER YOU.
THEY MUST BE BAD MAMAJAMAS BECAUSE YOU SHOW ALL THE SIGNS OF ADRENAL FATIGUE BROUGHT ON BY STRESS.
AS CRINGEY AS IT SOUNDS, WE NEED EACH OTHER.
SIMON? I'M PICKING UP A LOT OF POWER EXPENDITURE.
YOU FIND HER?
NOT YET, HAL.
COUPLE... DRUNKS DECIDED TO FLEX ON THE BIGGEST GUY AT THE BAR. YOU KNOW HOW IT GOES.
I'LL KEEP YOU POSTED.
DO THAT. OUT.
WE NEED TO GO. HAL COULD CHANGE HIS MIND ANY MINUTE AND HEAD THIS WAY. IF WE KNEW ABOUT THIS PLACE, SO DOES HE.
MY RING'S GOING DARK UNTIL WE GET THIS STRAIGHTENED OUT.
WHERE'S THE GOON?
PULLING HIS SHIP AROUND, SO...

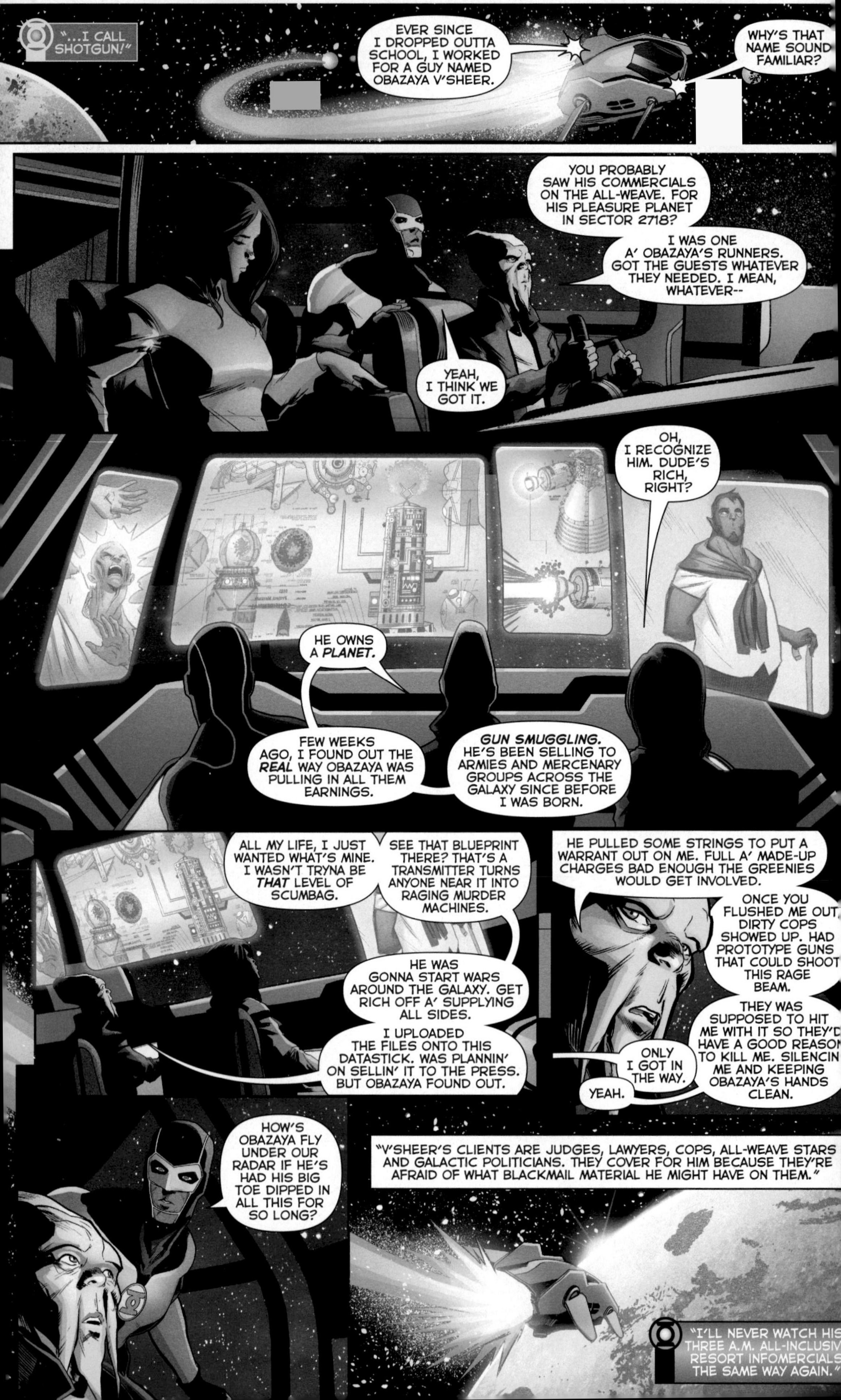
"...I CALL SHOTGUN!"
EVER SINCE I DROPPED OUTTA SCHOOL, I WORKED FOR A GUY NAMED OBAZAYA V'SHEER.
WHY'S THAT NAME SOUND FAMILIAR?
YOU PROBABLY SAW HIS COMMERCIALS ON THE ALL-WEAVE. FOR HIS PLEASURE PLANET IN SECTOR 2718?
I WAS ONE A' OBAZAYA'S RUNNERS. GOT THE GUESTS WHATEVER THEY NEEDED. I MEAN, WHATEVER--
YEAH, I THINK WE GOT IT.
OH, I RECOGNIZE HIM. DUDE'S RICH, RIGHT?
HE OWNS A *PLANET.*
FEW WEEKS AGO, I FOUND OUT THE *REAL* WAY OBAZAYA WAS PULLING IN ALL THEM EARNINGS.
*GUN SMUGGLING.* HE'S BEEN SELLING TO ARMIES AND MERCENARY GROUPS ACROSS THE GALAXY SINCE BEFORE I WAS BORN.
ALL MY LIFE, I JUST WANTED WHAT'S MINE. I WASN'T TRYNA BE *THAT* LEVEL OF SCUMBAG.
SEE THAT BLUEPRINT THERE? THAT'S A TRANSMITTER TURNS ANYONE NEAR IT INTO RAGING MURDER MACHINES.
HE WAS GONNA START WARS AROUND THE GALAXY. GET RICH OFF A' SUPPLYING ALL SIDES.
I UPLOADED THE FILES ONTO THIS DATASTICK. WAS PLANNIN' ON SELLIN' IT TO THE PRESS. BUT OBAZAYA FOUND OUT.
HE PULLED SOME STRINGS TO PUT A WARRANT OUT ON ME. FULL A' MADE-UP CHARGES BAD ENOUGH THE GREENIES WOULD GET INVOLVED.
ONCE YOU FLUSHED ME OUT, DIRTY COPS SHOWED UP. HAD PROTOTYPE GUNS THAT COULD SHOOT THIS RAGE BEAM.
THEY WAS SUPPOSED TO HIT ME WITH IT SO THEY'D HAVE A GOOD REASON TO KILL ME. SILENCIN' ME AND KEEPING OBAZAYA'S HANDS CLEAN.
ONLY I GOT IN THE WAY.
YEAH.
HOW'S OBAZAYA FLY UNDER OUR RADAR IF HE'S HAD HIS BIG TOE DIPPED IN ALL THIS FOR SO LONG?
"V'SHEER'S CLIENTS ARE JUDGES, LAWYERS, COPS, ALL-WEAVE STARS AND GALACTIC POLITICIANS. THEY COVER FOR HIM BECAUSE THEY'RE AFRAID OF WHAT BLACKMAIL MATERIAL HE MIGHT HAVE ON THEM."
"I'LL NEVER WATCH HIS THREE A.M. ALL-INCLUSIVE RESORT INFOMERCIALS THE SAME WAY AGAIN."

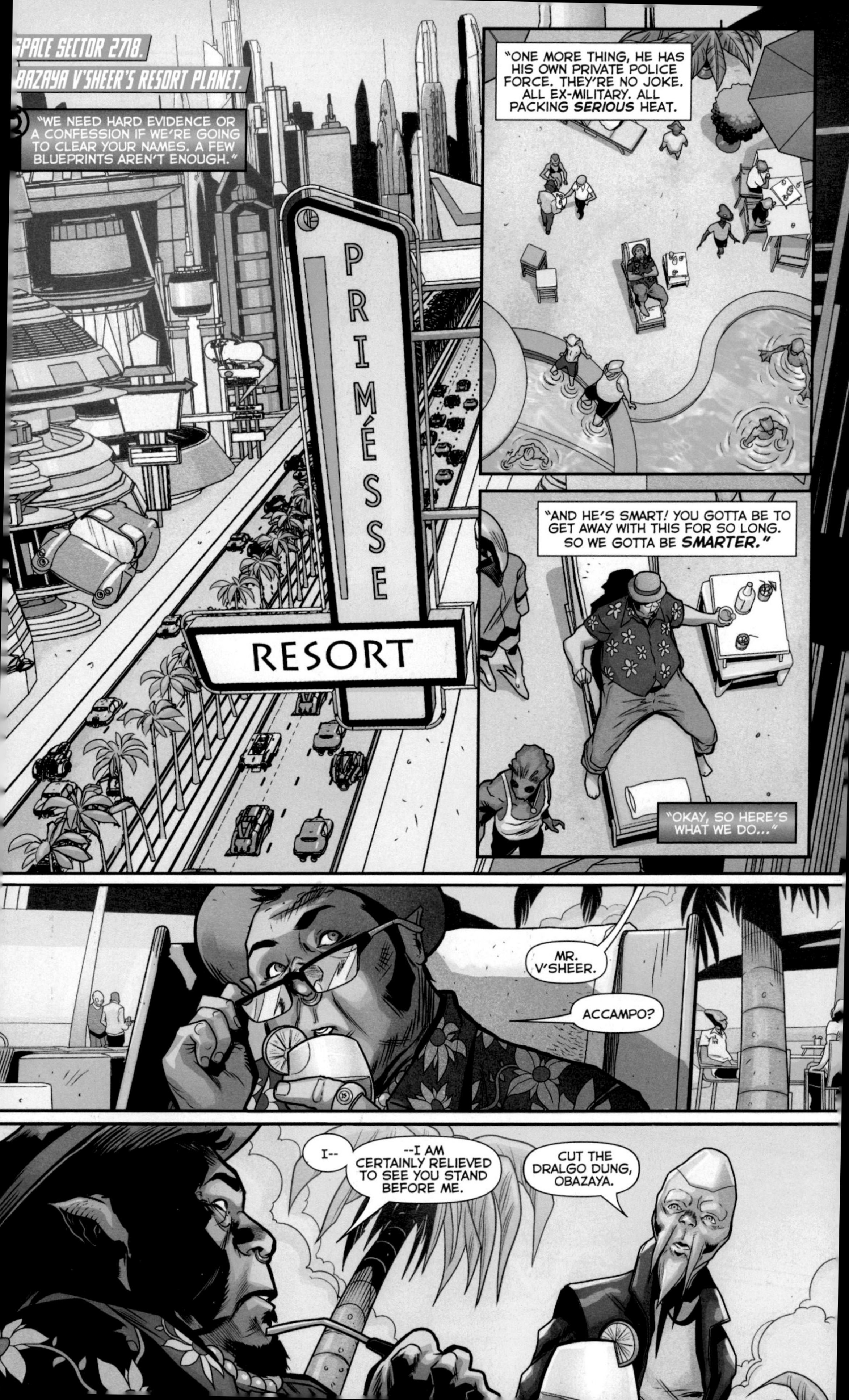

SPACE SECTOR 2718.
BAZAYA V'SHEER'S RESORT PLANET.
"WE NEED HARD EVIDENCE OR A CONFESSION IF WE'RE GOING TO CLEAR YOUR NAMES. A FEW BLUEPRINTS AREN'T ENOUGH."
PRIMÉSSE
RESORT
"ONE MORE THING, HE HAS HIS OWN PRIVATE POLICE FORCE. THEY'RE NO JOKE. ALL EX-MILITARY. ALL PACKING SERIOUS HEAT.
"AND HE'S SMART! YOU GOTTA BE TO GET AWAY WITH THIS FOR SO LONG. SO WE GOTTA BE SMARTER."
"OKAY, SO HERE'S WHAT WE DO..."
MR. V'SHEER.
ACCAMPO?
I--
--I AM CERTAINLY RELIEVED TO SEE YOU STAND BEFORE ME.
CUT THE DRALGO DUNG, OBAZAYA.

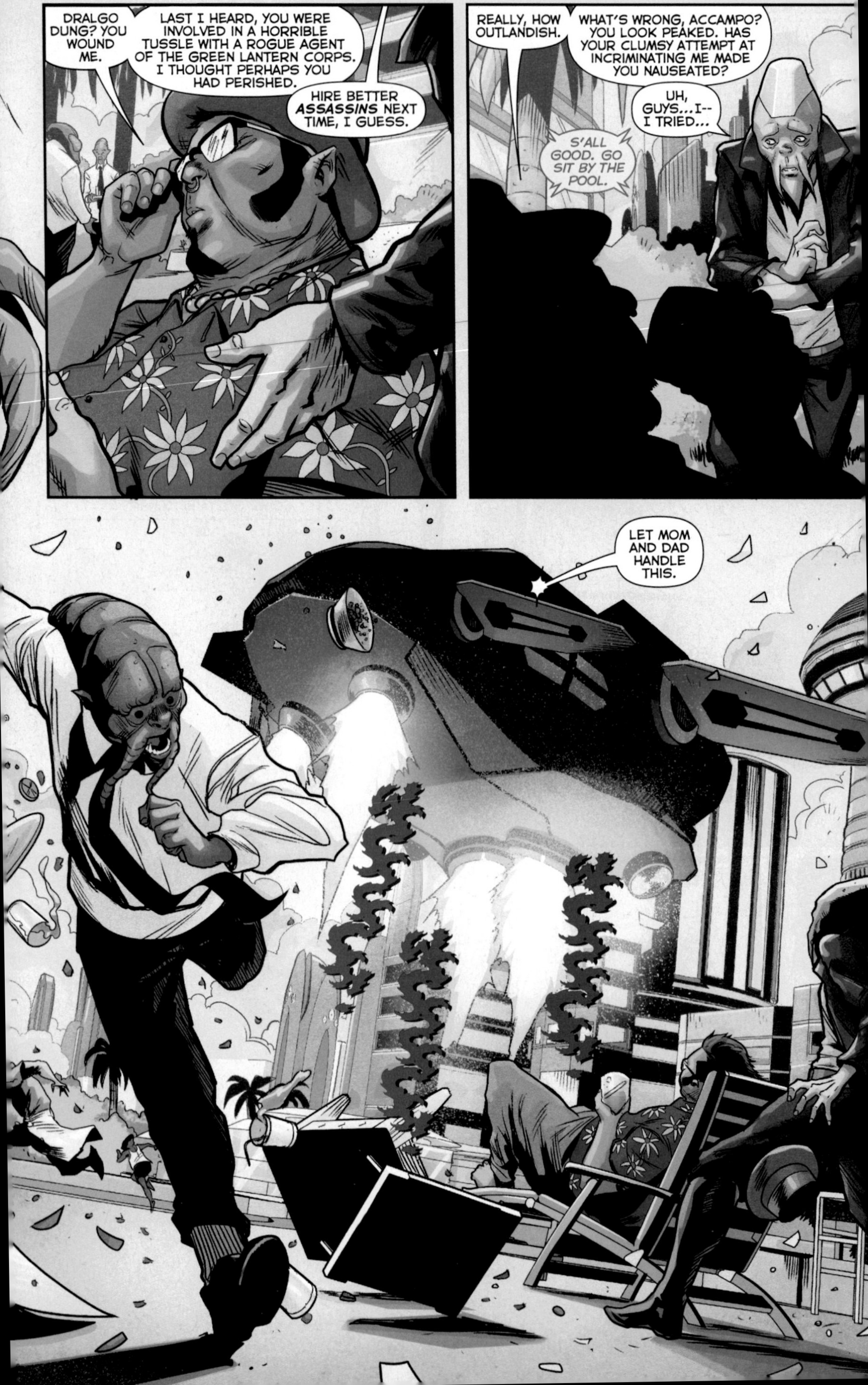
DRALGO DUNG? YOU WOUND ME.
LAST I HEARD, YOU WERE INVOLVED IN A HORRIBLE TUSSLE WITH A ROGUE AGENT OF THE GREEN LANTERN CORPS. I THOUGHT PERHAPS YOU HAD PERISHED.
HIRE BETTER ASSASSINS NEXT TIME, I GUESS.
REALLY, HOW OUTLANDISH.
WHAT'S WRONG, ACCAMPO? YOU LOOK PEAKED. HAS YOUR CLUMSY ATTEMPT AT INCRIMINATING ME MADE YOU NAUSEATED?
UH, GUYS... I-- I TRIED...
S'ALL GOOD. GO SIT BY THE POOL.
LET MOM AND DAD HANDLE THIS.

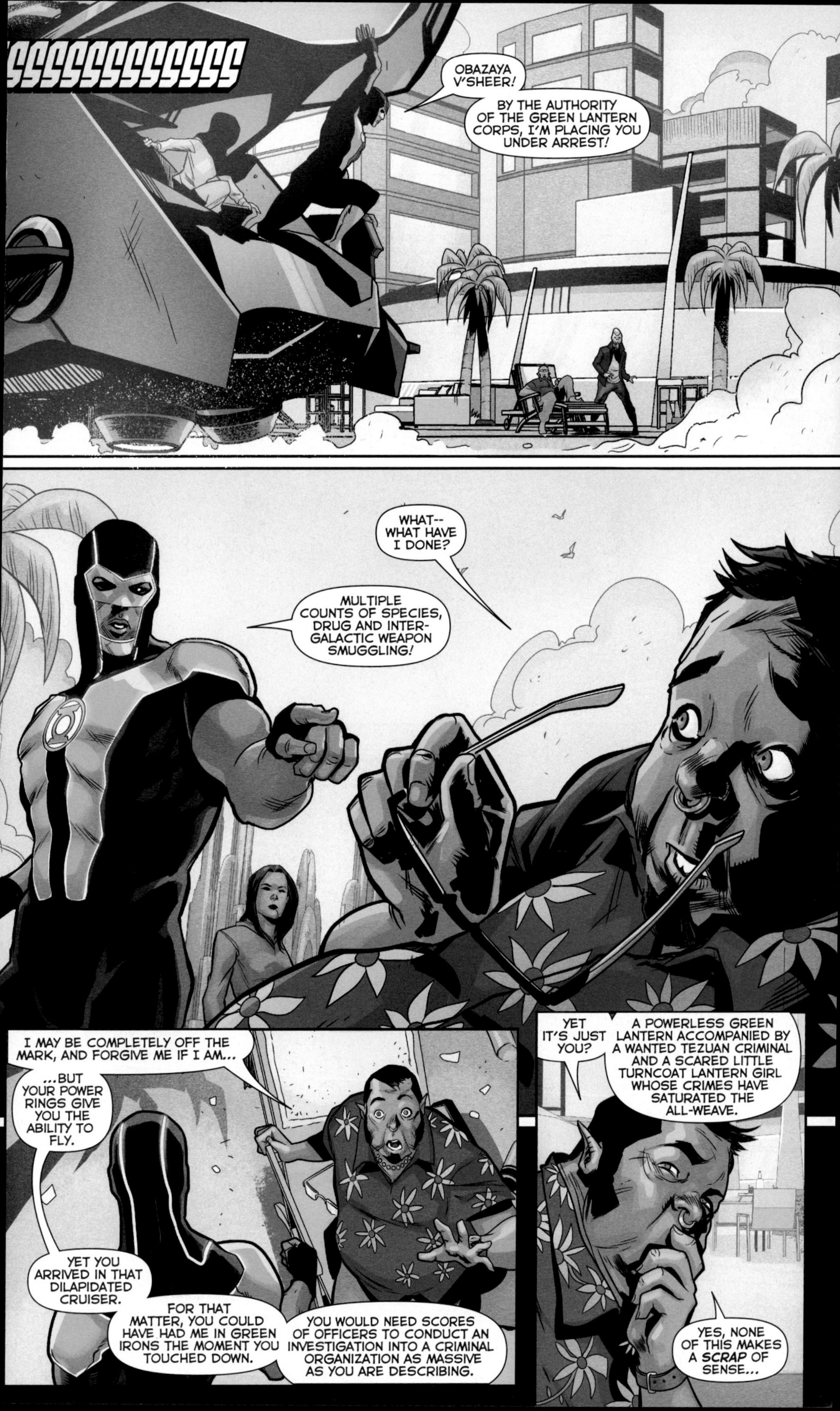
SSSSSSSSSSSS
OBAZAYA V'SHEER!
BY THE AUTHORITY OF THE GREEN LANTERN CORPS, I'M PLACING YOU UNDER ARREST!
WHAT-- WHAT HAVE I DONE?
MULTIPLE COUNTS OF SPECIES, DRUG AND INTER-GALACTIC WEAPON SMUGGLING!
I MAY BE COMPLETELY OFF THE MARK, AND FORGIVE ME IF I AM...
...BUT YOUR POWER RINGS GIVE YOU THE ABILITY TO FLY.
YET YOU ARRIVED IN THAT DILAPIDATED CRUISER.
FOR THAT MATTER, YOU COULD HAVE HAD ME IN GREEN IRONS THE MOMENT YOU TOUCHED DOWN.
YOU WOULD NEED SCORES OF OFFICERS TO CONDUCT AN INVESTIGATION INTO A CRIMINAL ORGANIZATION AS MASSIVE AS YOU ARE DESCRIBING.
YET IT'S JUST YOU?
A POWERLESS GREEN LANTERN ACCOMPANIED BY A WANTED TEZUAN CRIMINAL AND A SCARED LITTLE TURNCOAT LANTERN GIRL WHOSE CRIMES HAVE SATURATED THE ALL-WEAVE.
YES, NONE OF THIS MAKES A *SCRAP* OF SENSE...

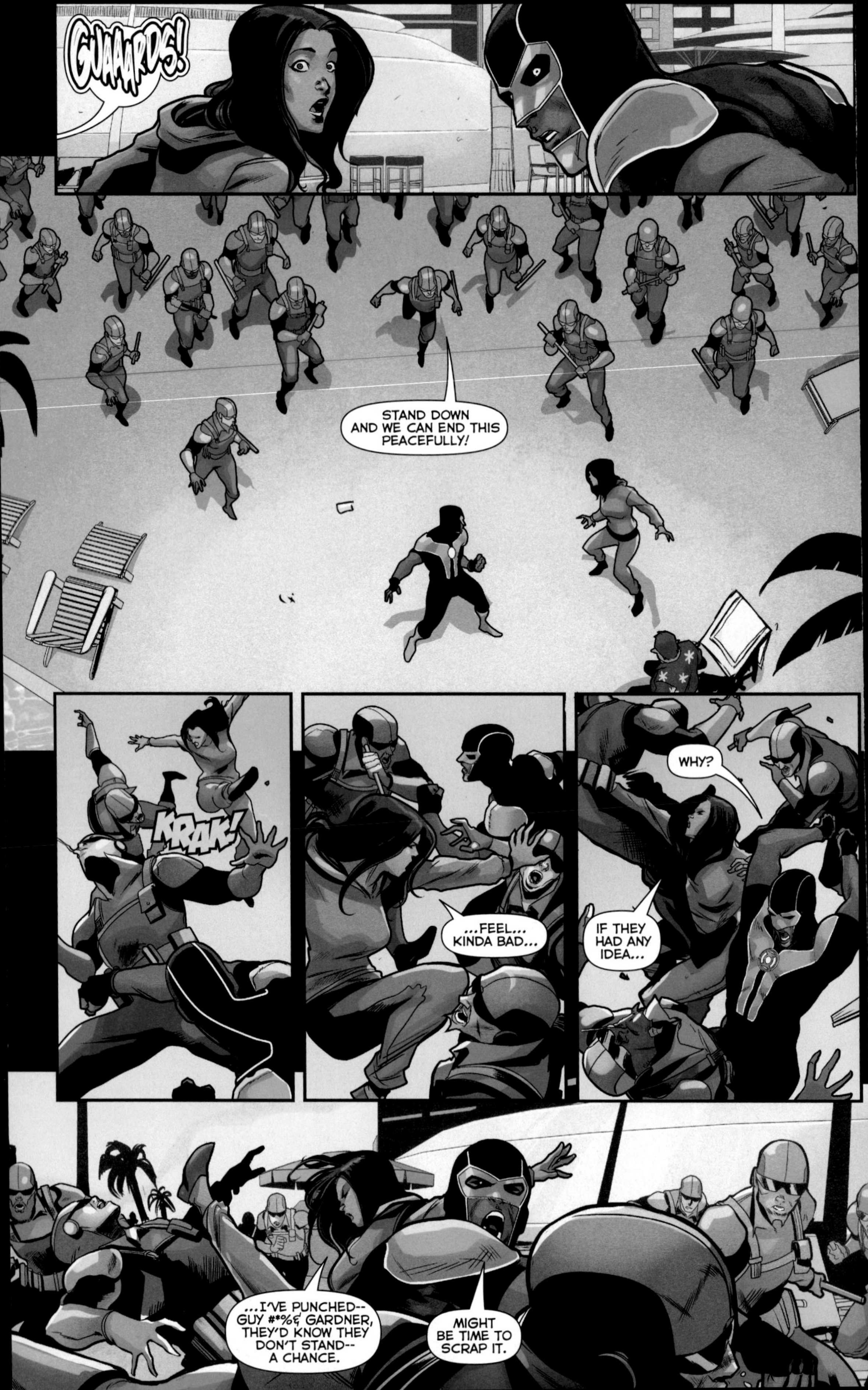
GUAAARDS!
STAND DOWN AND WE CAN END THIS PEACEFULLY!
KRAK!
...FEEL... KINDA BAD...
WHY?
IF THEY HAD ANY IDEA...
...I'VE PUNCHED-- GUY #*%& GARDNER, THEY'D KNOW THEY DON'T STAND-- A CHANCE.
MIGHT BE TIME TO SCRAP IT.

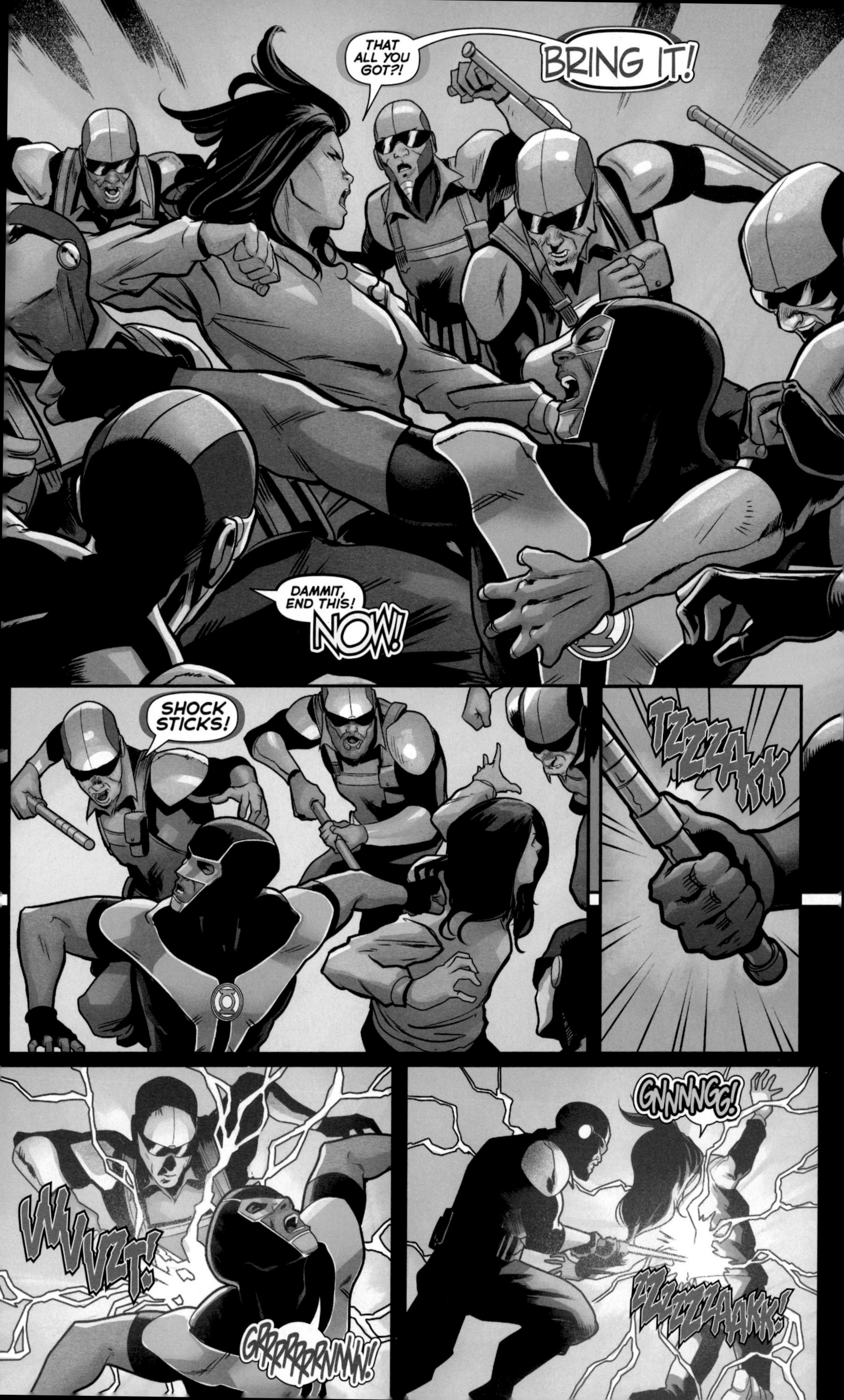
THAT ALL YOU GOT?!
BRING IT!
DAMMIT, END THIS! NOW!
SHOCK STICKS!
TZZZAKK
WVVZT!
GRRRRRRNNNN!
GNNNNGG!
ZZZZZZAAKK!

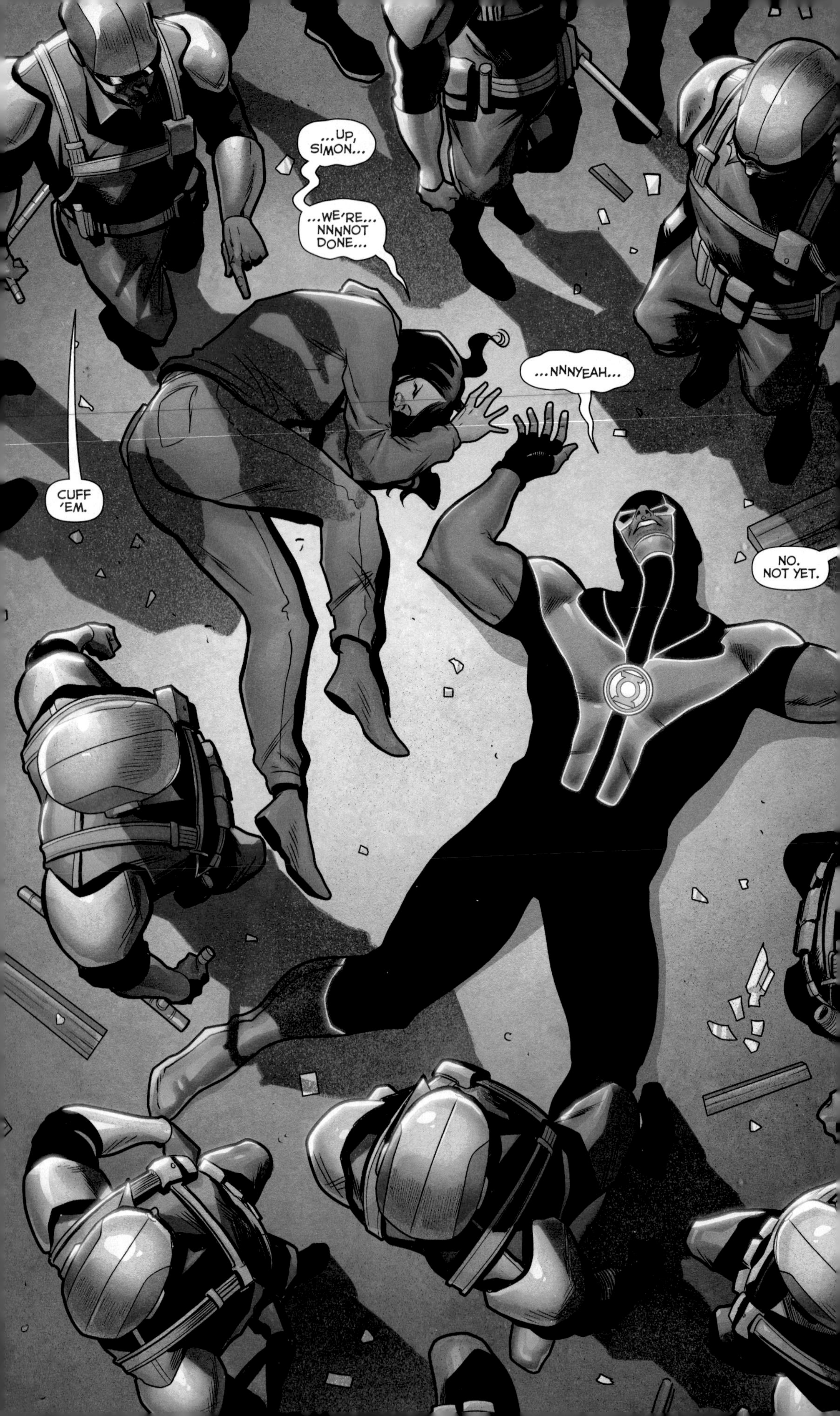
...UP, SIMON...
...WE'RE... NNNNOT DONE...
CUFF 'EM.
...NNNYEAH...
NO. NOT YET.

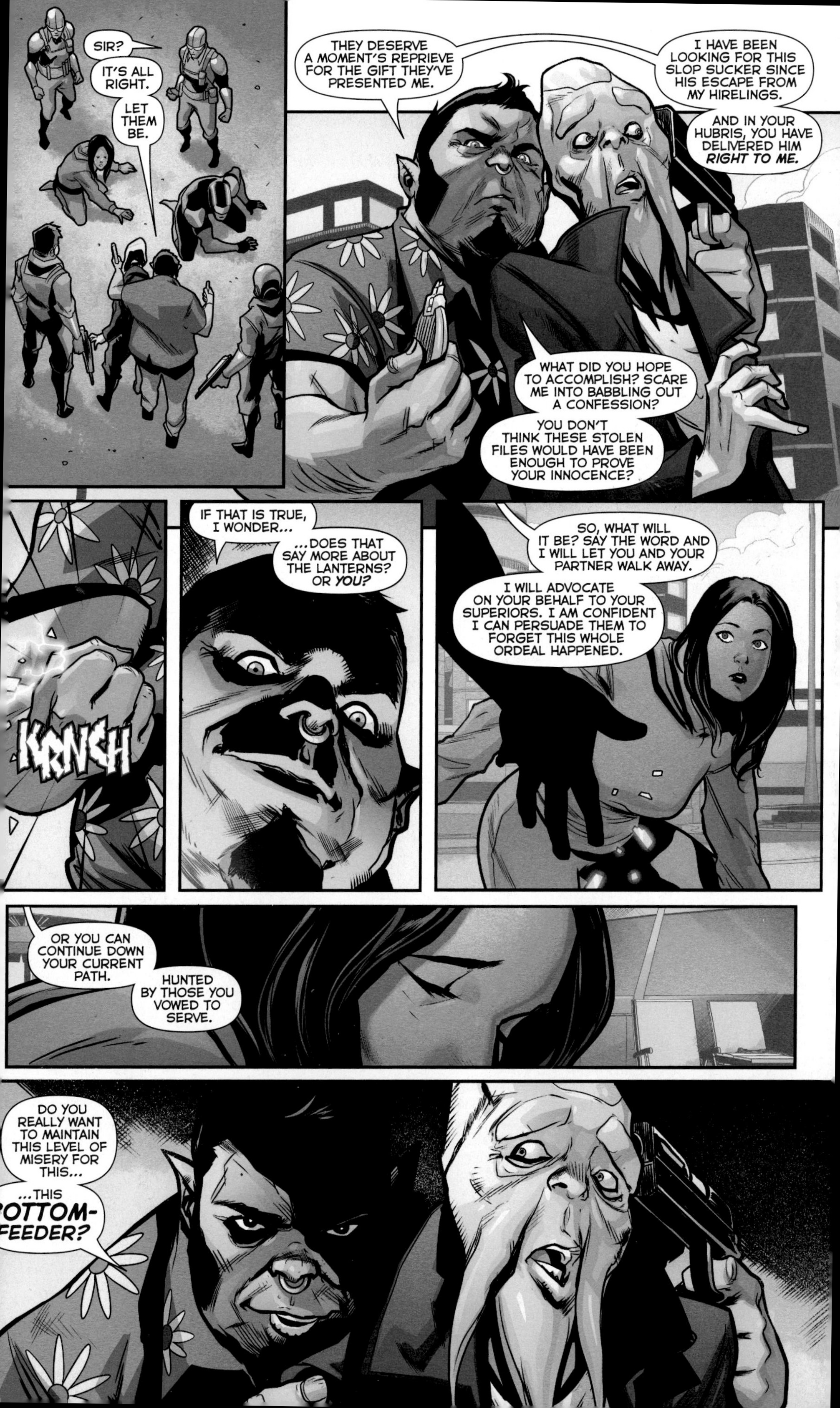
SIR?
IT'S ALL RIGHT.
LET THEM BE.
THEY DESERVE A MOMENT'S REPRIEVE FOR THE GIFT THEY'VE PRESENTED ME.
I HAVE BEEN LOOKING FOR THIS SLOP SUCKER SINCE HIS ESCAPE FROM MY HIRELINGS.
AND IN YOUR HUBRIS, YOU HAVE DELIVERED HIM RIGHT TO ME.
WHAT DID YOU HOPE TO ACCOMPLISH? SCARE ME INTO BABBLING OUT A CONFESSION?
YOU DON'T THINK THESE STOLEN FILES WOULD HAVE BEEN ENOUGH TO PROVE YOUR INNOCENCE?
KRNCH
IF THAT IS TRUE, I WONDER...
...DOES THAT SAY MORE ABOUT THE LANTERNS? OR YOU?
SO, WHAT WILL IT BE? SAY THE WORD AND I WILL LET YOU AND YOUR PARTNER WALK AWAY.
I WILL ADVOCATE ON YOUR BEHALF TO YOUR SUPERIORS. I AM CONFIDENT I CAN PERSUADE THEM TO FORGET THIS WHOLE ORDEAL HAPPENED.
OR YOU CAN CONTINUE DOWN YOUR CURRENT PATH.
HUNTED BY THOSE YOU VOWED TO SERVE.
DO YOU REALLY WANT TO MAINTAIN THIS LEVEL OF MISERY FOR THIS...
...THIS BOTTOM-FEEDER?

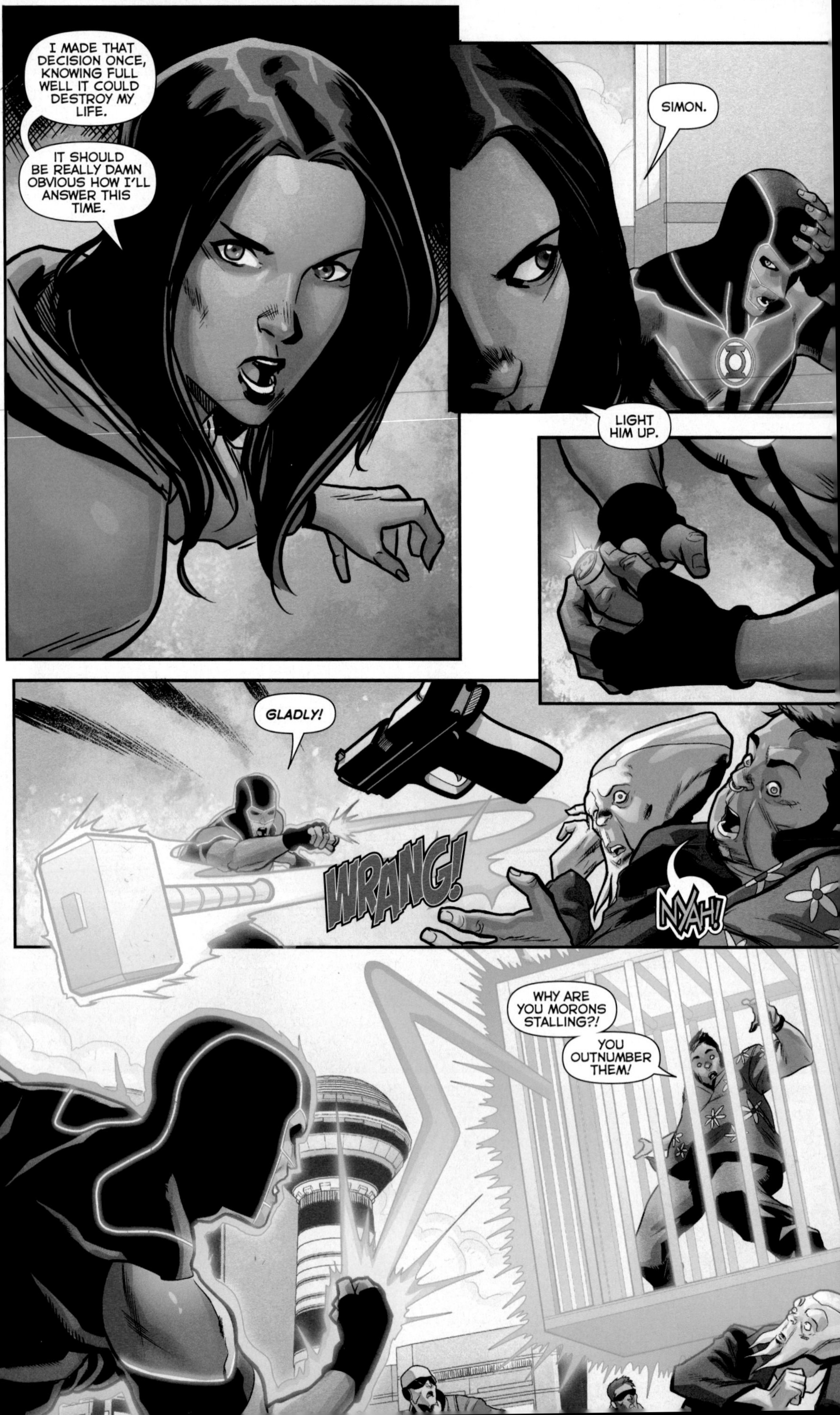
I MADE THAT DECISION ONCE, KNOWING FULL WELL IT COULD DESTROY MY LIFE.
IT SHOULD BE REALLY DAMN OBVIOUS HOW I'LL ANSWER THIS TIME.
SIMON.
LIGHT HIM UP.
GLADLY!
WRANG!
NYAH!
WHY ARE YOU MORONS STALLING?!
YOU OUTNUMBER THEM!

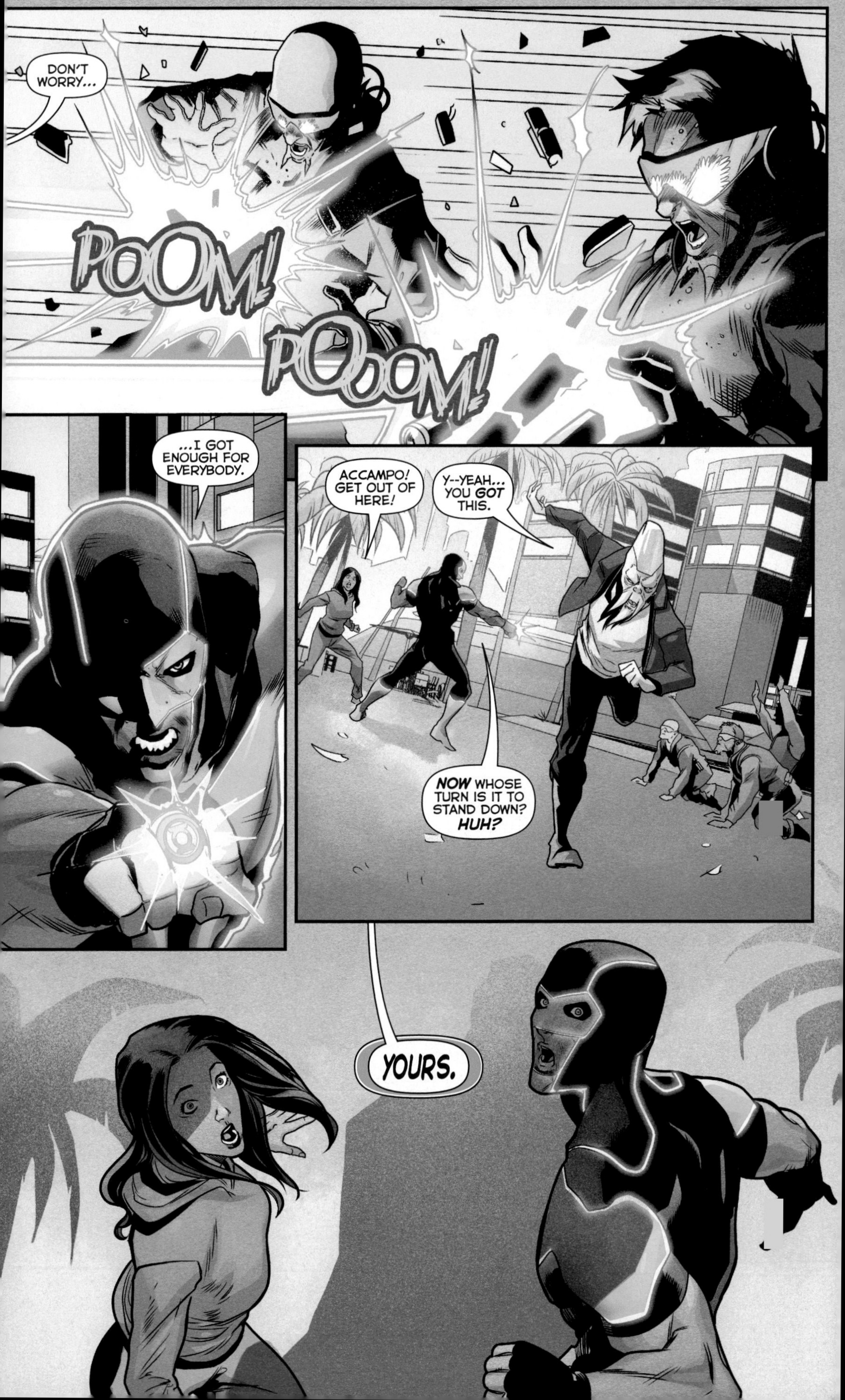
DON'T WORRY...
POOM!
POOOOM!
...I GOT ENOUGH FOR EVERYBODY.
ACCAMPO! GET OUT OF HERE!
Y--YEAH... YOU GOT THIS.
NOW WHOSE TURN IS IT TO STAND DOWN? HUH?
YOURS.

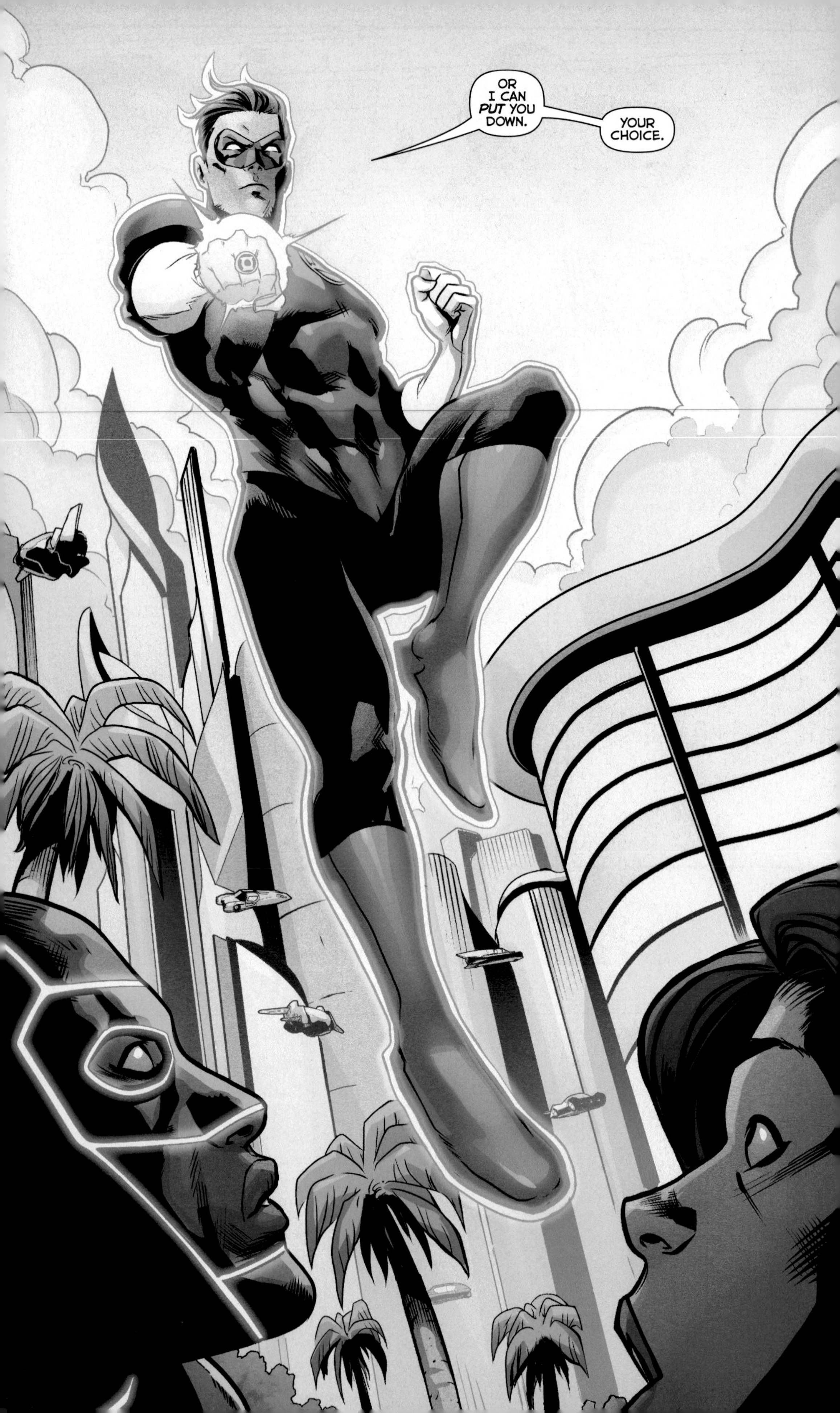
OR I CAN *PUT* YOU DOWN.
YOUR CHOICE.

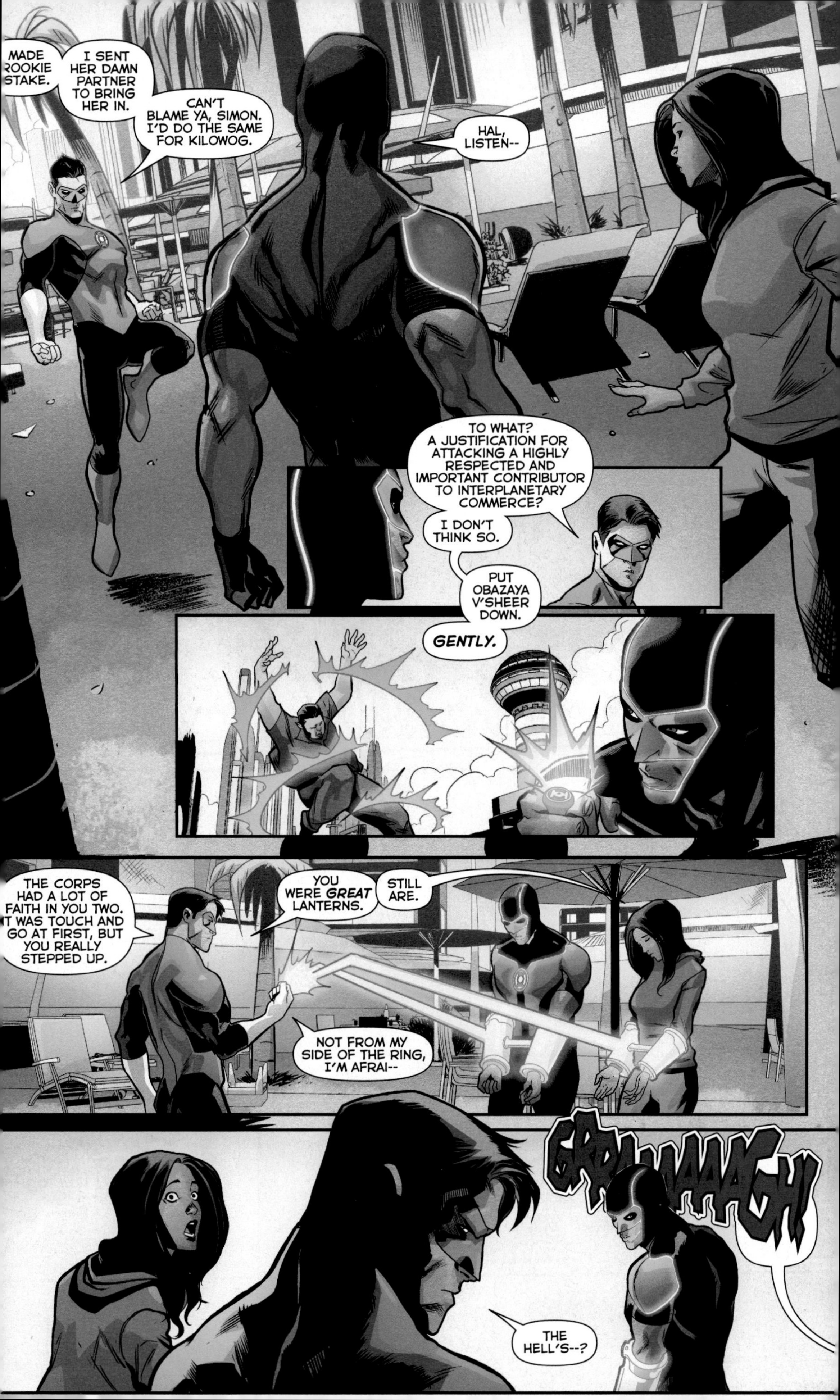
MADE ROOKIE STAKE.
I SENT HER DAMN PARTNER TO BRING HER IN.
CAN'T BLAME YA, SIMON. I'D DO THE SAME FOR KILOWOG.
HAL, LISTEN--
TO WHAT? A JUSTIFICATION FOR ATTACKING A HIGHLY RESPECTED AND IMPORTANT CONTRIBUTOR TO INTERPLANETARY COMMERCE?
I DON'T THINK SO.
PUT OBAZAYA V'SHEER DOWN.
GENTLY.
THE CORPS HAD A LOT OF FAITH IN YOU TWO. IT WAS TOUCH AND GO AT FIRST, BUT YOU REALLY STEPPED UP.
YOU WERE GREAT LANTERNS.
STILL ARE.
NOT FROM MY SIDE OF THE RING, I'M AFRAI--
GRAAAAAGH!
THE HELL'S--?

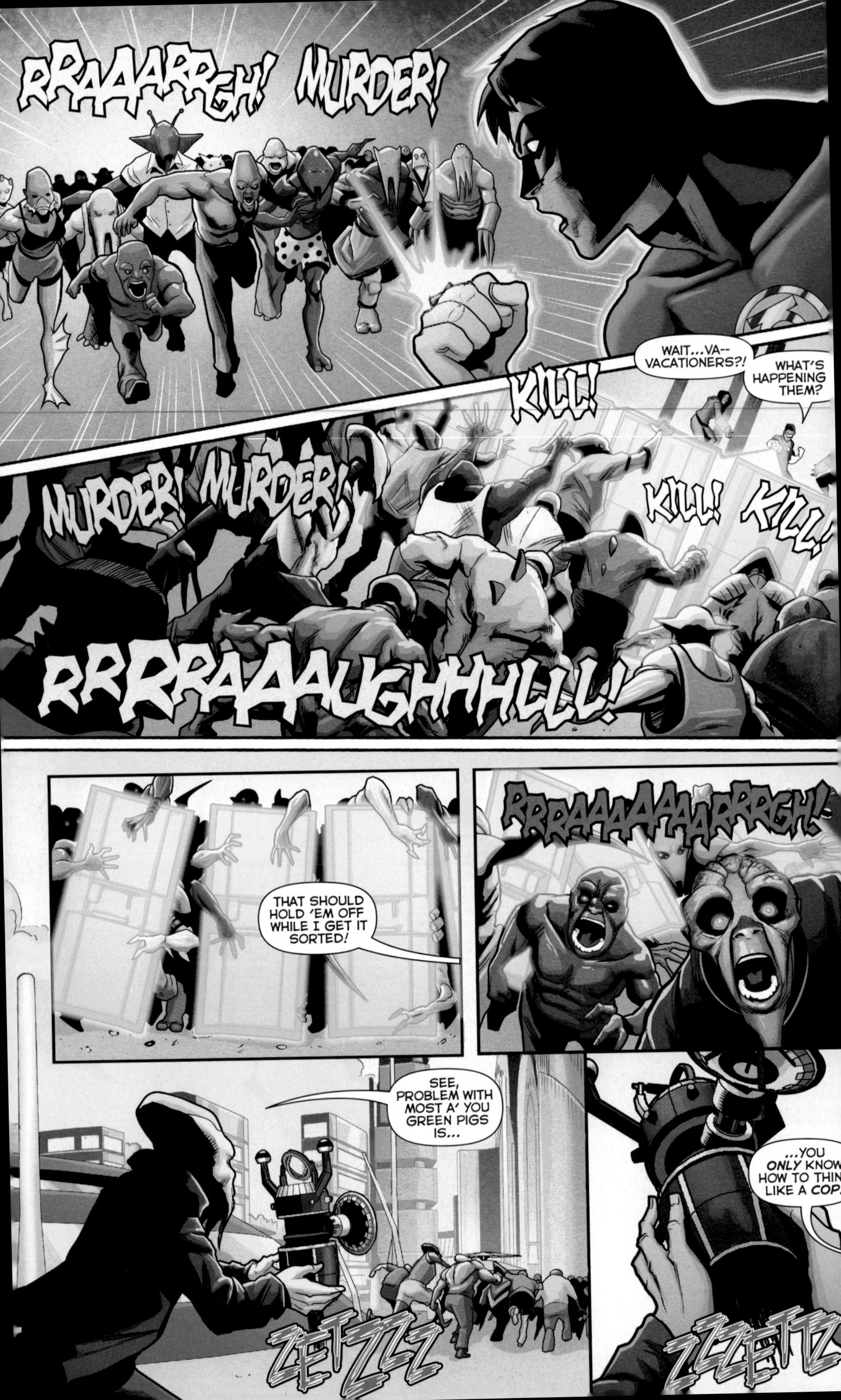
RRAAARRGH! MURDER!
WAIT...VA-- VACATIONERS?!
WHAT'S HAPPENING THEM?
KILL!
MURDER! MURDER!
KILL! KILL!
RRRRAAAUGHHHLLL!
THAT SHOULD HOLD 'EM OFF WHILE I GET IT SORTED!
RRRAAAAAAARRRGH!
SEE, PROBLEM WITH MOST A' YOU GREEN PIGS IS...
ZETZZZ
...YOU ONLY KNOW HOW TO THIN LIKE A COP.
ZZZETTZ

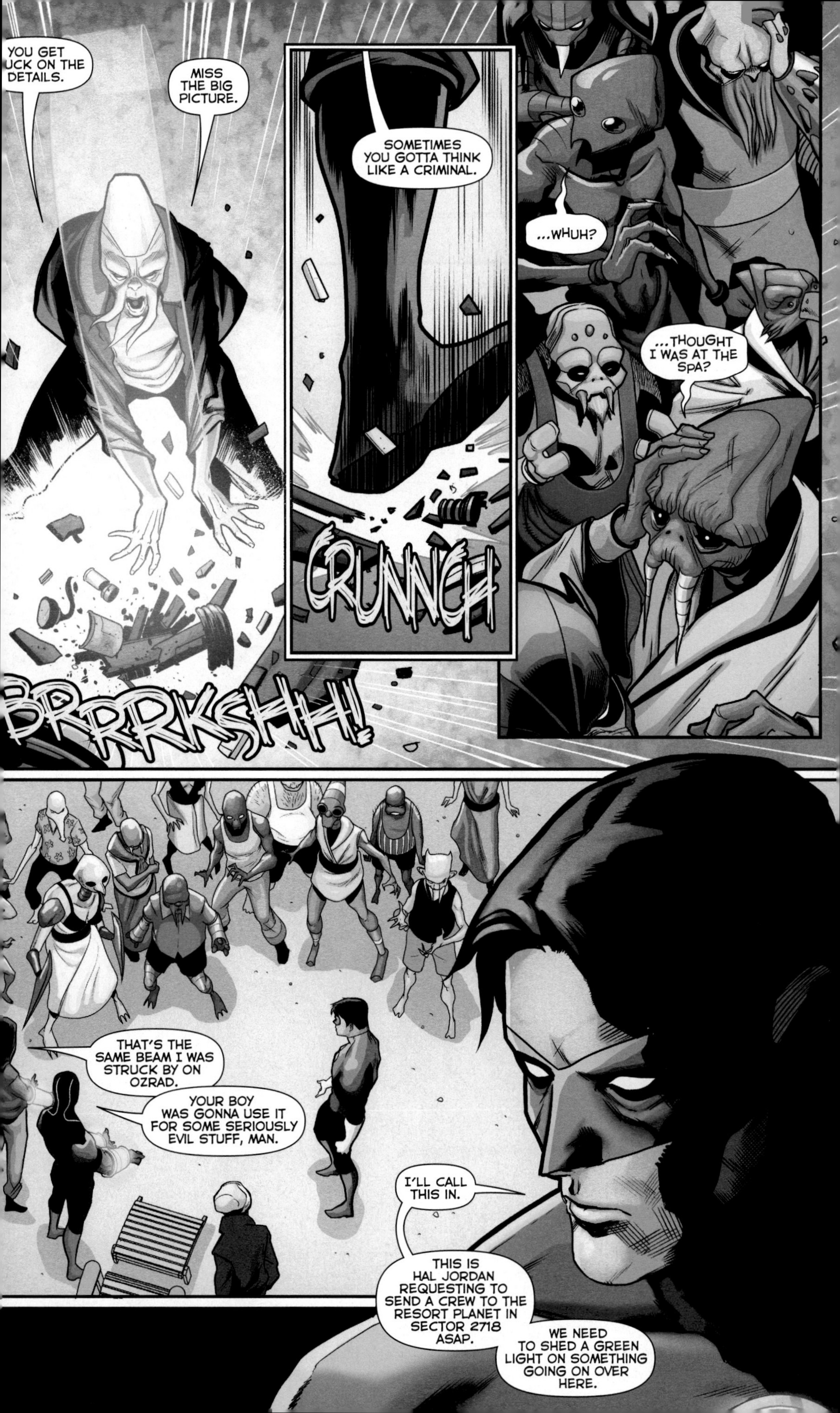
YOU GET
UCK ON THE
DETAILS.
MISS
THE BIG
PICTURE.
SOMETIMES
YOU GOTTA THINK
LIKE A CRIMINAL.
...WHUH?
...THOUGHT
I WAS AT THE
SPA?
CRUNNCH
BRRRKSHH!
THAT'S THE
SAME BEAM I WAS
STRUCK BY ON
OZRAD.
YOUR BOY
WAS GONNA USE IT
FOR SOME SERIOUSLY
EVIL STUFF, MAN.
I'LL CALL
THIS IN.
THIS IS
HAL JORDAN
REQUESTING TO
SEND A CREW TO THE
RESORT PLANET IN
SECTOR 2718
ASAP.
WE NEED
TO SHED A GREEN
LIGHT ON SOMETHING
GOING ON OVER
HERE.

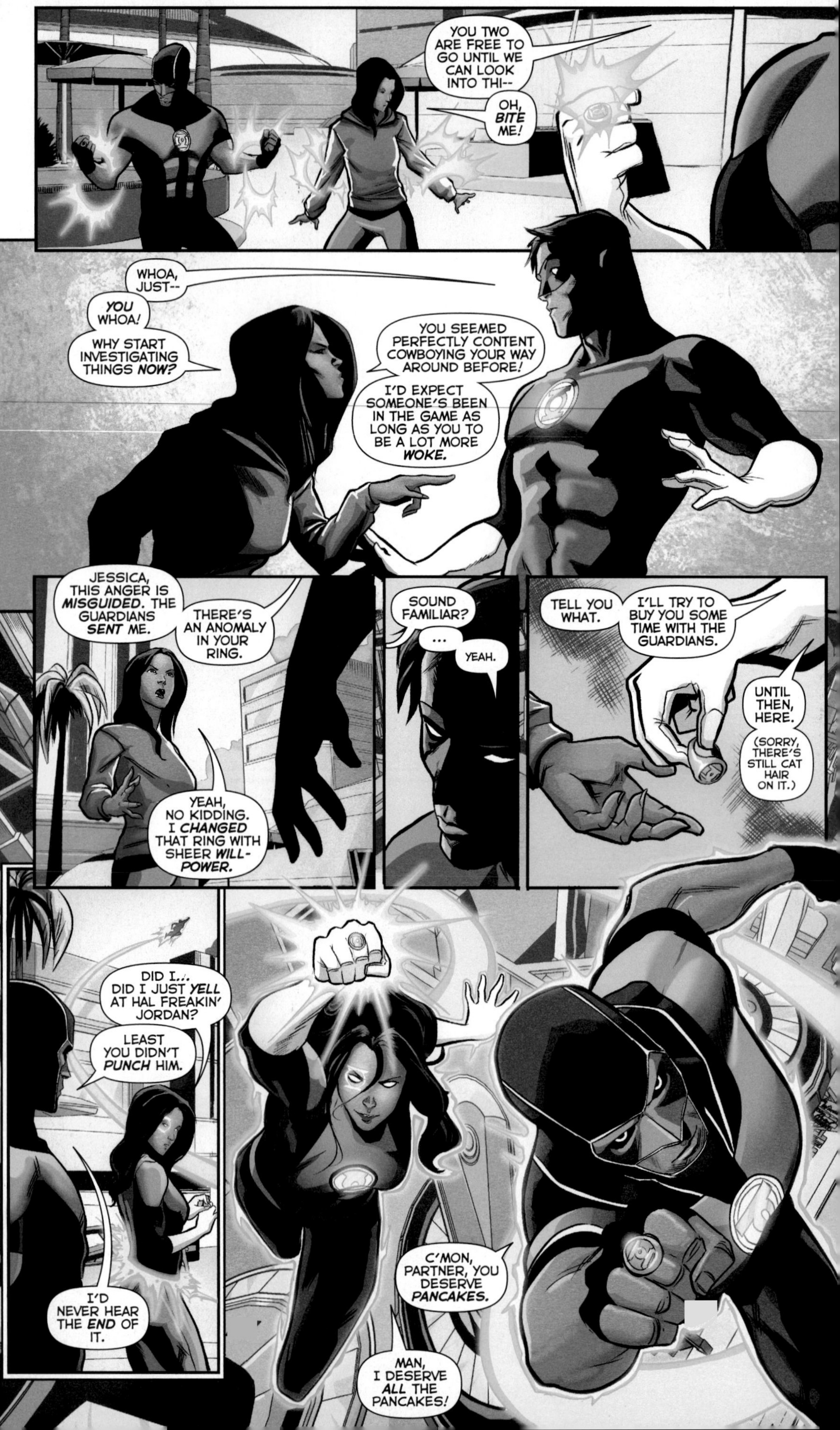
YOU TWO ARE FREE TO GO UNTIL WE CAN LOOK INTO THI--
OH, BITE ME!
WHOA, JUST--
YOU WHOA!
WHY START INVESTIGATING THINGS NOW?
YOU SEEMED PERFECTLY CONTENT COWBOYING YOUR WAY AROUND BEFORE!
I'D EXPECT SOMEONE'S BEEN IN THE GAME AS LONG AS YOU TO BE A LOT MORE WOKE.
JESSICA, THIS ANGER IS MISGUIDED. THE GUARDIANS SENT ME.
THERE'S AN ANOMALY IN YOUR RING.
YEAH, NO KIDDING. I CHANGED THAT RING WITH SHEER WILL-POWER.
SOUND FAMILIAR?
...
YEAH.
TELL YOU WHAT.
I'LL TRY TO BUY YOU SOME TIME WITH THE GUARDIANS.
UNTIL THEN, HERE.
(SORRY, THERE'S STILL CAT HAIR ON IT.)
DID I... DID I JUST YELL AT HAL FREAKIN' JORDAN?
LEAST YOU DIDN'T PUNCH HIM.
I'D NEVER HEAR THE END OF IT.
C'MON, PARTNER, YOU DESERVE PANCAKES.
MAN, I DESERVE ALL THE PANCAKES!

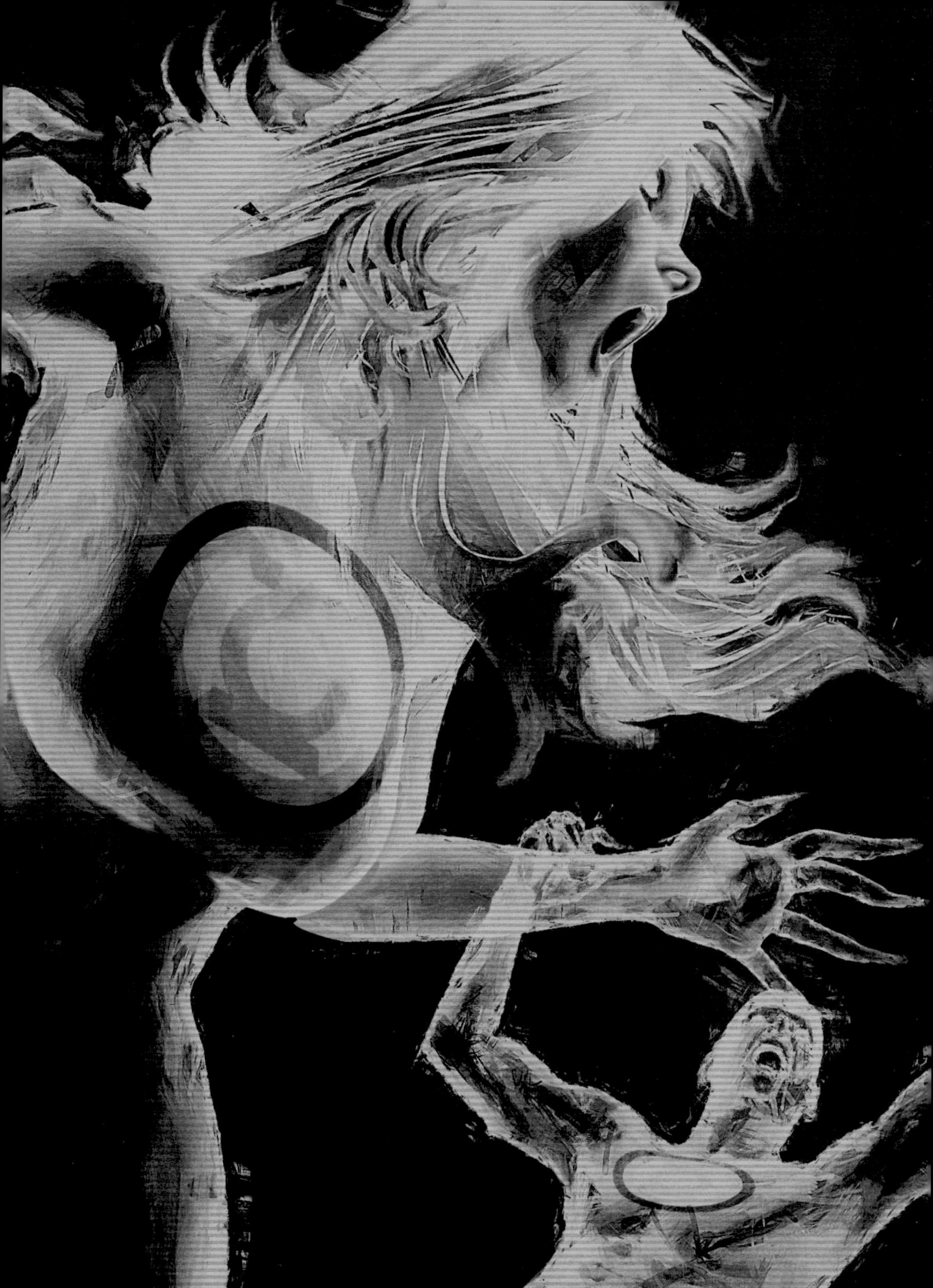

# VARIANT COVER GALLERY

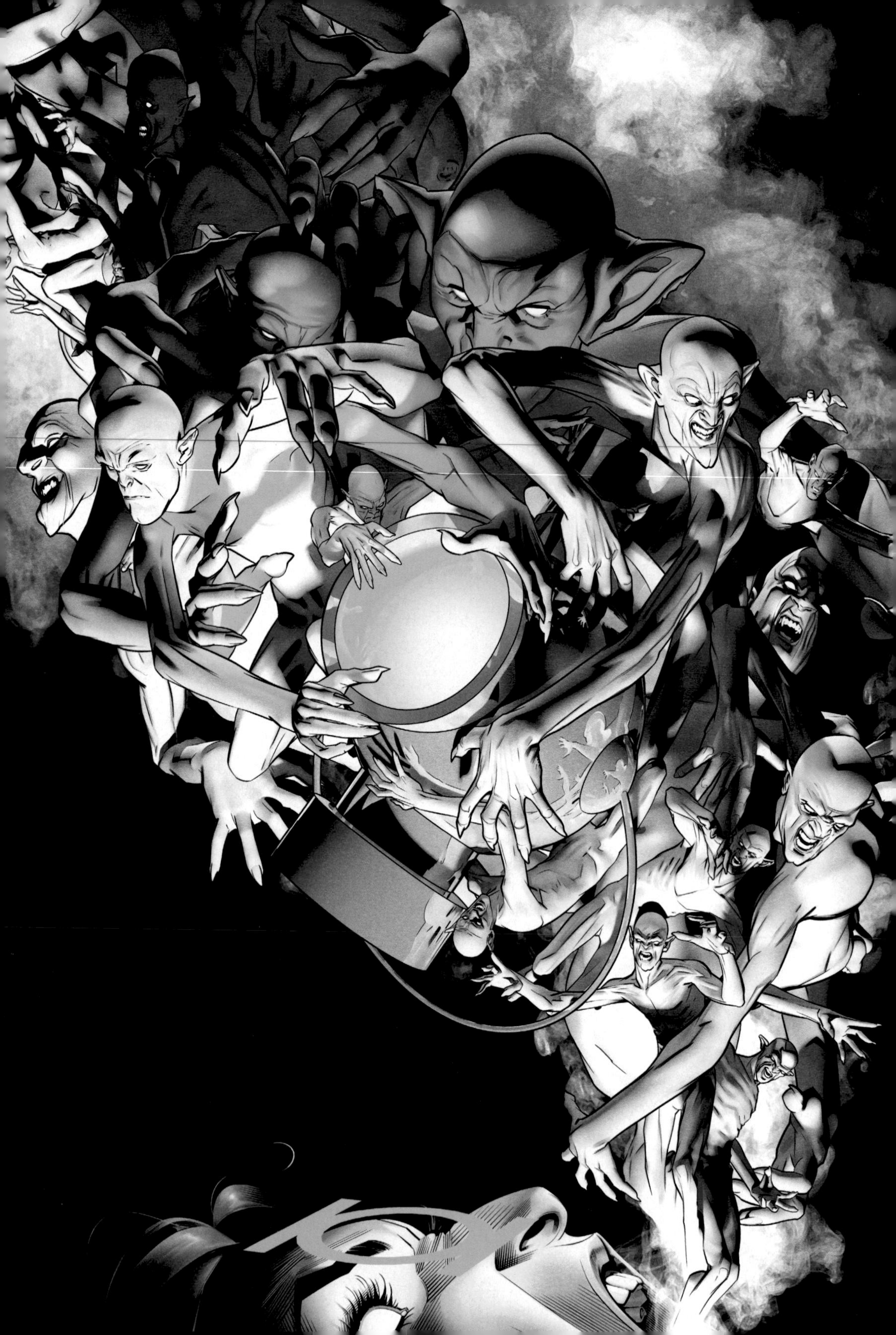

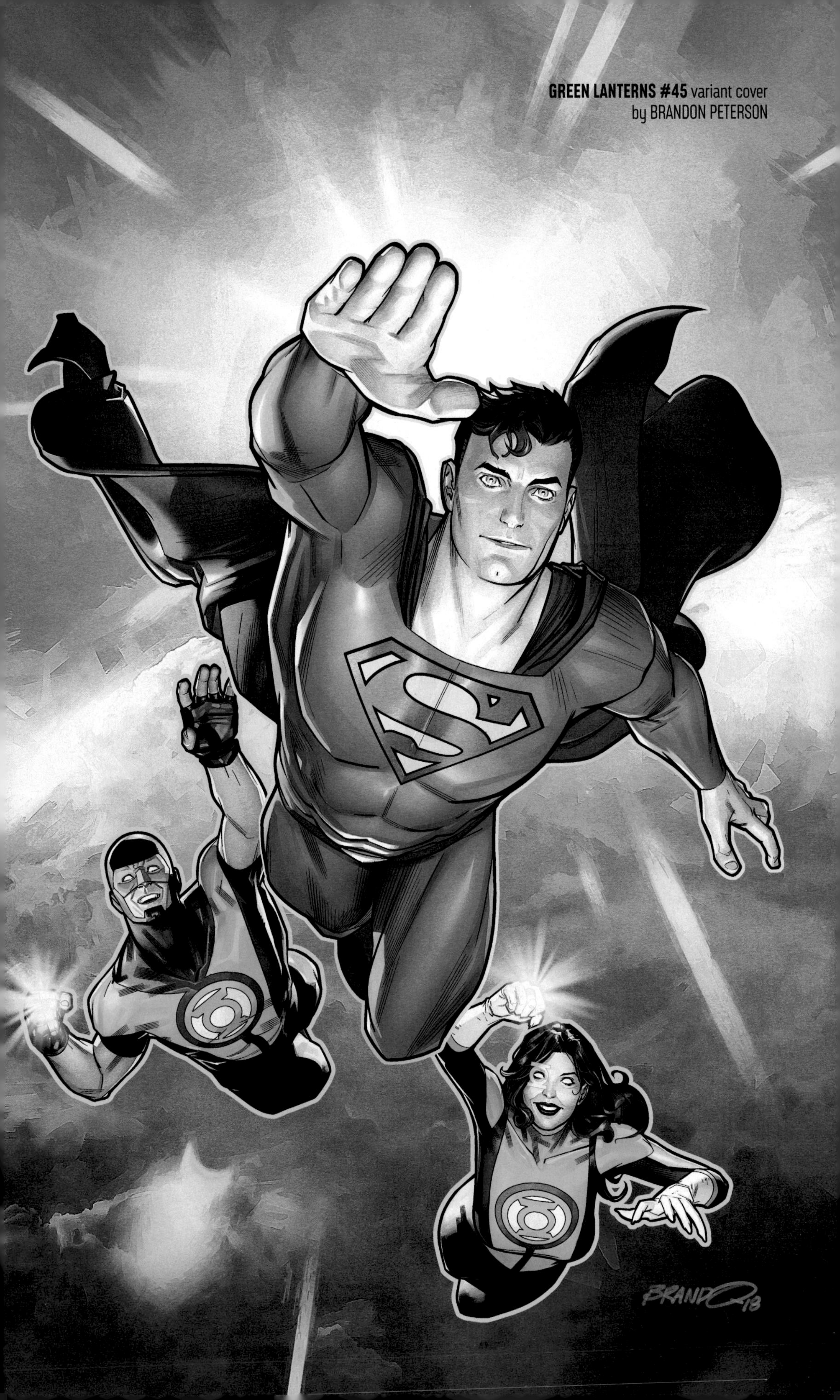

**GREEN LANTERNS #45** variant cover
by BRANDON PETERSON

**GREEN LANTERNS #46** variant cover
by BRANDON PETERSON

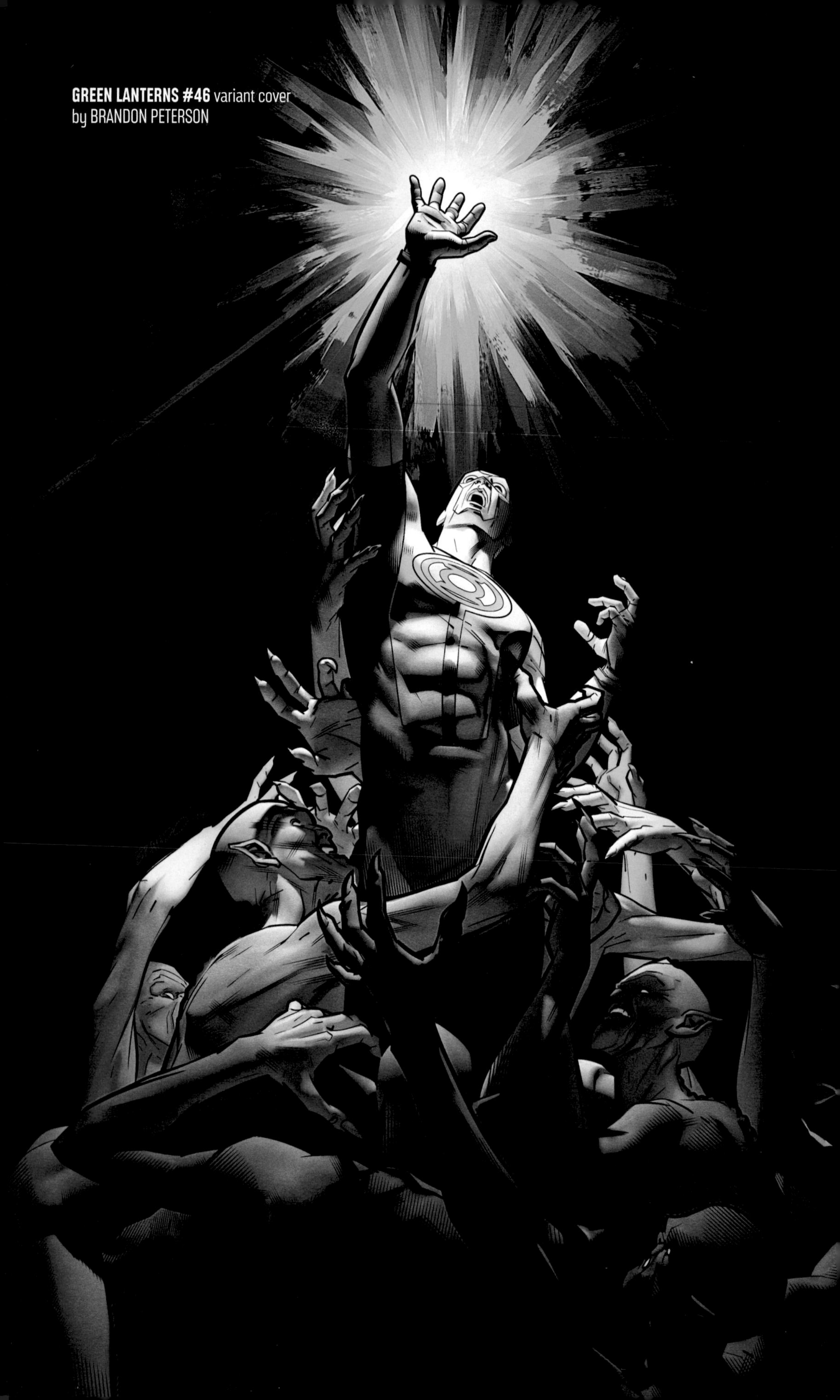

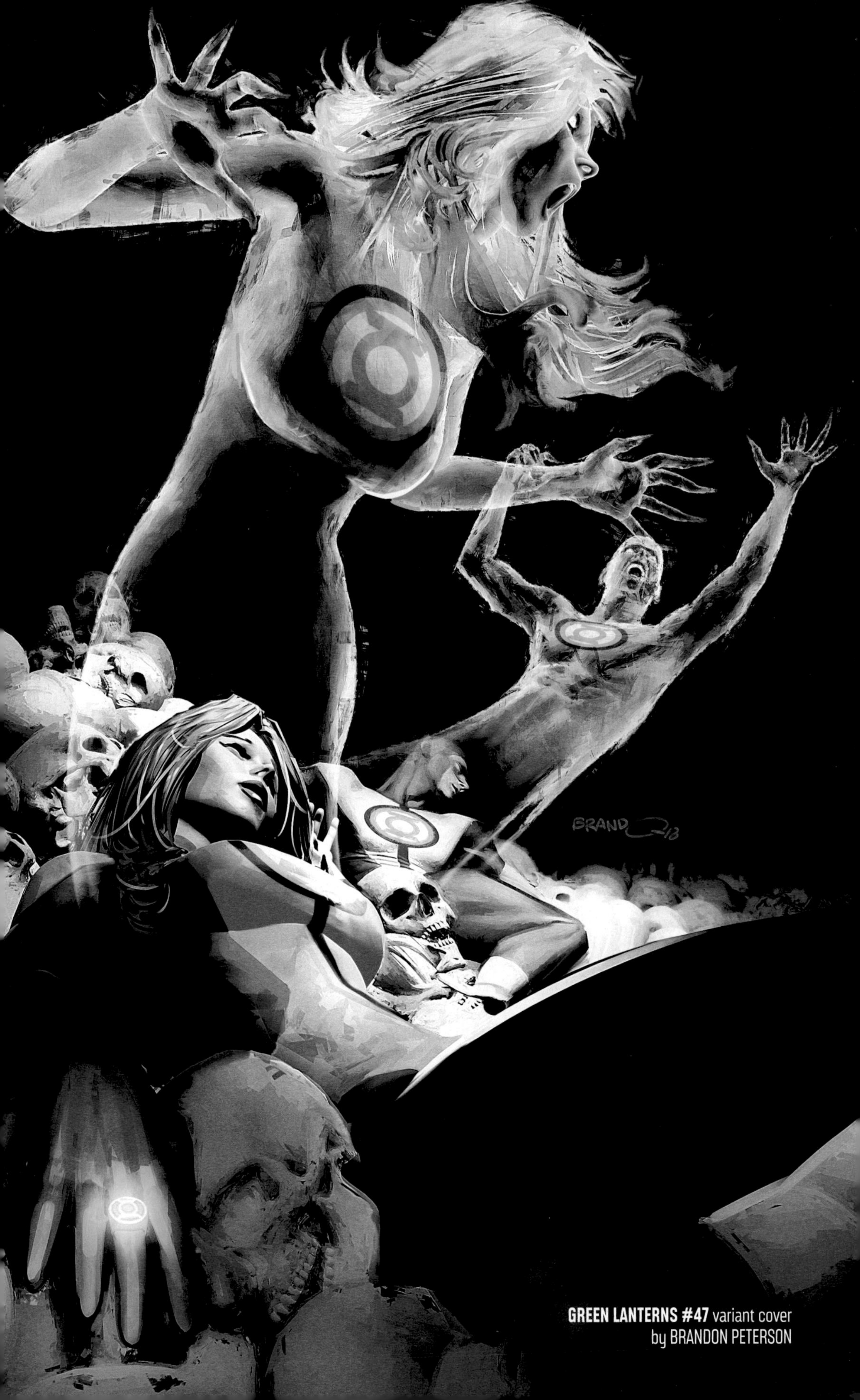

**GREEN LANTERNS #47** variant cover
by BRANDON PETERSON

**GREEN LANTERNS #48** variant cover
by WARREN LOUW

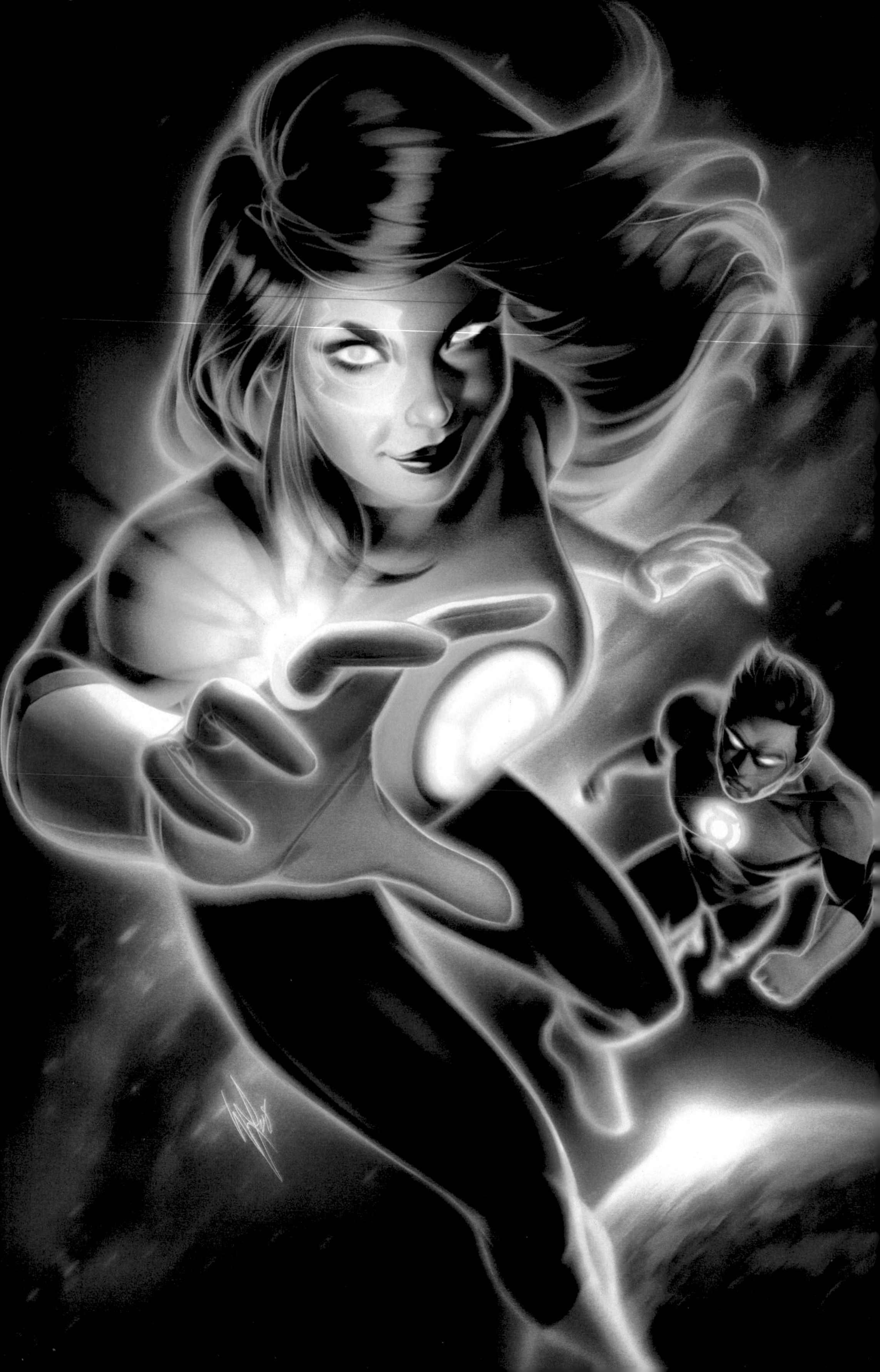

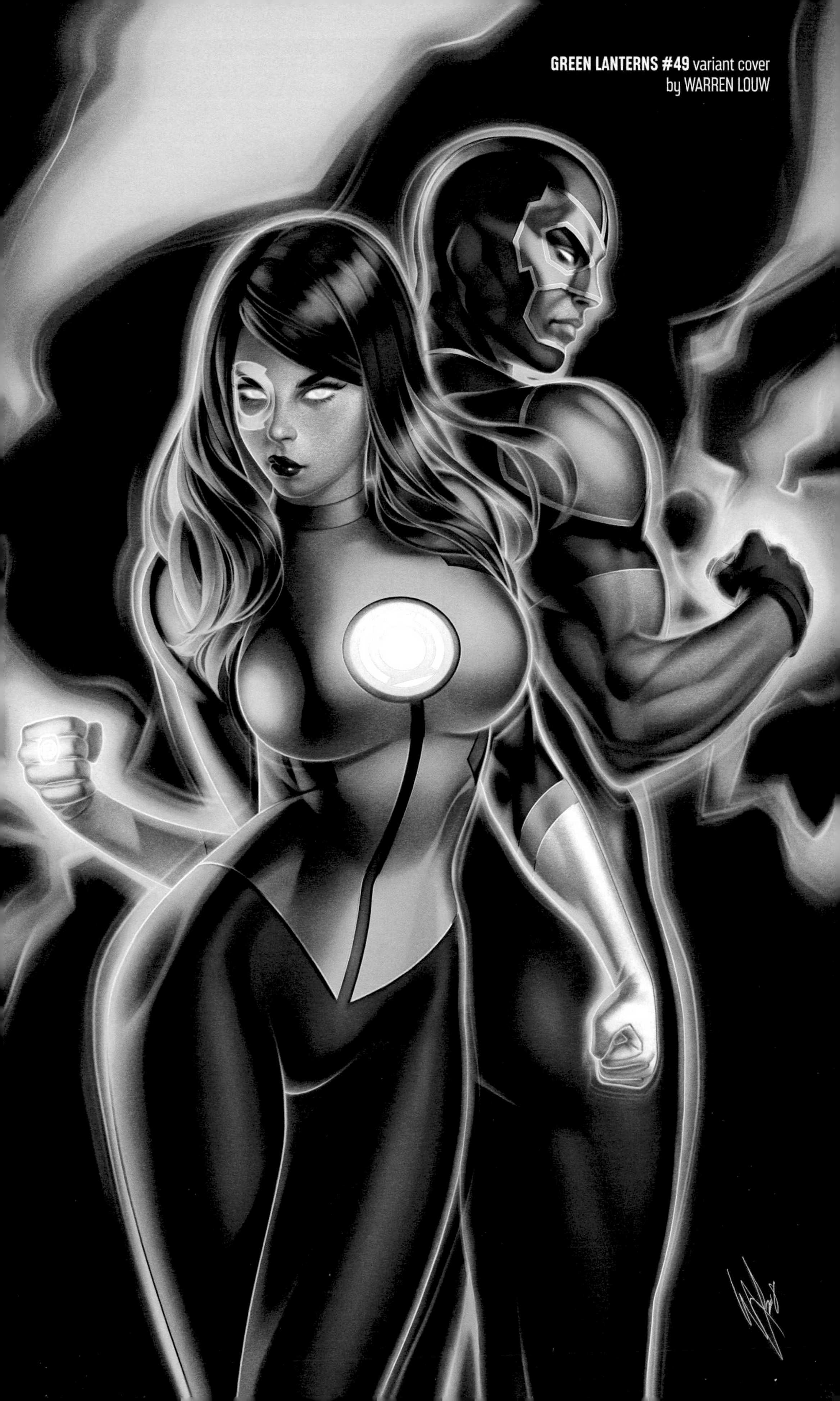

**GREEN LANTERNS #49** variant cover
by WARREN LOUW

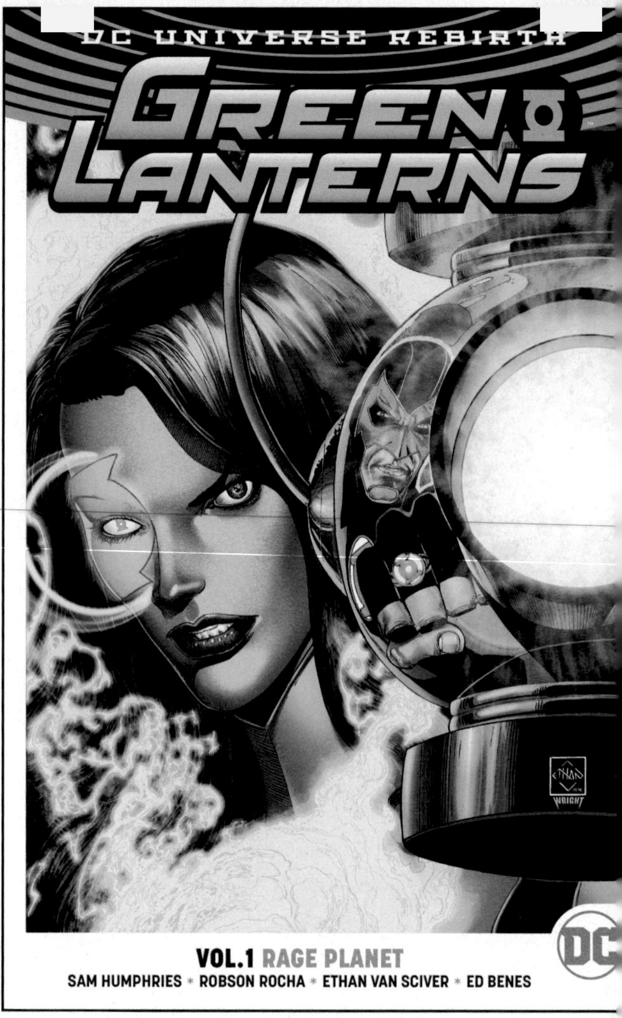

DC UNIVERSE REBIRTH
GREEN LANTERNS
VOL.1 RAGE PLANET
SAM HUMPHRIES * ROBSON ROCHA * ETHAN VAN SCIVER * ED BENES


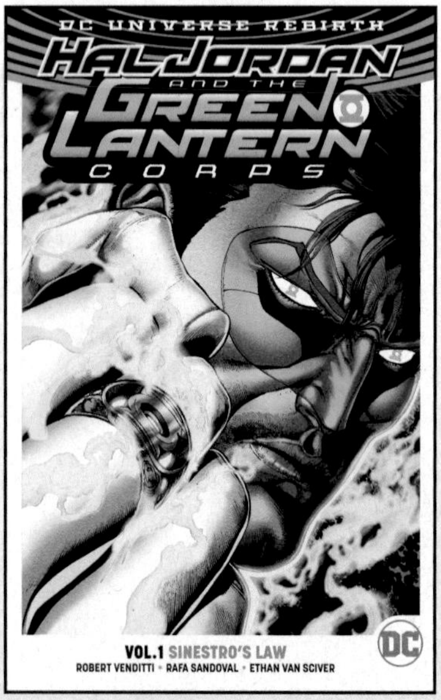

DC UNIVERSE REBIRTH
HAL JORDAN AND THE GREEN LANTERN CORPS
VOL.1 SINESTRO'S LAW
ROBERT VENDITTI * RAFA SANDOVAL * ETHAN VAN SCIVER




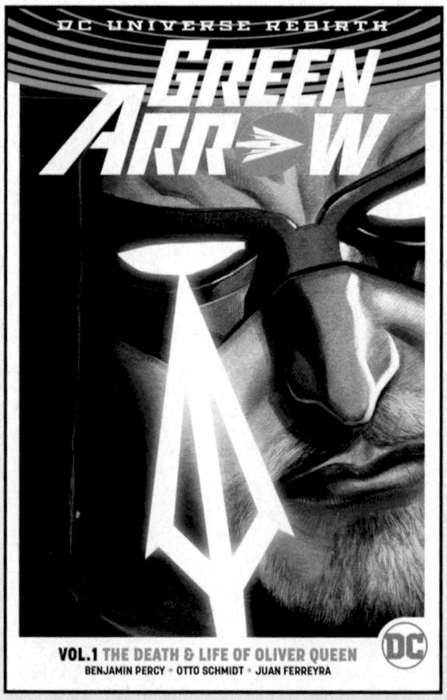

DC UNIVERSE REBIRTH
GREEN ARROW
VOL.1 THE DEATH & LIFE OF OLIVER QUEEN
BENJAMIN PERCY * OTTO SCHMIDT * JUAN FERREYRA




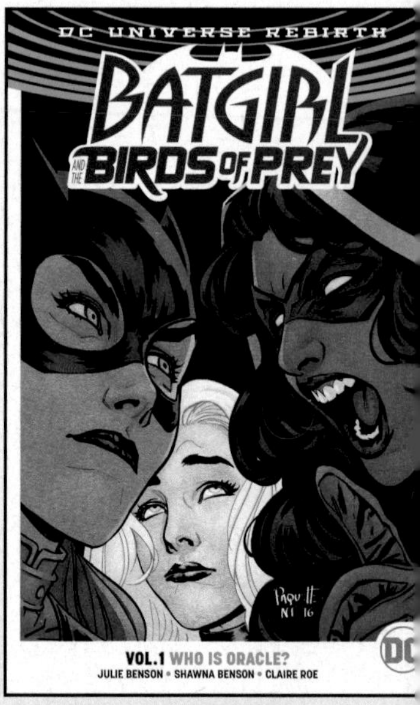

DC UNIVERSE REBIRTH
BATGIRL AND THE BIRDS OF PREY
VOL.1 WHO IS ORACLE?
JULIE BENSON * SHAWNA BENSON * CLAIRE ROE